I0088518

THE FALL OF
JERUSALEM

GREAT CHRISTIAN BOOKS
LINDENHURST, NEW YORK

THE FALL OF
JERUSALEM

G. A. HENTY

Great Christian Books
is an imprint of Rotolo Media
160 37th Street Lindenhurst, New York 11757
(631) 956-0998

©2015 Rotolo Media / Great Christian Books

All rights reserved under International and Pan-American Copyright Conventions. No part of this book maybe reproduced in any form, or by any means, electronic or mechanical, including photocopying, and informational storage and retrieval systems without the expressed written permission from the publisher, except in the case of brief quotations embodied in articles or reviews or promotional/advertising/catalog materials. For additional information or permissions, address all inquiries to the publisher.

Henty, George Alfred, 1832 – 1902
The Fall of Jerusalem/ by G. A. Henty
p. cm.
A "A Great Christian Book" book
GREAT CHRISTIAN BOOKS an imprint of Rotolo Media
ISBN 978-1-61010-033-5
Recommended Dewey Decimal Classifications: 200, 270
Suggested Subject Headings:
1. Religion—Christianity—Eschatology
2. History of Christianity & Christian church
I. Title

Book and cover design are by Michael Rotolo, www.michaelrotolo.com. This book is typeset in the Minion typeface by Adobe Inc. and is quality-manufactured on acid-free paper stock. To discuss the publication of your Christian manuscript or out-of-print book, please contact us.

Manufactured in the United States of America

CONTENTS

Chapter One

THE LAKE OF TIBERIAS

"Dreaming, John, as usual? I never saw such a joy. You are always in extremes, either tiring yourself out or lying half-asleep."

"I was not half-asleep, mother; I was looking at the lake."

"I cannot see much to look at, John; It's just as it has been ever since you were born or since I was born."

"No, I suppose there's no change, mother, but I am never tired of looking at the sun shining on the ripples, and the fishermen's boats, and the birds standing in the shallows or flying off in a desperate hurry without any reason that I can make out. Besides, mother, when one is looking at the lake one is thinking of other things."

"And very often thinking of nothing at all, my son."

"Perhaps so, mother; but there's plenty to think of in these times."

"Plenty, John; there are baskets and baskets of figs to be stripped from the trees and hung up to dry for the winter, and next week we are going to begin the grape harvest. But the figs are the principal matter at present, and I think that it would be far more useful for you to go and help old Isaac and his son in getting them in than in lying there watching the lake."

I suppose it would, mother," the lad said, rising briskly, for his fits of indolence were by no means common, and as a rule he was ready to assist at any work which might be going on.

"I do not wonder at John loving the lake," his mother said to herself when the lad had hurried away. "It is a fair scene, and it may be, as Simon thinks, that a change may come over it before long, and that ruin and desolation may fall upon us all."

There were, indeed, few scenes which could surpass in tranquil beauty that which Martha, the wife of Simon, was looking upon, the sheet of sparkling water with its low shores dotted with towns and villages. Down the lake, on the opposite shore, rose the walls and citadel of Tiberias, with many stately buildings, for although Tiberias was not now the chief town of Galilee, for Sephoris had usurped its place, it had been the seat of the Roman authority, and the kings who ruled the country for Rome generally dwelt there. Half a mile from the spot where Martha was standing rose the newly erected wall so Hippos.

Where the towns and villages did not engross the shore, the rich orchards and vineyards extended down to the very edge of the water. The plain of Galilee was a veritable garden; here flourished in the greatest abundance the vine and the fig; while the low hills were covered with olive groves, and the corn waved thickly on the rich, fat land. No region on the earth's face possessed a fairer climate. The heat was never extreme; the winds blowing from the Great Sea brought the needed moisture for the vegetation, and so soft and equable was the air that for ten months in the year grapes and figs could be gathered. The population, supported by the abundant fruits of the earth, was very large. Villages which could elsewhere be called towns, for those containing but a few thousand inhabitants were regarded as small indeed, were scattered thickly over the plain, and few areas of equal dimensions could show a population approaching that which inhabited the plains and slopes between the Sea of Galilee and the Mediterranean. None could have been dreamed of the dangers that were to come, or believe that this rich cultivation and teeming population would disappear, and that in time a few flocks of wandering sheep would be scarce to be able to find herbage growing on the wastes of land which would take the place of this fertile soil. Certainly no such thought as this occurred to Martha as she re-entered the house, though she did fear that trouble and ruin might be approaching.

John was soon at work among the fig-trees, aiding Isaac and his son Reuben, a lad of some fifteen years, to pick the soft, luscious fruit, and carry it to the little courtyard shaded from the rays of the sun by an overhead trellis-work covered with vines and almost bending beneath the purple bunches of grapes. Miriam, the old nurse, and four or five maid-servants, under the eye of Martha, tied them in rows on strings and fastened them to pegs driven into that side of the house upon which the sun beat down most hotly. It was only the best fruit that was so served, for that which had been damaged in the picking and all of smaller size were laid on trays in the sun. The girls chatted merrily as they worked, for Martha, although a good housewife, was a gentle mistress, and so long as fingers were busy heeded not if the tongue ran on.

"Let the damsels be happy while they may, "she would say if Miriam scolded a little when the laughter rose louder than usual. "Let them be happy while they can; who knows what lies in the future?"

But at present the future cast no shade upon the group, nor upon a girl of about fourteen years old who danced in and out of the courtyard in the highest spirits, now stopping a few minutes to string the figs, then scampering away with an empty basket, which, when she reached the gatherers, she placed on her head and supported demurely for a little while at the foot of the ladder upon which John was perched, so that he could lay the figs in it without bruising them; but long ere the basket was filled she would tire of the work, and setting it on the ground run back into the house.

"And so you think you are helping, Mary," John said, laughing, when the girl returned for the fourth time with an empty basket.

"Helping, John! Of course I am, ever so much; helping you and helping them at the house, and carrying empty baskets. I consider myself the most active of the party."

"Active, certainly, Mary! But if you do not help them in stringing and hanging the figs more than you help me, I think you might as well leave it alone."

"Fie, John! That is most ungrateful, after my standing here like a statue with the basket on my head ready for you to lay the figs in."

"That is all very fine!" John laughed; "but before the basket is half-full away you go, and I have to get down the ladder and bring up the basket and fix it firmly, and that without shaking the figs, whereas ha you left it alone altogether I could have brought up the empty basket and fixed it close by my hand without any trouble at all."

"You are an ungrateful boy, and you know how bad it is to be ungrateful! And after my making myself so hot, too!" Miriam said. "My face is as red as fire, and that is all the thanks I get. Very well, then, I shall go into the house and leave you to your own bad reflections."

"You need not do that, Mary; you can sit down in the shade there and watch us at work, and eat figs and get yourself cool, all at the same time. The sun will be down in another half hour and then I shall be free to amuse you."

"Amuse me, indeed!" the girl said indignantly as she sat down on the bank to which John had pointed. "You mean that I shall amuse you; that is what it generally comes to. If it wasn't for me I am sure very often there would not be a word said when we are out together."

"Perhaps that is true," John agree; "but you see there is so much to think about."

"And so you choose the time when you are with me to think! Thank you, John! You had better think at present;" and rising from the seat she had just taken, she walked back to the house again, regardless of John's explanations and shouts.

Old Isaac chuckled on his tree close by.

"They are ever so sharp for us in words, John. The damsel is younger than you by full two years, and yet she can always put you in the wrong with her tongue."

"She puts meanings to my words which I never thought of," John said, "and is angered, or pretends to be, for I never know which it is, at things which she has coined out of her own mind, for they had no place in mine."

"Boys' wits are always slower than girls'," the old man said; "a girl has more fancy in her little finger than a boy in his whole body. Your cousin laughs at you because she sees that you take it seriously, and wonders in her mind how it is her thoughts run ahead of yours. But I love the damsel, and so do all in the house, for if she be a little wayward at times, she is bright and loving, and has cheered the house since she came here. Your father is not a man of many words, and Martha, as becomes her age, is staid and quiet, though she is no enemy of mirth and cheerfulness; but the loss of all her children save you has saddened her, and I think she must often have pined that she had not a girl, and she has brightened much since the damsel came here three years ago. But the sun is sinking and my basket is full; there will be enough for the maids to go on with in the morning until we can supply them with more."

John's basket was not full, but he was well content to stop, and descending their ladders the three returned to the house.

Simon of Cadez, for that was the name of his farm and the little fishing village close by on the shore was a prosperous and well-to-do man. His land, like that of all around him, had come down from father to son through long generations, for the law by which all mortgages were cleared off every seven years prevented those who might be disposed to idleness and extravagance from ruining themselves and their children. Every man dwelt upon the land which, as eldest son, he had inherited, while the younger sons, taking their smaller share, would settle in the towns or villages and become traders or fishermen according to their bent and means.

There were poor in Palestine, for there will be poor everywhere so long as human nature remains as it is, and some men are idle and self-indulgent while others are industrious and thrifty; but taking it as a whole there were, thanks to the wise provisions of their laws, no people on the face of the earth so generally comfortable and well-to-do. They grumbled, of course, over the exactions of the tax-collectors—exactions due not to the contributions which was paid by the province to imperial Rome, but to the luxury and extravagance of their kings and to the greed and corruption of the officials. But in spite of this the people of rich and prosperous Galilee could have lived in contentment and happiness had it not been for the factions in their mist.

On reaching the house, John found that his father had just returned from Hippos, whither he had gone on business. He nodded when the lad entered with his basket.

"I have hired eight men in the market to-day to come out tomorrow to aid in gathering in the figs," he said, "and your mother has just sent down to get some of the fishermen's maidens to come in to help her; it is time that we had done with them, and we will then set about the vintage. Let us reap while we can' there is no saying what the morrow will bring forth. Wife, add something to the evening mean, for the Rabbi Solomon Ben Masassch will sup with us and sleep here tonight."

John saw that his father looked graver than usual; but he knew his duty as a son too well to think of asking any questions, and he busied himself for the time in laying out the figs on trays, knowing that otherwise their own weight would crush the soft fruit before the morning, and bruise the tender skins.

A quarter of an hour later the quick footsteps of a donkey were heard approaching. John ran out, and having saluted the rabbi, held the animal while his father assisted him to alight, and welcoming him to his house, led him within. The meal was soon served. It consisted of fish from the lake, kid's flesh seethed in milk, and fruit. Only the men sat down; the rabbi sitting upon Simon's right hand, John on his left, and Isaac and his son at the other end of the table. Martha's maids waited upon them, for it was not the custom for the women to sit down with the men; and although in the country this usage was not strictly observed, and Martha and little Mary generally took their meals with Simon and John, they did not do so if any guest was present.

In honor of the visitor a white cloth had been laid on the table. All ate with their fingers, two dishes of each kind being placed on the table— one at each end. But few words were said during the meal. After it was concluded Isaac and his son withdrew, and presently Martha and Mary, having taken their meals in the women's apartments, came into the room. Mary made a little face at John to signify her disapproval of the visitor, whose coming would compel her to keep silent all the evening. But though John smiled, he made no sign of sympathy, for indeed he was anxious to hear the news from without, and doubted not that he should learn much from the rabbi.

Solomon Ben Manasseh was a man of considerable influence in Galilee. He was a tall, stern-looking old man, with bushy black eyebrows, deep-set eyes, and a long beard of black hair streaked with gray. He was said to have acquired much of the learning of the Gentiles, among whom at Antioch he had dwelt for some years; but it was to his powers as a speaker that he owed his influence. It was the tongue in those days that ruled men, and there were few who could lash a crowd to fury, or still their wrath when excited, better than Solomon Ben Manasseh. For some time they talked upon different subjects—on the corn-harvest and vintage, the probable amount of taxation, the marriage feast which was to take place in the following week at the house of one of the principal citizens of Hippos, and other matters. But at last Simon broached the subject which was uppermost in all their thoughts.

"And the news from Tiberias, you say, is bad, rabbi?"

"The news from Tiberias is always bad, friend Simon; in all the land there is not a city which will compare with it in the wrong-headedness of its people and the violence of its seditions, and little can be hoped, as far as I can see, so long as our good governor, Josephus, continues to treat the malefactors so leniently. A score of times they have conspired against his life, and as often has he eluded them, for the Lord has been ever with him. But each time, instead of punishing those who have brought about these disorders, he lets them go free, trusting always that they will repent them of their ways, although he sees that his kindness is thrown away and that they grow even bolder and more bitter against him after each failure.

"All Galilee is with him. Whenever he gives the word every man takes up his arms and follows him; and did he but give the order they would level those proud towns Tiberias and Sepphoris to the ground, and tear down stone by stone the stronghold of John of Gischala. But he will suffer them to do nothing—not a hair of these traitors' heads is to be touched, nor their property to value of a penny be interfered with. I call such lenity culpable. The law ordains punishment for those who disturb people. We know what befell those who rebelled against Moses. Josephus has the valor and the wisdom of King David, but it were well if he had, like our great king, a Joab by his side, who would smite down traitors and spare not."

"It is his only fault," Simon said. "What a change has taken place since he was sent hither from Jerusalem to take up our government! All abuses have been repressed, extortion has been put down, taxes have been lightened. We eat our bread in peace and comfort and each man's property is his own. Never was there such a change as he has wrought, and were it not for John of Gischala, Justus the son of Piscus, and Jesus the son of Sapphias all would go quietly and well; but these men are continually stirring up the people, who in their folly listen to them, and conspiring to murder Josephus and seize upon his government.

"Already he has had more than once to reduce to submission Tiberias and Sepphoris, happily without bloodshed. For when the people of these cities saw that all Galilee was with Josephus, they opened their gates and submitted themselves to his mercy. Truly in Leviticus it is said: "Thou shalt not avenge nor bear any grudge against the children of they people, but thou shalt love thy neighbor as thyself." But Josephus carries this beyond reason. Seeing that his adversaries by no means observe this law, he should remember that it is also said that "He that taketh the sword shall fall by the sword," and that the law lays down punishments for the transgressors. Our judges and kinds slew those who troubled the land and destroyed them utterly, and Josephus does wrong to depart from their teaching."

"I know not where he could have learned such notions of mercy to his enemies and to the enemies of the land," Simon said. "He has been to Rome, but it is not among the Romans that he will have found that it is right to forgive those who rise up in rebellion."

"Yes, he was in Rome when he was twenty-six years old," Simon said.

"He went thither to plead the case of certain priests who had been thrown into bonds by Felix and sent to Rome. It was a perilous voyage, for his ship was wrecked in the Adriatic, and of six hundred men who were aboard only eighty were picked up, after floating and swimming all night, by a ship of Cyrene. He was not long in Rome, for being introduced to Popæa, the wife of Cæsar, he used his interest with her and obtained the release of those for whose sake he went there. No, if he gained these ideas from any one, he learned them from one Banus, and Ascetic, of the sect of the Essenes, who lived in the desert with no other clothing than the park and leaves of trees, and no other food save that which grew wild."

"Josephus lived with him in like fashion for three years, and doubtless learned all that was in his heart. Banus was a follower, they say, of that John whom Herod put to death, and, for aught I know, of that Jesus who was crucified two years afterward at Jerusalem, and in whom many people believed, and who has many followers to this day. I have conversed with some of them, and from what they tell me this Jesus taught doctrines similar to those which Josephus practices, and which he may have learned from Banus, without accepting the doctrines which the members of this sect hold as to their founder being the promised Messiah who was to restore Israel."

"I too have talked with many of the sect," Simon said, "and have argued with them on the folly of their belief, seeing that their founder by no means saved Israel, but was himself put to death. From what I could see there was much that was good in the doctrines they hold; but they have exaggerated ideas, and are opposed to all wars, even to fighting for their country. I hear that since there has been trouble with Rome most of them have departed altogether out of the land so as to avoid the necessity of fighting."

"They are poor creatures," Solomon Ben Manasseh said scornfully; "but we need not talk of them now, for they affect us in no way, save that it may be that Josephus has learned somewhat of their doctrines from Banus, and that he is thus unduly, and as I think, most unfortunately for the country, inclined too much to mercy instead of punishing the evil-doers as they deserve."

"But, nevertheless, rabbi, it seems to me that there has been good policy as well in the mercy which Josephus has shown his foes. You know that John has many friends in Jerusalem, and that if he could accuse Josephus of slaughtering any, he would be able to make so strong a party there that he could obtain the recall of Josephus."

"We would not let him go," Solomon said hotly. "Since the Romans have gone we submit to the supremacy of the council at Jerusalem, but it is only on sufferance. For long ages we have had nothing to do with Judah, and we are not disposed to put our necks under their yoke now. We submit to unity because in the Romans we have a common foe, but we are not going to be tyrannized. Josephus has shown himself a wise ruler. We are happier under him than we have been for generations under the men who call themselves kings, but who are nothing but Roman satraps, and we are not going to suffer him to be taken from us. Only let the people of Jerusalem try that, and they will have to deal with all the men of Galilee."

"I am past the age at which men are bound to take up the sword, and John has not yet attained it, but if there were need we would both go out and fight. What should they do? For the population of Galilee is greater than that of Judah. And while we would fight every man to the death, the Jews would few of them care to hazard their lives only to take from us the man we desire to rule over us. Still Josephus does wisely perhaps to give no occasion for accusation by his enemies. There is no talk, is there, rabbi, of any movement on the part of the Romans to come against us in force?"

"None so far as I have heard," the rabbi replied. "King Agrippa remains in his country to the east, but he has no Roman force with him sufficient to attempt any great enterprise, and so long as they leave us alone we are content."

"They will come sooner or later," Simon said, shaking his head. "They are busy elsewhere. When they have settled with their other enemies they will come here to avenge the defeat of Cestius, to restore Florus, and to reconquer the land. Where Rome has once laid her paw she never lets slip her prey."

"Well, we can fight," Solomon Ben Manasseh said sternly. "Our forefathers won the land with the sword, and we can hold it by the sword."

"Yes," Martha said quietly, joining in the conversation for the first time, "if God fights for us as He fought for our forefathers."

"Why should He not?" the rabbi asked sternly. "We are still His people. We are faithful to his law."

"But God has many times in the past suffered us to fall into the hands of our enemies as a punishment for our sins," Martha said quietly. "The tribes were carried away into captivity, and are scattered we know not where. The temple was destroyed, and the people of Judah dwelt long as captives in Babylon. He suffered us to fall under the yoke of the Romans. In his right time he will fight for us again, but can we say that that time has come, rabbi, and that he will smite the Romans as he smote the host of Sennacherib?"

"That no man can say," the rabbi answered gloomily; "time only will show; but whether or no, the people will fight valiantly."

"I doubt not that they will fight," Simon said; "but many other nations, to whom we are but as a bandful, have fought bravely, but have succumbed to the might of Rome. It is said that Josephus and many of the wisest in Jerusalem were heartily opposed to the tumults against the Romans, and that they only went with the people because they were in fear of their lives; and even at Tiberias many men of worth and gravity, such as Julius Capellus, Herod the son of Miarus, Herod the son of Gamalus, Compsus, and others, are all strongly opposed to hostility against the Romans. And it is the same elsewhere. Those who know best what is the might and power of Rome would fain remain friendly with her. It is the ignorant and violent classes have led us into this strait, from which, as I fear, naught but ruin can arise."

"I thought better things of you, Simon," the rabbi said angrily.

"But you yourself have told me," Simon urged, "that you thought it a mad undertaking to provoke the vengeance of Rome."

"I thought so at first," Solomon admitted, "but now our hand is placed on the plow we must not draw back; and I believe that the God of our fathers will show his might before the heathen."

"I trust that it may be so," Simon said gravely. "In his hand is all power. Whether he will see fit to put it forth now in our behalf remains to be seen. However, for the present we need not concern ourselves greatly with the Romans. It may be long before they bring an army against us, while these seditions here are at our very door and ever threaten to involve us in civil war."

"We need fear no civil war," the rabbi said. "The people of all Galilee, save the violent and ill-disposed in a few of the towns, are all for Josephus. If it comes to force, John and his party know that they will be swept away like a straw before the wind. The fear is that they may succeed in murdering Josephus, either by the knife of an assassin or in one of these tumults. They would rather the latter, because they would then say that the people had torn him to pieces in their fury at his misdoings. However, we watch over him as much as we can, and his friends have warned him that he must be careful, not only for his own sake but for that of all the people, and he has promised that as far as he can he will be on his guard against these traitors."

"The governor should have a strong body-guard," John exclaimed impetuously, "as the Roman governors had. In another year I shall be of age to have my name inscribed in the list of fighting men, and I would gladly be one of his guards."

"You are neither old enough to fight nor to express an opinion unasked," Simon said, "in the presence of your elders."

"Do not check the boy," the rabbi said; "he has fire and spirit, and the days are coming when we shall not ask how old or how young are those who would fight, so that they can but hold arms. Josephus is wise not to have a military guard, John, because the people love not such appearance of state. His enemies would use this as an argument that he is setting himself up above them. It is partly because he behaves himself discreetly and goes about among them like a private person of no more account than themselves that they love him. None can say he is a tyrant, because he has no means of tyrannizing. His enemies cannot urge it against him at Jerusalem, as they would doubtless do if they could, that he is seeking to lead Galilee away from the rule of Jerusalem, and to set himself up as its master; for to do this he would require to gather an army, and Josephus has not a single armed man at his service, save and except that when he appears to be in danger many out of love of him assemble and provide him escort. No, Josephus is wise in that he affects neither pomp nor state, that he keeps no armed men around him, but trusts to the love of the people. He would be wiser, however, did he seize one of the occasions when the people have taken up arms for him, to destroy all those who make sedition, and to free the country once and for all from the trouble.

"Sedition should be always nipped in the bud. Lenity in such a case is the most cruel course, for it encourages men to think that those in authority fear them, and that they can conspire without danger; and whereas at first the blood of ten men will put an end to sedition, it needs at last the blood of as many thousands to restore peace and order. It is good for a man to be merciful, but not for a ruler, for the good of the whole people is placed in his hands. The sword of justice is given to him, and he is most merciful who uses it the most promptly against those who work sedition. The wise ruler will listen to the prayers of his people, and will grant their petitions when they show that their case is hard; but he will grant nothing to him who asketh with his sword in his hand, for he knows full well that when he yields once he must yield always, until the time comes, as come it surely will, when he must resist with the sword. Then the land will be filled with blood, whereas in the beginning he could have avoided all trouble by refusing so much as to listen to those who spoke with threats. Josephus is a good man, and the Lord has given him great gifts. He has done great things for the land, but you will see that many woes will come and much blood will be shed from this lenity of his toward those who stir up tumults among the people."

A few minutes later the family retired to bed, the hour being a late one for Simon's household, which generally retired to rest a short time after the evening meal.

The next day the work of gathering in the figs was carried on earnestly and steadily, with the aid of the workers whom Simon had hired in the town, and in two days the trees were all stripped, and strings of figs hung to dry from the boughs of all the trees round the house. Then the gathering of the grapes began. All the inhabitants of the little fishing village lent their aid—men as well as women and children, for the vintage was looked upon as a holiday, and Simon was regarded as a good friend by his neighbors, being ever ready to aid them when there was need, judging any disputes which arouse between them, and lending them money without interest if misfortune came upon their boats or nets, or if illness befell them; while the women in times of sickness or trouble went naturally to Martha with their griefs, and were assured of sympathy, good advice, and any drugs or dainty food suited to the case. The women and girls picked the grapes and laid them in baskets; these were carried by men and emptied into the vat, where other men trod them down and pressed out the juice. Martha and her maids saw to the cooking and laying out on the great table in the courtyard of the meals, to which all sat down together. Simon superintended the crushing of the grapes, and John worked now at one task and now at another. It was a pretty scene, and rendered more gay by the songs of the women and girls as they worked, and the burst of merry laughter which at times arose.

It lasted four days, by which time the last bunch, save those on a few vines preserved for eating, was picked and crushed, and the vats in the cellar, sunk underground for coolness, were full to the brim. Simon was much pleased with the result, and declared that never in his memory had the vine and fig harvest turned out more abundant. The corn had long before been gathered, and there remained now only the olives, but it would be some little time yet before these were fit to be gathered and their oil extracted, for they were allowed to hang on the trees until ready to drip. The last basket of grapes was brought in with much ceremony, the gatherers forming a little procession and singing a thanksgiving hymn as they walked; the evening meal was more bounteous even than usual, and all who helped carried away with them substantial proofs of Simon's thankfulness and satisfaction.

For the next few days Simon and his men and Martha's maids lent their assistance in getting in the vintage of their neighbors, for each family had its patch of ground and grew sufficient grapes and fruits for its own needs. Those in the village brought their grapes to a vat which they had in common, the measures of the grapes being counted as they were put in, and the wine afterward divided in like proportion; for wine to be good must be made in considerable quantities.

And now there was a time little to do on the farm. Simon superintended the men who were plowing up the corn stubbles ready for the sowing in the spring, sometimes putting his hand to the plow and driving the oxen. Isaac and his son worked in the vineyard and garden near the house, aided to some extent by John, who, however, was not yet called upon to take a man's share of the work of the farm, he having but lately finished his learning with the rabbi at the school in Hippos. Still he worked steadily every morning, and in the afternoon generally went out on the lake with the fishermen, with whom he was a great favorite. This was not to last long, for at seventeen he was to join his father regularly in the management of the farm, and indeed the Rabbi Solomon, who was a frequent guest, was of opinion that Simon gave the boy too much license, and that he ought already be doing man's work; but Simon when urged by him said:

"I know that at his age I was working hard, rabbi, but the lad has studied diligently and I have a good report of him, and I think it well that at his age the bow should be unbent somewhat; besides, who know what is before us! I will let the lad have as much pleasure from his life as he can. The storm is approaching; let him play while the sun shines."

Chapter Two

A STORM ON GALILEE

One day after the midday meal John said: "Mary, Raphael and his brother have taken the big boat and gone off with fish to Tiberias, and have told me that I can take the small boat if I will. Ask my mother to let you off your task and come out with me. It is a fortnight since we had a row on the lake together."

"I was beginning to think that you were never going to ask me again, John; and only I should punish myself, I would say you nay. There have you been going out fishing every afternoon, and leaving me at home to spin; and it is all the worse because your mother has said that the time is fast coming when I must give up wandering about like a child, and must behave myself like a woman. Oh, dear, how tiresome it will be when there will be nothing to do but to sit and spin, and to look after the house, and to walk instead of running when I am out, and to behave like grown-up person altogether."

"You are almost grown-up," John said; "you are taller now than any of the maids except Zillah; but I shall be sorry to see you growing staid and solemn. And it was selfish of me not to ask you to go out before, but I really did not think of it. The fishermen have been working hard to make up for the time lost during the harvest, and I have really been useful helping them with their nets, and this is the last year I shall have my liberty. But come, don't let's be wasting time in talking; run in and get my mother's permission, and then join me on the shore. I will take some grapes down for you to eat, for the sun is hot to-day and there is scarce a breath of wind on the water."

A few minutes later the young pair stood together by the side of the boat.

"Your mother made all sorts of objections," Mary said, laughing; "and I do think she won't let me come again. I don't think she would have done it to-day if Miriam had not stood up for me and said that I was but a child though I was so tall, and that, as you are very soon going to work with your father, she thought that it was no use in making the change before that."

"What nonsense it all is!" John said. "Besides, you know it is arranged that in a few months we are to be betrothed according to the wish of your parents and mine. It would have been done long ago only my father and mother do not approve of young betrothals, and think it better to wait to see if the young ones like each other; and I think that it is quite right, too, in most cases' only, of course, living here as you have done for the last three years, since your father and mother died, there was no fear of our not liking each other."

"Well, you see," Mary said as she sat in the stern of the boat while John rowed it quietly along, "it might have been just the other way: when people don't see anything of each other till they are betrothed by their parents, they can't dislike each other very much; whereas when they get to know each other, if they are disagreeable they might get to almost hate each other."

"Yes, there is something in that," John agreed. "Of course, in our case it is all right, because we do like each other we couldn't have liked each other more, I think, if we had been brother and sister; but it seems to me that sometimes it must be horrid when a boy is told by his parents that he is to be betrothed to a girl he has never seen. You see, it isn't as if it were for a short time, but for all one's life. It must be awful!"

"Awful!" Mary agreed heartily, "but of course it would have to be done."

"Of course," John said, the possibility of a lad refusing to obey his parents' commands not even occurring to him "Still, it doesn't seem to me quite right that one should have no choice in so important a matter. Of course when one's got a father and mother like mine, who would be sure to think only of making me happy, and not of the amount of dowry or anything of that sort, it would be all right; but with some parents it would be dreadful."

For some time not a word was spoken, both of them meditating over the unpleasantness of being forced to marry some one they disliked. Then, finding the subject too difficult for them, they began to talk about other things, stopping sometimes to see the fishermen haul up their nets, for there were a number of boats out on the lake. They rowed down as far as Tiberias, and there John ceased rowing, and they sat chatting over the wealth and beauty of that city, which John had often visited with his father, but which Mary had never entered. Then John turned the head of the boat up the lake and again began to row, but scarcely had he dipped his oar into the water when he exclaimed:

"Look that that black cloud rising at the other end of the lake! Why did you not tell me, Mary?"

"How stupid of me," she exclaimed, "not to have kept my eyes open!"

He bent to his oars and made the boat move through the water at a very different rate to that at which she had before traveled.

"Most of the boats have gone," Mary said presently, "and the rest are all rowing to the shore, and the clouds are coming up very fast," she added looking around.

"We are going to have a storm," John said, "it will be upon us long before we get back. I shall make for the shore, Mary. We must leave the boat there and take shelter for awhile, and then walk home. It will not be more than four miles to walk."

But though he spoke cheerfully, John knew enough of the sudden storms that bursts upon the Sea of Galilee to be aware that long before he could cross the mile and a half of water which separated them from the eastern shore the storm would be upon them; and indeed they were not more than half-way when it burst.

The sky was already covered with black clouds; a great darkness gathered round them; then came a heavy downpour of rain; and then with a sudden burst the wind smote them. It was useless now to try to row, for the oars would have been twisted from his hands in a moment; and John took the helm, and told Mary to lie down in the bottom of the boat. He had already turned the boat's head up the lake, the direction in which the storm was traveling.

The boat sprang forward as if it had received a blow when the gale struck it. John had more than once been out on the lake with the fishermen when sudden storms had come up, and knew what was best to be done. When he had laid in his oars he had put them so that the blades stood partly up above the bow and caught the wind somewhat, and he himself crouched down in the bottom, with his head below the gunwale and his hand on the tiller; so that the tendency of the boat was to drive straight before the wind. With a strong crew he knew that he could have rowed obliquely toward the sore, but alone his strength could have done nothing to keep the heavy boat off her course.

The sea rose as if by magic, and the spray was soon dashing over them; each wave, as it followed the boat, rising higher and higher. The shores were no longer visible, and the crests of the waves seemed to gleam with a pallid light in the darkness which surrounded them. John sat quietly in the bottom of the boat, with one hand on the tiller and the other hand around Mary, who was crouched up against him. She had made no cry or exclamation from the moment the gale struck them.

"Are we getting near the shore?" she asked at last.

"No, Mary; we are running straight before the wind, which is blowing right up the lake. There is nothing to be done but to keep straight before it."

Mary had seen many storms on the lake, and knew into what a fury its waters were lashed in a tempest such as was now upon them.

"We are in God's hands, John," she said with the quiet resignation of her race. "He can save us if he will; let us pray to him."

John nodded, and for a few minutes no word was spoken.

"Can I do anything?" Mary asked presently as a wave struck the stern and threw a mass of water into the boat.

"Yes," John replied; "take that earthen pot and bail out the water."

John had no great hope that they would live through the gale, but he thought it better for the girl to be kept busily employed. She bailed steadily; but fast as she worked the water came in faster, for each wave, as it swept past them, broke on board. So rapidly were they traveling that John had the greatest difficulty in keeping the boat from broaching to, in which case the flowing waves would have filled or overturned her.

"I don't think it's any use, John," Mary said quietly as a great wave broke on board, pouring in as much water in a second as she could have bailed out in ten minutes.

"No use, dear. Sit quietly by me; but first pull those oars aft; now tie them together with that piece of rope. Now when the boat goes down keep tight hold of them. Cut off another piece of rope and give it me. When we are in the water I will fasten you to the oars. They will keep you afloat easily enough. I will keep close to you. You know I am a good swimmer; and whenever I feel tired I can rest my hands on the oars too. Keep up your courage and keep as quiet as you can. These sudden storms seldom last long, and my father will be sure to get the boats out as soon as he can to look for us."

John spoke cheerfully, but he had no great hope of their being able to live in so rough a sea. Mary had still less, but she quietly carried out John's instruction. The boat was half-filled of water now and rose but heavily upon the waves. John raised himself and looked round, in hopes that he wind might unnoticed have shifted a little and blown them toward shore. As he glanced around him he gave a shout. Following almost in their tracks and some fifty yards away, was a large galley running before the wind, with a rag of sail set on its mast.

"We are saved, Mary!" he exclaimed. "Here is a galley close to us."

He shouted loudly, though he knew that his voice could not be heard many yards away on the teen of the gale; but almost directly he saw two or three men stand up in the bow of the galley. One was pointing toward them, and he saw that they were seen. In another minute the galley came sweeping along close to the boat. A dozen figures appeared over her side, and two or three ropes were thrown. John caught one, twisted it rapidly round Mary's body and his own, knotted it, and, taking her in his arms, jumped overboard. Another minute they were drawn alongside the galley and pulled on board. As soon as the ropes were unfastened John rose to his feet, but Mary lay insensible on the deck.

"Carry the damsel into the cabin," a man who was evidently in authority said. "She has fainted, but will soon come around. I will see to her myself."

The suddenness of the rescue, the plunge in the water, and the sudden revulsion of his feelings, affected John so much that it was two or three minutes before he could speak.

"Come along with me, lad," one of the sailors said, laying his hand on his shoulder. "Some dry clothes and a draught of wine will set you all right again; but you have had a narrow escape of it. That boat of yours was pretty nearly water-logged, and in another five minutes we should have been too late."

John hastily changed his clothes in the forecastle, took a draught of wine, and then hurried back again toward the aft cabin. Just as he reached it the man who had ordered Mary to be carried in came out.

"The damsel has opened her eyes," he said, "and you need not be uneasy about her. I have given her some woolen cloths, and bade her take off her wet garments and wrap herself in them. Why did you not make for the shore before the tempest broke' It was foolish of you indeed to be out on the lake when any one could see that this gale was coming."

"I was rowing down and did not notice it until I turned," John replied. "I was making for the shore when the gale struck her."

"It was well for you that I noticed you. I was myself thinking of making for the shore, although in so large and well-manned a craft as this there is little fear upon the lake. It is not like the Great Sea, where I myself have seen a large ship as helpless before the waves as that small boat we picked you from. I had just set out from Tiberias when I marked the storm coming up; but my business was urgent, and, moreover, I marked your little boat and saw that you were not likely to gain the shore, so I bade the helmsman keep his eye on you until the darkness fell upon us, and then to follow straight in your wake, for you could but run before the wind; and well he did it, for when we first caught sight of you you were right ahead of us."

The speaker was a man of about thirty years of age, tall, and with a certain air of command.

"I thank you, indeed, sir," John said, "for saving my life and that of my cousin Mary, the daughter of my father's brother. Truly my father and mother will be grateful to you for having saved us, for I am their only son. Whom are they to thank for our rescue.?"

"I am Joseph, the son of Matthias, to whom the Jews have entrusted the governorship of this province."

"Josephus!" John exclaimed in a tone of surprise and reverence.

"So men call me," Josephus replied with a smile.

It was indeed the governor. Flavius Josephus, as the Romans afterward called him, came of a noble Jewish family, his father, Matthias, belonging to the highest of the twenty-four classes into which the sacerdotal families were divided. Matthias was eminent for his attainments and piety, and had been one of the leading men in Jerusalem. From his youth Josephus had carefully prepared himself for public life, mastering the doctrines of the three leading sects among the Jews: the Pharisees, Sadducees, and Essenes -- and having spent three years in the desert with Banus the Ascetic. The fact that at only twenty-six years of age he had gone as the leader of a deputation to Rome on behalf of some priests sent there by Felix shows that he was early looked upon as a conspicuous person among the Jews, and he was but thirty when he was intrusted with the important position of governor of Galilee.

Contrary to the custom of the times, he had sought to make no gain from his position. He accepted neither presents nor bribes, but devoted himself entirely to ameliorating the condition of the people, and in repressing the turbulence of the lower classes of the great towns, and of the robber chieftains who, like John of Gischala, took advantage of the authority caused by the successful rising against the Romans to plunder and tyrannize over the people.

The expression of the face of Josephus was lofty and at the same time gentle. His temper was singularly equable, and whatever the circumstances he never gave way to anger, but kept his passions well under control. His address was soft and winning, and he had the art of attracting respect and friendship from all who came in contact with him. Poppæa, the wife of Nero, had received him with much favor; and bravely as he fought against them, Vespasian and Titus were afterward as much attached to him as were the Jews of Galilee. There can be no doubt that had he been otherwise placed than as one of a people on the verge of destruction, Josephus would have been one of the great figures of history.

John had been accustomed to hear his father and his friends speak in tones of such admiration for Josephus as the man who was regarded not only as the benefactor of the Jews of Galilee, but as the leader and mainstay of the nation, that he has long ardently desired to see him; and to find that he had now been rescued from death by him, and that he was now talking to him face to face, filled him with confusion.

"You are a brave lad," Josephus said, "for you kept your head well in a time when older men might have lost their presence of mind. You must have kept your boat dead before the wind, and you were quick and ready in seizing the rope and knotting it round yourself and the maid with you. I feared you might try and fasten it to the boat. If you had, full of water as she was, and fast as we were sailing before the wind, the rope would barely have stood the strain."

"The clouds are breaking," the captain of the boat said, coming up to Josephus, "and I think that we are past the worst of the gale. And well it is so, for even in so stanch a craft there is much peril in such a sea as this."

The vessel, although one of the largest on the lake, was indeed pitching and rolling very heavily, but she was light and buoyant, and each time that she plunged bows under, as the following waves lifted her stern high in the air, she rose lightly again, and scarce a drop fell into her deep waist, the lofty erections fore and aft throwing off the water.

"Where do you belong, my lad?" Josephus asked. "I fear that it is impossible for us to put you ashore until we reach Capernaum; but once there, I will see that you are provided with means to take you home."

"Our farm lies three miles above Hippos."

"That is unfortunate," Josephus said, "since it lies on the opposite side of the lake to Capernaum. However, we shall see. If the storm goes down rapidly I may be able to get a fishing-boat to take you across this evening, for your parents will be in sore trouble. If not, you must wait till early morning."

In another hour they reached Capernaum. The wind had by this time greatly abated, although the sea still ran high. The ship was soon alongside a landing-jetty which ran out a considerable distance, and formed a breakwater protecting the shipping from the heavy sea which broke there when the wind was, as at present, from the south. Mary came out from the cabin, as the vessel entered the harbor, wrapped up from head to food in the woolen cloths with which she had been furnished. John sprang to her side.

"Are you quite well, Mary?"

"Quite well," she said, "only very ashamed of having fainted, and very uncomfortable in these wrappings. But, oh! John, how thankful we ought to be to God for having sent this ship to our aid when all seemed lost!"

"We ought indeed, Mary. I have been thanking him as I have been standing here watching the waves, and I am sure you have been doing the same in the cabin."

"Yes, indeed, John. But what am I to do now' I do not like going on shore like this, and the officer told me I was on no account to put on my wet clothes."

"Do you know, it is Josephus himself, Mary think of that the great Josephus, who has saved us! He marked our boat before the storm broke and seeing that we could not reach the shore, had his vessel steered so as to overtake us."

Mary was too surprised to utter more than an exclamation. The thought that the man who had been talking so kindly and pleasantly to her was the great leader of whom she had heard so much quite took away her breath.

At that moment Josephus himself came up.

"I am glad to see you have got your color again, maiden," he said. "I am just going to land. Do you with your cousin remain on board here. I will send a woman down with some attire for you. She will conduct you both to the house where I shall be staying. The sea is going down, and the captain tells me that he thinks in another three or four hours I shall be able to get a boat to send you across to your home. It will be late, but you will not mind that, for they are sure not to retire to rest at home, but to be up all night searching for you."

A crowd assembled on the jetty, for Josephus was expected, and the violent storm had excited the fears of all for his safety, and the leading inhabitants had all flocked down to welcome him when his vessel was seen approaching.

"Isn't he kind and good?" Mary said enthusiastically as she watched the greeting which he received as he landed. "He talked to me just as if he had been of my own family."

"He is grand!" John agreed with equal enthusiasm. "He is just what I pictured to myself that a great leader would be, such as Joshua, or Gideon, or the Prince of the Maccabees."

"Yes, but more gentle, John."

"Brave men should always be gentle," John said positively.

"They ought to be, perhaps," Mary agreed, "but I don't think they are." They chatted then about the storm and the anxiety which they would be feeling at home until an officer, accompanied by a woman carrying attire for Mary, came on board.

Mary soon came out of the cabin dressed, and the officer conducted them to the house which had been placed at the disposal of Josephus. The woman led them up to a room where a meal has been prepared for them.

"Josephus is in council with the elders," she said; "he bade me see that you had all that you required. He has arranged that a bark shall start with you as soon as the sea goes down, but if by eight o'clock it is still too rough, I shall take the maiden home to my house to sleep, and they will arouse you as soon as it is safe to put out, whatever the hour may be, as your friends will be in great anxiety concerning you."

The sun had already set, and just as they finished their meal the man belonging to the boat came to say that it would be midnight before he could put out.

Mary then went over with the woman, and John lay down on some mats to sleep until it was time to start. He slept soundly until he was aroused by the entry of some one with lights. He started to his feet, and found that it was Josephus himself with an attendant.

"I had not forgotten you," he said; "but I have been until now in council. It is close upon midnight, and the boat is in readiness I have sent to fetch the damsel, and have bidden them take plenty of warm wraps so that the night air may do her no harm."

Mary soon arrived, and Josephus himself went down with them to the shore and saw them on board the boat, which was a large one with eight rowers. The wind had died away to a gentle breeze, and the sea had gone down greatly. The moon was up and the stars shining brightly. Josephus chatted kindly to John as they made their way to the shore.

"Tell your father," he said, "that I hope he will come over to see me ere long, and that I shall bear you in mind. The time is coming when every Jew who can bear arms will be needed in the service of his country, and if your father consents I will place you near my person for I have seen that you are brave and cool in danger, and you will have plenty of opportunities of winning advancement."

With many thanks for his kindness John and Mary took their places in the stern of the boat. Mary enveloped herself in the wraps that had been prepared for her, for the nights were chilly. Then the sail was hoisted, and the boat sailed away from the land. The wind had shifted round somewhat to the west, and they were able to lay their course across toward Hippos, but their progress was slow, and the master bade the crew out their oars and aid the sail.

In three hours they neared the land, John pointing out the exact position of the village, which was plainly enough marked out by a great fire blazing on the shore. As they approached it they could see several figures, and presently there came a shout which John recognized as that of Isaac.

"Any news?"

"Here we are, Isaac, safe and well."

There was a confused sound of shouts and cries of pleasure. In a few minutes the boat grated on the shallow shore. The moment she did so John leaped out over the bow and waded ashore, and was at once clasped in his mother's arms, while one of the fishermen carried Mary to land. She received from Martha a full share of her caresses, for she loved the girl almost as dearly as she did her son. Then Miriam and the maids embraced and kissed her, while Isaac folded John in his arms.

"The God of Israel be thanked and praised, my children!" Mary exclaimed. "He has brought you back to us as from the dead, for we never thought to see you again. Some of the fishermen returned and told us that they saw your boat far on the lake before the storm burst, and none held out hope that you could have weathered such a storm."

"Where is father?" John asked.

"He is out on the lake, as are all the fishermen of their village, searching for you. That reminds me, Isaac set fire to the other piles of wood that we have prepared. If one of the boats returned with any sure news of you we were to light them to call the others back: one fire if the news was bad, tow if it was good; but we hardly even dared to hope that the second would be required."

A brand from the fire was soon applied to the other piles, and the three fires shone out across the lake with the good news. In a quarter of an hour a boat was seen approaching, and soon came a shout:

"Is all well?"

"All is well," John shouted in reply, and soon he was clasped in his father's arms.

The other boats came in one by one, the last to arrive towing in the boat, which had been found bottom upward far up the lake, its discovery destroying the last hope of its late occupants being found alive. As soon as Simon landed the party returned to the house. Miriam and the maids hurried to prepare a meal, of which all were sorely in need, for no food had been eaten since the gale burst on the lake, while their three hours in the boat had again sharpened the appetite of John and Mary. A quantity of food was cooked and a skin of old wine brought up from the cellar, and Isaac remained down on the shore to bid all who had been engaged in the search come up and feast as soon as they landed.

John related to his parents the adventure which had befallen them, and they wondered greatly at the narrowness of their deliverance. When the feasting was over, Simon called all together, and solemnly returned thanks to God for the mercies which he had given them. It was broad daylight before all sought their beds for a few hours before beginning the work of the day.

A week later Josephus himself came to Hippos, bringing with him two nobles who had fled from King Agrippa and sought refuge with him; he had received them hospitably, and had allotted a home to them at Tarichea, where he principally dwelt. He had just before had another narrow escape, for six hundred armed men (robbers and others) had assembled round his house, charging him with keeping some spoils which had been taken by a party of men of that town from the wife of Ptolemy, King Agrippa's procurator, instead of dividing them among the people.

For a time he pacified them by telling them that this money was destined for strengthening the walls of their town and for walling other towns at present undefended, but the leaders of the evil-doers were determined to set his house on fire and slay him. He had but twenty armed men with him. Closing the doors he went to an upper room and told the robbers to send in one of their number to receive the money. Directly he entered the door was closed. One of his hands was cut off and hung round his neck, and he was then turned out again. Believing that Josephus would not have ventured to act so boldly had he not had a large body of armed men with him, the crowd were seized with panic and fled to their homes.

After this the enemies of Josephus persuaded the people that the nobles he had sheltered were wizards, and demanded that they should be given up to be slain, unless they would change religion to that of the Jews. Josephus tried to argue them out of their belief, saying that there were no such things as wizards, and if the Romans had wizards who could work them wrong they would not need to send an army to fight against them; but as the people still clamored he got the men privately on board a ship, and sailed across the lake with them to Hippos, where he dismissed them with many presents.

As soon as the news came that Josephus had come to Hippos, Simon set out with Martha, John, and Mary to see him. Josephus received them kindly, and would permit no thanks for what he had done.

"Your son is a brave youth," he said to Simon, "and I would gladly have him near me if you would like to have it so. This is the time when there are greater things than planting vineyards and gathering in harvests to be done, and there is a need for brave and faithful men. If, then, you and your wife will give the lad to me I will see to him and keep him near me. I have need of faithful men with me, for my enemies are ever trying to slay me. If all goes well with the land he will have a good opportunity to rise to honor. What say you? Do not give an answer hastily, but think it over among yourselves, and if you agree to my proposal send him across the lake to me."

"It need no thought, sir," Simon said. "I know well that there are more urgent things now than sowing and reaping, and that much trouble and peril threaten the land. Right glad am I that my son should serve one who is the hope of Israel, and his mother will not grudge him for such service. As to advancement, I wish nothing better than that he should till the land of his fathers; but none can say what the Lord hath in store for us, or whether strangers may not reap what I have sown. Thus, then, the wisdom which he will gain in being with you is likely to be a far better inheritance than any I can give him. What say you, Martha?"

"I say as you do, Simon. It will grieve me to part with him, but I know that such an offer as that which my Lord Josephus makes is greatly for his good. Moreover, the manner in which he was saved from death seems to show that the Lord has something for his hand to do and that his path is specially marked out for him. To refuse to let him go would be to commit the sin of withstanding God' therefore, my lord, I willingly give up my son to follow you."

"I think that you have decided wisely," Josephus said. "I tarry here for tonight, and tomorrow cross to Tiberias, therefore let him be here by noon."

Mary was the most silent of the party on the way home. Simon and his wife felt convinced the decision they had made was a wise one, and although they were not ambitious, they yet felt that the offer of Josephus was a most advantageous one, and opened a career of honor to their son.

John himself was in a state of the highest delight. To be about the person of Josephus seemed to him the greatest honor and happiness. It opened the way to the performance of great actions which would bring honor to his father's name; and although he had been hitherto prepared to settle down to the life of a cultivator of the soil, he had had his yearnings for one of more excitement and adventure, and these were now likely to be gratified to the fullest. Mary, however, felt the approaching loss of her friend and playmate greatly, though even she was not insensible to the honor which the offer of Josephus conferred upon him.

"You don't seem glad of my good fortune, Mary," John said as, after they returned home, they strolled together as usual down to the edge of the lake.

"It may be your good fortune, but it's not mine," the girl said pettishly. "It will be very dull here without you. I know what it will be. Your mother will always be full of anxiety, and will be fretting whenever we get news of any disturbances, and that is often enough, for there seem to be disturbances continually. Your father will go about silently, Miriam will be sharper than usual with the maids, and everything will go wrong. I can't see why you couldn't have said that in a year or two you would go with the governor, but that at present you thought you had better stop with your own people."

"A nice milksop he would have thought me!" John laughed. "No. If he thought I was man enough to do him service it would have been a nice thing for me to say that I thought I was too young. Besides, Mary, after all it is your good fortune as well as mine, for is it not settled that you are to share it' Josephus is all-powerful, and if I please him and do my duty he can, in time, raise me to a position of great honor. I may even come to be the governor of a town, or a captain over troops, or a councilor!"

"No, no!" Mary laughed; "not a councilor, John, a governor perhaps, and a captain perhaps, but never, I should say, a councilor." John laughed good-temperedly.

"Well, Mary, then you shall look forward to be the wife of a governor or captain, but you see I might even fill the place of a councilor with credit, because I could always come to you for advice before I gave an opinion, then I should be sure to be right. But, seriously, Mary, I do think it great honor to have had such an offer made me by the governor."

"Seriously, so do I, John, though I wish in my heart he had not made it. I had looked forward to living here all my life, just as your mother has done, and now there will be nothing fixed to look forward to. Besides, where there is honor there is danger. There seems to be always tumults, always conspiracies, and then, as your father says, above all, there are the Romans to be reckoned with; and, of course, if you are near Josephus you run a risk, going wherever he does."

"I shall never be in greater risk, Mary, than we were together on the lake the other day. God helped us then and brought us through it, and I have faith that he will do so again. It may be that I am meant to do something useful before I die. At any rate, when the Romans come every one will have to fight, so I shall be in no greater danger than any one else.'"

"I know, John; and I am not speaking quite in earnest. I am sorry you are going, that is only natural; but I am proud that you are to be near our great leader, and I believe that our God will be your shield and protector. And now we had better go in. Your father will doubtless have much to say to you this evening, and your mother will grudge every minute you are out of her sight."

Chapter Three

THE REVOLT AGAINST ROME

That evening the Rabbi Solomon Ben Manasseh came in, and was informed of the offer which Josephus had made.

"You are present, rabbi," Simon said, "at the events which took place in Jerusalem, and at the defeat of Cestius. John has been asking me to tell him more about these matters; for now that he is to be with the governor it is well that he should be well acquainted with public affairs."

"I will willingly tell him the history, for, as you say, it is right that the young man should be well acquainted with the public events and the state of parties, and though the story must be somewhat long, I will try and not make it tedious. The first tumult broke out in Cæsarea, and began by frays between our people and the Syrian Greeks. Felix, the governor, took the part of the Greeks, and many of our people were killed and more plundered. When Felix was recalled to Rome we sent a deputation there with charges against him; but the Greeks, by means of bribery, obtained a decree against us, depriving the Jews of Cæsarea of rights of equal citizenship. From this constant troubles arouse; but outside Cæsarea Festus kept all quiet, putting down robbers as well as impostors who led the people astray.

"Then there came trouble in Jerusalem. King Agrippa's palace stood on Mount Zion, looking toward the temple, and he built a lofty story from whose platform he could command a view of the courts of the Temple, and watch the sacrifices. Our people resented this impious intrusion, and built a high wall to cut off the view. Agrippa demanded its destruction on the ground that it intercepted the view of the Roman guard. We appealed to Nero, and sent to him a deputation headed by Ismael, the high-priest, and Hilkiah, the treasurer. They obtained an order for the wall to be allowed to stand; but Ismael and Hilkiah were detained in Rome. Agrippa thereupon appointed another high-priest, Joseph, but soon afterward nominated Annas in his place.

"When Festus, the Roman governor, was away Annas put to death many of the sect called Christians to gratify the Sadducees. The people were indignant, for these men had done no harm, and Agrippa deprived him of the priesthood and appointed Jesus, son of Damnai. Then, unhappily, Festus, who was a just and good governor, died, and Albinus succeeded him. He was a man greedy of money, and ready to do anything for gain; he took bribes from robbers and encouraged rather than repressed evil-doers. There was open war in the streets between the followers of various chief robbers. Albinius opened the prisons and filled the city with malefactors, and at the completion of the works at the Temple eighteen thousand workmen were discharged, and thus the city was filled with men ready to sell their services to the highest bidder.

"Albinus was succeeded by Gessius Florus, who was even worse than Albinus. This man was a great friend of Cestius Gallus, who commanded the Roman troops in Syria, and who therefore scoffed at the complaints of the people against Florus. At this time strange prodigies appeared in Rome. A sword of fire hung above the city for a whole year. The inner gate of the Temple, which required twenty men to move it, opened by itself, chariots and armed squadrons were seen in the heavens, and, worse than all, the priests in the Temple heard a great movement and a sound of many voices, which said, "Let us depart hence!"

"So things went on in Jerusalem until the old feud at Cæsarea broke out afresh. The trouble this time began about one of our synagogues. The land around it belonged to the Greek, and for this our people offered a high price. The heathen who owned it refused, and to annoy us raised mean houses round the synagogue. The Jewish youths interrupted the workmen, and the wealthier of the community, headed by John, a publican, subscribed eight talents and sent them to Florus as a bribe, that he might order the building to be stopped.

"Forus took the money and made many promises; but the evil man desired that a revolt should place in order that he might gain great plunder. So he went away from Cæsarea and did nothing, and a great tumult arose between the heathen and our people. In this we were worsted and went away from the city, while John, with twelve of the highest rank, went to Samaria to lay the matter before Florus, who threw them into prison, doubtless the more to excite the people, and at the same time sent to Jerusalem and demanded seventeen talents from the treasure of the Temple.

"The people burst into loud outcries, and Florus advanced upon the city with all his force. But we knew that we could not oppose the Romans, and so received Florus on his arrival with acclamations. But this did not suit the tyrant. The next morning he ordered his troops to plunder the upper market and put to death all they met. The soldiers obeyed, and slew thirty-six hundred men, women, and children.

"You may imagine, John, the feelings of grief and rage which filled every heart. The next day the multitude assembled in the market-place, wailing for the dead and cursing Florus. But the principal men of the city, with the priests, tore their robes, and went among them praying them to disperse and not to provoke the anger of the governor. The people obeyed their voices and went quietly home.

"But Florus was not content that matters should end so. He sent for the priests and leaders and commanded them to go forth and receive with acclamations of welcome two cohorts of troops who were advancing from Cæsarea. The priests called the people together in the Temple, and with difficulty persuaded them to obey the order. The troops, having orders from Florus, fell upon the people and trampled them down, and driving the multitude before them entered the city, and at the same time Florus sallied out from his palace with his troops, and both parties pressed forward to gain the castle of Antonia, whose possession would lay the

Temple open to them, and enable Florus to gain the sacred treasures deposited there. But as soon as the people perceived their object they ran together in such vast crowds that the Roman soldiers could not cut their way through the mass which blocked up the streets, while the more active men, going up on to roofs, hurled down stones and missiles upon the troops.

"What a scene was that, John! I was on the portico near Antonia and saw it all. It was terrible to hear the shouts of the soldiers as they strove to hew their way through the defenseless people, the war-cries of our own youths, the shrieks and wailings of the women. While the Romans were still striving our people broke down the galleries connecting Antonia with the Temple, and Florus, seeing that he could not carry out his objective, ordered his troops to retire to their quarters, and calling the chief priests and the rulers proposed to leave the city, leaving behind min one cohort to preserve the peace.

"As soon as he had done so he sent to Cestius Gallus lying accounts of the tumults, laying all the blame upon us, while we and Bernice, the sister of King Agrippa, who had tried in vain to obtain mercy for the people from Florus, sent complaints against him. Cestius was moving to Jerusalem, to inquire into the matter, as he said, but really to restore Florus, when fortunately King Agrippa arrived from Egypt.

"While he was yet seven miles from the city a procession of the people met him, headed by the women whose husbands had been slain; these, with cries and wailings called on Agrippa for protection, and related to a centurion, whom Cestius had sent forward and who met Agrippa on the way, the cruelty of Florus. When the king and the centurion arrived in the city they were taken to the market-place and shown the houses where the inhabitants had been massacred.

"Agrippa called the people together, and taking his seat on the lofty dais, with Bernice by his side, harangued them. He assured them that when the emperor heard what had been done he would send a better governor to them in the place of Florus. He told them that it was vain to hope for independence, for that the Romans had conquered all the nations in the world, and that the Jews could not contend against them, and that war would bring about the destruction of the city and the Temple.

"The people exclaimed they had taken up arms, not against the Romans, but against Florus. Agrippa urged us to pay our tribute and repair the galleries. This was willingly done. We sent out leading men to collect the arrears of tribute, and these soon brought in forty talents. All was going well until Agrippa tried to persuade us to receive Florus till the emperor should send another governor. At the thought of the return of Florus a mad rage seized the people. They poured abuse upon Agrippa, threw stones at him, and ordered him to leave the city. This he did, and retired to his own kingdom.

"The upper class, and all those who possessed wisdom enough to know how great was the power of Rome, still strove for peace. But the people were beyond control. They seized the fortress of Masada, a very strong place near the Dead Sea, and put the Roman garrison to the sword. But what was even worse, Eleazar, son of Ananias, the chief priest, persuaded the priests to reject the offerings regularly made in the name of the emperor to the God of the Hebrews, and to make a regulation that from that time no foreigner should be allowed to sacrifice in the Temple. The chief priests, with the heads of the Pharisees, addressed the people in the quadrangle of the Temple before the eastern gate. I myself was one of those who spoke. We told them that the Temple had long benefited by the splendid gifts of strangers, and that it was not only inhospitable, but impious to preclude them from offering victims and worshipping God there.

"We, who were learned in the law, showed them that it was an ancient and immemorial usage to receive the offerings of strangers, and that this refusal to accept the Roman gifts was nothing short of a declaration of war. But all we could do or say availed nothing. The influence of Eleazar was too great. A madness had seized the people, and they rejected all our words; but the party of peace made one more effort. They sent a deputation, headed by Simon, son of Ananias, to Florus, and another to Agrippa, praying them to march upon Jerusalem and reassert their authority before it was too late. Florus made no reply, for things were going just as he wished; but Agrippa, anxious to preserve the city, sent three thousand horsemen, commanded by Darius and Philip. When these troops arrived the party of peace took possession of the upper city, while Eleazar and the war party held the Temple.

"For a week fighting went on between the two parties. Then at the festival of the Wood Carrying great numbers of the poorer people were allowed by the party of the chief priest to pass through their lines and go as usual to the Temple. When there these joined the party of Eleazar, and a great attack was made on the upper city. The troops of Darius and Philip gave way. The house of Ananias, the high-priest, and the palaces of Agrippa and Bernice were burned, and also the public archives. Here all the bonds of the debtors were registered, and thus at one blow the power of the rich over the poor was destroyed. Ananias himself and a few others escaped into the upper towers of the palace, which they held.

"The next day Eleazar's party attacked the fortress of Antonia, which was feebly garrisoned, and after two days' fighting captured it and slew the garrison. Manahem, the son of Judas the Zealot, arrived two days later, while the people were besieging the palace. He was accepted as general by them, and took charge of the siege. Having mined under one of the towers they brought it to the ground, and the garrison asked for terms. Free passage was granted to the troops of Agrippa and the Jews, but none was granted to the Roman soldiers, who were few in number and retreated to the three great towers, Hippicus, Phasaelus, and Mariamne.

"The palace was entered and Ananias and Hezekiah his brother, were found in hiding and put to death. Manahem now assumed the state of a king; but Eleazar, unwilling that, after having led the enterprise, the fruits should be gathered by another, stirred up the people against him, and he was slain. The three towers were now besieged, and Metilius, the Roman commander, finding he could no longer hold out, agreed to surrender, on the condition that his men should deliver up their arms and be allowed to march away unharmed.

"The terms were accepted and ratified, but as soon as the Roman soldiers marched out and laid down their arms Eleazar and his followers fell upon them and slew them, Metilius himself being alone spared.

"After this terrible massacre a sadness fell on the city; all felt that there was no longer any hope of making condition with Rome. We had placed ourselves beyond the pale of forgiveness. It was war to death with Rome. Up to this time, as I have told you, I was one of those who had labored to maintain peace. I had fought in the palace by the side of Ananias, and had left it only when the troops, and we of their party, were permitted to march out when it surrendered; but from this time I took another part. All hope of peace, of concessions, or of conditions was at an end. There remained nothing now but to fight; and as the vengeance of Rome would fall on the whole Jewish people, it was for the whole Jewish People to unite in the struggle for existence.

"On the very day and hour in which the Romans were put to death retribution began to fall upon the nation, for the Greeks of Cæsarea rose suddenly and massacred the Jews. Twenty thousand were slain in a single day. The news of these two massacres drove the whole people to madness. They rose throughout the land, laid waste the country all round the cities of Syria—Philadelphia, Sebonitis, Gerasa, Pella, and Scythopolis—and burned and destroyed many places.

"The Syrians in turn fell upon the Jewish inhabitants of all their towns, and a frightful carnage everywhere took place. Then our people made an inroad into the domains of Scythopolis, but though the Jewish inhabitants there joined the Syrians in defending their territory, the Syrians doubted their fidelity, and falling upon them in the night, slew them all and seized their property. Thirteen thousand perished here. In many other cities the same things were done; in Ascalon twenty-five hundred were put to the sword; in Ptolemais two thousand were killed. The land was deluged with blood, and despair fell upon all.

"Even in Alexandria our countrymen suffered. Breaking out into a quarrel with the Greeks, a tumult arose, and Tiberias Alexander, the governor, by faith a Jew, tried to pacify matters, but the madness which had seized the people here had fallen also upon the Jews of Alexandria.

They heaped abuse upon Alexander, who was forced to send the troops against them. The Jews fought, but vainly, and fifty thousand men, women, and children fell.

"While blood was flowing over the land, Cetius Gallus the prefect was preparing for invasion. He had with him the Twelfth Legion, forty-two hundred strong; two thousand picked men taken from the other legions; six cohorts of foot, about twenty-five hundred; and four troops of horse, twelve hundred. Of allies he had from Antonichus two thousand horse and three thousand foot; Sohemus joined him with four thousand men, a third of whom were horse, the rest archers. Thus he had ten thousand Roman troops and thirteen thousand allies, besides many volunteers who joined him from the Syrian cities. After burning and pillaging Zebulon, and wasting the district, Cestius returned to Ptolemais, and then advanced to Cæsarea.

"He sent forward a part of his army to Joppa. The city was open and no resistance was offered; nevertheless the Romans slew all to the number of eighty-five hundred. The cities of Galilee opened their gates without resistance, and Cetius advanced against Jerusalem. When he arrived within six miles of the town the Jews poured out and fell upon them with such fury that if the horse and light troops had not made a circuit and fallen upon us in the rear, I believe we should have destroyed the whole army. But we were forced to fall back, having killed over five hundred.

"As the Romans moved forward, Simon, son of Gioras, with a band pressed them closely in rear, and slew many and carried off numbers of their beasts of burden. Agrippa now tried once more to make peace, and sent a deputation to persuade us to surrender, offering in the name of Cestius pardon for all that had passed; but Eleazar's party, fearing the people might listen to him, fell upon the deputation, slew some and drove the others back.

"Cestius advanced within a mile of Jerusalem, and after waiting three days in hopes that the Jews would surrender, and knowing that many of the chief persons were friendly to him, he advanced to the attack, took the suburb of Bezetha, and encamped opposite the palace in the upper city. The people discovered that Ananias and his friends had agreed to open the gates, and so slew them and threw the bodies over the wall. The Romans for five days attacked, and on the sixth Cestius with the flower of his army made an assault, but the people fought bravely, and disregarding the flights of arrows which the archers shot against them, held the walls and poured missiles of all kinds upon the enemy, until at last, just as it seemed to all that the Romans would succeed in mining the walls and firing the gates, Cestius called off his troops.

"Had he not done so he would speedily have taken the city, for the peace party were on the point of seizing one of the gates and opening it. I no longer belonged to this party, for it seemed to me that it was altogether too late now to make terms, nor could we expect that the Romans would keep to their conditions after we had set them the example of breaking faith. Cestius fell back to his camp, a mile distant, but he had no rest there. Exultant at seeing a retreat from their walls, all the people poured out and fell upon the Romans with fury.

"The next morning Cestius began to retreat, but we swarmed around him, pressing upon his rear and dashing down from the hills upon his flanks, giving him no rest. The heavy-armed Romans could do nothing against us, but marched steadily on, leaving numbers of dead behind them, till they reached their former camp at Gabao, six miles away.

"Here Cestius waited two days, but seeing how the hills around him swarmed with our people, who flocked in from all quarters, he gave word for a further retreat, killing all the beasts of burden and leaving all the baggage behind, and taking on only those animals which bore the arrows and engines of war. Then he marched down the valley toward Bethoron. The multitude felt now that their enemy was delivered into their hands. Was it not in Bethoron that Joshua had defeated the Canaanites while the sun stayed his course? Was it not here that Judas the Maccabean had routed the host of Nicanor? As soon as the Romans entered the defile the Jews rushed down upon them, sure of their prey.

"The Roman horse were powerless to act; the men of the legions could not climb the rocky sides, and from every point javelins, stones, and arrows were poured down upon them, and all would have been slain had not night come on and hidden them from us, and enabled them to reach Bethoron. What rejoicings were there not on the hills that night as we looked down on their camp there, and thought that in the morning they would be ours! Fires burned on every crest; hymns of praise and exulting cries arose everywhere in the darkness, but the watch was not kept strictly enough. Cestius left four hundred of his bravest men to mount guard and keep the fires alight, so that we might think that all his army was there, and then with the rest he stole away.

"In the morning we saw that the camp was well-nigh deserted; and furious at the escape of our foes, rushed down, slew the four hundred whom Cestius had left behind, and then set out in pursuit. But Cestius had many hours' start, and though we followed as far as Antipatris, we could not overtake him, and so returned with such rich spoil and all the Roman engines of war to Jerusalem, having, with some scarcely any loss, defeated a great Roman army and slain fifty-three hundred foot and three hundred and eighty horse.

"Such is the history of events which have brought about the present state of things. As you see, there is no hope of pardon or mercy from Rome. We have offended beyond forgiveness. But the madness against which I fought so hard at first is still upon the people. They provoked the power of Rome, and then by breaking the terms and massacring the Roman garrison, they went far beyond the first offense of insurrection. By the destruction of the army of Cestius they struck a heavy blow against the pride of the Romans. For generations no such misfortune had fallen upon their arms.

"What, then, would a sane person have done since? Surely they would have spent every moment in preparing themselves for the struggle. Every man should have been called to arms; the passes should have been all fortified, for it is among the hills that we can best cope with the heavy Roman troops; the cities best calculated for defense should have been strongly walled; preparations made for places of refuge among the mountains for the women and children; large depots of provisions gathered up in readiness for the strife.

"That we could ever in the long run hope to resist successfully the might of Rome was out of the question; but we might so sternly and valiantly have resisted as to be able to obtain fair terms on our submission. Instead of this men go on as if Rome had no existence, and we only show an energy in quarreling among ourselves. At bottom it would seem that the people rely upon our God doing great things for us, as he did when he smote the Assyrian army of Sennacherib; and such is my hope also, seeing that so far a wonderful success has attended us. And yet how can one expect the divine assistance in a war so begun and so conducted; for a people who turn their swords against each other, who spend their strength in civil feuds, who neither humble themselves nor repent of the wickedness of their ways?

"Alas! My son, though I speak brave words to the people, my heart is very sad, and I fear that troubles like those which fell upon us when we were carried captive into Babylon await us now!"

There was a silence as the rabbi finished. John had of course heard something of the events which had been taking place, but as he now heard them in sequence, the gravity and danger of the situation came freshly upon him.

"What can be done?" he asked after a long pause.

"Nothing save to pray to the Lord," the rabbi said sorrowfully. "Josephus is doing what he can toward building walls to the towns, but it is not walls, but soldiers that are wanted; and so long as the people remain blind and indifferent to the danger, thinking of naught save tilling their ground and laying up money, nothing can be done."

"Then will destruction come upon all?" John asked, looking round in a bewildered and hopeless way.

"We may hope not," the rabbi said. "Here in Galilee we have had no share in the events in Jerusalem, and many towns even now are faithful to the Romans; therefore it may be that in this province all will not be involved in the lot of Jerusalem. There can be, unless a mighty change takes place, no general resistance to the Romans, and it may be, therefore, that no general destruction will fall upon the people. As to this none can say.

"Vespasian, the Roman general who has been charged by Nero with the command of the army which is gathering against us, is said to be a merciful man as well as a great commander. The Roman mercies are not tender, but it may be that the very worst may not fall upon this province. The men of spirit and courage will doubtless proceed to Jerusalem to share in the defense of the Holy City. If we cannot fight with success here it is far better that the men should fight at Jerusalem, leaving their wives and families here, and doing naught to call down the vengeance of the Romans upon this province.

"In Galilee there have, as elsewhere, been risings against the Romans, but these will count for little in their eyes in comparison to the terrible deeds at Jerusalem; and I pray, for the sake of all my friends here, that the Romans may march through the land on their way to Jerusalem without burning and wasting the country. Here on the eastern shore of Galilee there is much more hope of escape than there is across the lake.

"Not only are we out of the line of the march of the army, but there are few important cities on this side, and the disposition of the people has not been so hostile to the Romans. My own opinion is that when the Romans advance it will be the duty of every Jew who can bear arms to go down to the defense of the Holy City. Its position is one of vast strength. We shall have numbers and courage, though neither order nor discipline; and it may be that at the last the Lord will defend his sanctuary and save it from destruction at the hands of the heathen. Should it not be so we can but die, and how could a Jew better die than in defense of God's Temple?"

"It would have been better," Simon said, "had we not by our evil doings have brought God's Temple into danger."

"He has suffered it," the rabbi said, "and his ways are not the ways of man. It may be that he has suffered such madness to fall upon us in order that his name may at last be glorified."

"May it be so!" Simon said piously; "and now let us to bed, for the hour is growing late."

The following morning Simon, his wife, and the whole household accompanied John to the shore, as Simon had arranged with one of the boatmen to take the lad to Hippos. The distance was but short, but Simon, when his wife had expressed surprise at his sending John in a boat, said:

"It is not the distance, Martha. A half-hour's walk is naught to the lad; but I had reasons altogether apart from the question of distance. John is going out to play a man's part. He is young, but since my Lord Josephus has chosen to place him among those who form his bodyguard, he has a right to claim to be regarded as a man. That being so, I would not accompany him to Hippos, for it would seem like one leading a child, and it were best to let him go by himself. Again, it were better to have but one parting. Here he will receive my blessing, and say good-bye to us all. Doubtless he will often be with us, for Tiberias lies within sight, and so long as Josephus remains in Galilee he will never be more than a long day's journey from home. The lad loves us, and will come as often as he can; but surrounded as Josephus is by dangers, the boy will not be able to get away on his own business. He must take the duties as well as the honor of the office, and we must not blind ourselves to the fact that in one of these popular tumults great danger and even death may come upon him.

"This seems to you terrible," he went on in answer to an exclamation of alarm from Martha; "but it does not seem so terrible to me. We go on planning and gathering in as if no danger threatened us and the evil day were far off, but it is not so; the Roman hosts are gathering, and we are wasting our strength in party strife and are doing naught to prepare against the storm. We have gone to war without counting the cost; we have affronted and put to shame Rome, before whom all nations bow; and assuredly she will take a terrible vengeance. Another year, and who can say who will be alive and who dead—who will be wandering over the wasted fields of our people or who will be a slave in Rome!

"In the times that are at hand no man's life will be worth anything; and therefore I say, wife, that though there is danger and peril about the lad, let us not trouble overmuch, for he is, like all of us, in God's hands."

Therefore the parting took place on the shore. Simon solemnly blessed John, and his mother cried over him. Mary was a little surprised at these demonstrations at what she regarded as a very temporary separation, but her merry spirits were subdued at the sight of her aunt's tears, although she herself saw nothing to cry about. She brightened up, however when John whispered, as he said good-bye to her:

"I shall come across the lake as often as I can to see how you are getting on, Mary."

Then he took his place in the stern of the boat, the fishermen dipped their oars in the water, and the boat drew away from the little group who stood watching it as it made its way across the sparkling waters to Hippos.

Upon landing John at once went to the house where Josephus was lodging. The latter gave him in charge to the leader of the little group of men who attached themselves to him as his body-guard.

"Joab," he said, "this youth will henceforth make one of your party. He is brave and, I think, ready and quick witted. Give him arms and see that he has all that is needful. Being young, he will be able to mingle unsuspected among the crowds, and may obtain tidings of evil intended me, when men would not speak maybe before others whom they might judge my friends. He will be able to bear messages unsuspected, and may prove of great service to the cause."

John found at once that there was nothing like discipline or regular duties among the little band who constituted the body-guard of Josephus. They were simply men who, from affection for the governor and a hatred for those who, by their plots and conspiracies, would un do the good work he was accomplishing, had left their farms and occupations to follow and guard him.

Every Jew boy received a certain training in the use of weapons in order to be prepared to fight in the national army when the day of deliverance should arrive, but beyond that the Jews had no military training whatever. Their army would be simply a gathering of the men capable of bearing arms throughout the land—each ready to give his life for his faith and his country, relying like their forefathers on the sword of the Lord and Israel, but without the slightest idea of military drill, discipline, or tactics. Such an army might fight bravely, might die nobly, but it could have little chance of victory over the well-trained legions of imperial Rome.

At noon Josephus embarked in a galley with his little band of followers, eight in number, and sailed across the lake to Tiberias. Here they landed and went up to the house in which Josephus always dwelt when in that city. His stay there was generally short, Tarichea being his general abode, for there he felt in safety, the inhabitants being devoted to him; while those of Tiberias were ever ready to follow the advice of the disaffected, and a section were eager for the return of the Romans and the renewal of the business and trade which had brought wealth to the city before the troubles began. That evening Josephus sent for John, and said:

"I purpose in two days to go to Tarichea, where I shall spend the Sabbath. I hear that there is a rumor that many of the citizens have privately sent to King Agrippa asking him to send hither Roman troops, and promising them a good reception. The men with me are known to many in the city and would be shunned by my enemies, and so would hear naught of what is going on; therefore I purpose to leave you here. In the morning go early to the house of Samuel, the son of Gideon. He dwells in the street called that of Tarichea, for it leadeth in the direction of that town. He is a tanner by trade, and you will have no difficulty in finding it. He has been here this evening, and I have spoken to him about you, and when you present yourself to him he will take you in. Thus no one will know that you are of my company. Pass your time in the streets, and when you see groups of people assemble join yourself to them and gather what they are saying. If it is aught that is important for me to know, come here and tell me; or if it be after I have departed for Tarichea, bring me the news there. It is but thirty furlongs distant."

John followed up the instructions given him, and was hospitably received by Samuel the tanner.

In the course of the day a number of the citizens called upon Josephus and begged him at once to set about building walls for the town, as he had already built them for Tarichea. When he assured them that he had already made preparations for doing so, and that the builders should set to work forthwith, they appeared satisfied, and the city remained perfectly tranquil until Josephus left the next morning for Tarichea.

Chapter Four

THE LULL BEFORE THE STORM

The galley which carried Josephus from Tiberias was scarcely out of sight when John, who was standing in the market-place watching the busy scene with amusement, heard the shout raised: "The Romans are coming!" At once people left their business and all ran to the outskirts of the city. John ran with them, and on arriving there saw a party of Roman horsemen riding along at no great distance. The people began to shout loudly to them to come into the town, calling out that all the citizens were loyal to King Agrippa and the Romans, and that they hated the traitor Josephus.

The Romans halted, but made no sign of entering the town, fearing that treachery was intended, and remembering the fate of their comrades who had trusted to Jewish faith when they surrendered the towers of Hippicus, Phasaelus, and Mariamne. The movement, however, spread through the city; the people assembled in crowds shouting "Death to Josephus!" and exclaimed for the Romans and King Agrippa.

Such as were loyal to Josephus did not venture to raise their voices, so numerous and furious were the multitude; and the whole city was soon in open revolt, the citizens arming themselves in readiness for war. As soon as he saw the course which affairs were taking, John made way out of the town and ran at the top of his speed to Tarichea, where he arrived in a little over half an hour. He was directed at once to the house of Josephus, who rose in surprise at the table at which he was seated writing at John's entry.

"Scarcely had you left, my lord, than some Roman horsemen approached near the town, whereupon the whole city rose in revolt, shouting to them to enter and take possession in the name of the king, and breathing out threats against yourself. The Romans had not entered as I came away; but the populace were all in arms, and your friends did not venture to lift up a voice. Tiberias has wholly revolted to the Romans."

"This is bad news, indeed," Josephus said gravely. "I have but the seven armed men who accompanied me from Tiberias here. All those who were assembled in the city I bade disperse so soon as I arrived, in order that they might go to their towns or villages for the Sabbath. Were I to send round the country I could speedily get a great force together; but in a few hours the Sabbath will begin, even though the necessity be great. And yet if the people of Tiberias march hither we can hardly hope to resist successfully, for the men of the town are too few to man the full extent of the walls. It is most necessary to put down this rising before King Agrippa can send large numbers of troops into Tiberias; and yet we can do nothing until the Sabbath is past.

"Nor would I shed blood if it can be avoided. Hitherto I have put down every rising, and caused Sepphoris, Tiberias, and other cities to expel the evil-doers and return to obedience by tact and by the great force which I could bring against them, and without any need of bloodshed. But this time, I fear, great trouble will come of it, since I cannot take prompt measures, and the enemy will have time to organize their forces and to receive help from John of Gischala and other robbers, to say nothing of the Romans."

Josephus walked up and down the room in agitation, and then stood looking out into the harbor.

"Ah!" he exclaimed suddenly, "we may yet frighten them into submission. Call in Joab."

When Joab entered Josephus explained to him in a few words the condition of things in Tiberias and then proceeded:

"Send quickly to the principal men of the town and bid them put trusty men at each of the gates and let none pass out; order the fighting men to man the walls in case those of Tiberias should come hither at once; then let one or two able fellows embark on board each of the boats and vessels in the port, taking with them two or three of the infirm and aged men. Send a fast galley across to Hippos and bid the fishermen set out at once with all their boats and join us off Tiberias. We will not approach close enough to the city for the people to see how feebly we are manned, but when they perceive all these ships making toward them they will think that I have with me a great army with which I propose to destroy their city."

The orders were quickly carried out. Josephus embarked with his eight companions in one ship, and followed by two hundred and thirty vessels of various sizes, sailed toward Tiberias. As they approached the town they saw a great movement among the population. Men and women were seen crowding down to the shore—the men holding up their hands to show that they were unarmed, the women wailing and uttering loud cries of lamentation.

Josephus waited for an hour until the ships from Hippos also came up and then caused them all to anchor off the town, but at such a distance that the number of those on board could not be seen. Then he advanced in his own ship to within speaking distance of the land. The people cried out to him to spare the city and their wives and children, saying that they had been misled by evil men and regretted bitterly what they had done.

Josephus told them that assuredly they deserved that city should be wholly destroyed, for that now when there was so much that had to be done to prepare for the war which Rome would make against the country they troubled the country with their seditions. The people set up a doleful cry for mercy, and Josephus then said that this time he would spare them, but that their principal men must be handed over to him.

To this the people joyfully agreed, and a boat with ten of their senate came out to the vessel. Josephus had them bound and sent them on board one of the other ships. Another and another boat-load came off, until all the members of the senate and many of the principal inhabitants were prisoners. Some of the men had been drawn from the other ships and put on board those with the prisoners, and these then sailed away to Tarichea.

The people of Tiberias, terrified at seeing so man taken away and not knowing how many more might be demanded, now denounced a young man named Clitus as being the leader of the revolt. Seven of the body-guard of Josephus had gone down the lake with the prisoners and one Levi alone remained. Josephus told him to go ashore and to cut off one of the hands of Clitus. Levi was, however, afraid to land alone among such a number of enemies, whereupon Josephus addressed Clitus, and told him that he was worthy of death, but that he would spare his life, if his two hands were sent on board a ship.

Clitus begged that he might be permitted to keep one hand, to which Josephus agreed. Clitus then drew his sword and struck off his left hand. Josephus now professed to be satisfied, and after warning the people against again listening to evil advisers sailed away with the whole fleet. Josephus that evening entertained the principal persons among the prisoners, and in the morning allowed all to return to Tiberias.

The people there had already learned that they had been duped, but with time had come reflection, and knowing that in a day or two Josephus could have assembled the whole population of Galilee against them and have destroyed them before any help could come, there were few who were not well content that their revolt had been so easily and bloodlessly repressed, and Josephus rose in their estimation by the quickness and boldness of the stratagem by which he had, without bloodshed, save in the punishment of Clitus, restored tranquillity.

Through the winter Josephus was incessantly active. He endeavored to organize an army, enrolled a hundred thousand men, appointed commanders and captains, and strove to establish something like military drill and order. But the people were averse to leaving their farms and occupations, and but little progress was made. Moreover, a great part of the time Josephus was occupied in suppressing the revolts which were continually breaking out in Sepporis Tiberias, and Galama, and in thwarting the attempts of John of Gischala and his other enemies, who strove by means of bribery at Jerusalem to have him recalled, and would have succeeded but had it not been that the Gilileans, save those of the great cities, were always ready to turn out in all their force to defend him, and by sending deputations to Jerusalem counteracted the efforts there of this enemies.

John was incessantly engaged as he accompanied Josephus in his rapid journeys through the province either to suppress the risings or to see to the work of organization; and only once or twice was he able to pay a short visit to his family.

"You look worn and fagged, John," his cousin said on the occasion of his last visit, when spring was close at hand.

"I am well in health, Mary, but it does try one to see how all the efforts of Josephus are marred by the turbulence of the people of Tiberias and Sepphoris. All his thought sand time are occupied in keeping order, and the work of organizing the army makes but little progress. Vespasian is gathering a great force at Antioch. His son Titus will soon join him with another legion, and they will together advance against us."

"But I hear that the walling of the cities is well-nigh finished."

"That is so, Mary, and doubtless many of them will be able to make a long defense; but, after all, the taking of a city is a mere question of time. The Romans have great siege engines which nothing can withstand; but even if the walls were so strong that they could not be battered down, each city could in time be reduced by famine. It is not for me, who am but a boy, to judge the doings of my elders, but it seems to me that this walling of cities is altogether wrong. They can give no aid to each other, and one by one must fall and all within perish or be made slaves, for the Romans give no quarter when they capture a city by storm.

"It seems to me that it would be far better to hold Jerusalem only with a strong force of fighting men, and for all the rest of the men capable of carrying arms to gather among the hills and there to fight the Romans. When the legion of Cestius was destroyed we showed that among defiles and on rocky ground our active lightly armed men were a match for the Roman soldiers in their heavy armor, and in this way I think that we might check even the legions of Vespasian.

"Them women and the old men and children could gather in the cities and admit the Romans when they approached. In that case they would suffer no harm, for the Romans are clement when not opposed. As it is, it seems to me that in the end destruction will fall on all alike. Here in Galilee we have a leader, but he is hampered by dissensions and jealousies. Samaria stands neutral. Jerusalem, which ought to take the lead, is torn by faction. There is war in her streets; she thinks only of herself and naught of the country, although she must know that when the Romans have crushed down all opposition elsewhere she must sooner or later fall. The country seems possessed with madness, and I see no hope in the future."

"Save in the God of Israel," Mary said gently; "that is what Simon and Martha say."

"Save in him," John assented; "but, dear, he suffered us to be carried away to Babylon, and how are we to expect his aid now when the people do naught for themselves, when his city is divided in itself, when its streets are wet with blood, and its very altars defiled by conflict? When evil men are made high-priests and all rule and authority is at an end, what right have we to expect aid at the hands of Jehovah? My greatest comfort, Mary, is that we lie here on the east of the lake, and that we are within the jurisdiction of King Agrippa. On this side his authority has never been altogether thrown off, though some of the cities have made common cause with those of the other side. Still we may hope that on this side of Jordan we may escape the horrors of the war."

"You are out of spirits, John, and take a gloomy view of things; but I know that Simon, too, thinks that everything will end badly, and I have heard him say that he too is glad that his farm lies on this side of the lake, and that he wishes Gamala had not thrown off the authority of the king, so that there might be naught to bring the Romans across Jordan. Our mother is more hopeful; she trusts in God, for, as she says, though the wealthy and powerful may have forsaken him, the people still cling to him, and he will not let us fall into the hands of our enemies."

"I hope it will be so, Mary, and I own I am out of spirits and look at matters in the worse light; however, I will have a talk with father tonight."

That evening John had a long conversation with Simon, and repeated the forebodings he had expressed to Mary.

"At any rate, father, I hope that when the Romans approach you will at least send away my mother, Mary and the women to a place of safety. We are but a few miles from Gamala, and if the Romans come there and besiege it they will spread through the country, and will pillage, even if they do not slay, in all the villages. If, as we trust, God will give victory to our arms, they can return peace; if not, let them at least be free from the dangers which are threatening us."

"I have been thinking of it, John. A fortnight since I sent old Isaac to your mother's brother, whose farm, as you know, lies upon the slopes of Mount Hermon, a few miles from Neve, and very near the boundary of Manasseh, to ask him if he will receive Martha, and Mary, and the women until the troubles are over. He will gladly do so, and I purpose sending them away as soon as I hear that the Romans have crossed the frontier."

"I am indeed rejoiced to hear it, father; but do not let them tarry for that, let them go as soon as the snows have melted on Mount Hermon, for the Roman cavalry will spread quickly over the land. Let them go as soon as the roads are fit for travel. I shall feel a weight off my mind when I know that they are safe. And does my mother know what you have decided?"

"She knows, John, but in truth she is reluctant to go. She says at present that if I stay she also will stay."

"I trust, father, that you will overrule my mother; and that you will either go with her, or if you stay you will insist upon her going; should you not overcome her opposition and finally suffer her with Miriam, and the older women, to remain with you, I hope that you will send Mary and the young ones to my uncle. The danger with them is vastly greater; the Romans, unless their blood is heated by opposition, may not interfere with the old people, who are valueless as slaves, but the young ones—" and he stopped.

"I have thought it ever, my son, and even if your mother remains here with me I will assuredly send off Mary and the young maidens to the mountain. Make your mind easy on that score. We old people have taken root on the land which was our fathers'. I shall not leave, whatever may befall, and it may be that your mother will tarry here with me, but the young women shall assuredly be sent away until the danger is over. Not that I think the peril is as great as it seems to you. Our people have ever shown themselves courageous in great danger; they know the fate that awaits them after provoking the anger of Rome. They know they are fighting for faith, for country, and their families, and will fight desperately. They greatly outnumber the Romans, at least the army by which we shall first be attacked, and maybe if we can resist that we may make terms with Rome, for assuredly in the long run she must overpower us."

"I should think with you, father," John said, shaking his head, "if I saw anything like union among the people, but I lose all heart when I see how divided they are, how blind to the storm that is coming against us, how careless as to anything but trouble of the day, how intent upon the work of their farms and businesses, how disinclined to submit to discipline and to prepare themselves for the day of battle."

"You are young, my son, and full of enthusiasm, but it is hard to stir men whose lives have traveled in one groove from their ordinary course. In all our history, although we have been ready to assemble and meet the foe, we have ever been ready to lay by the sword when the danger is past, and to return to our homes and families. We have been a nation of fighting men, but never a nation with an army."

"Yes, father, because we trusted in God to give us victory on the day of battle. He is our army. When he fought with us we conquered, when he abstained we were beaten. He suffered us to fall into the hands of the Romans, and instead of repenting of our sins we have sinned more and more. The news from Jerusalem is worse and worse. There is civil war in its streets. Robbers are its masters. The worst of the people sit in high place."

"That is so, my son. God's anger burns fiercely, and the people perish; yet it may be that he will be merciful in the end."

"I hope so, father, for assuredly our hope is only in him."

Early in the spring Vespasian was joined by King Agrippa with all his forces, and they advanced to Ptolemais, and here Titus joined his father, having brought his troops from Alexandria by sea. The force of Vespasian now consisted of the Fifth, Tenth, and Fifteenth legions. Beside these he had twenty-three cohorts, ten of which numbered a thousand footmen, the rest each six hundred footmen and a hundred and fifty horse.

The allied force contributed by Agrippa and others consisted of two thousand archers and a thousand horse; while Malchus, King of Arabia, sent a thousand horse and five thousand archers. The total force amounted to sixty thousand regular troops, beside great numbers of camp-followers, who were all trained to military service and could fight in case of need. Vespasian had encountered no resistance on his march down to Ptolemais. The inhabitants of the country which he passed forsook the villages and farms, and retired, according to the orders they had received, to the fortified towns.

There was no army to meet the Romans in the field. The efforts at organization which Josephus had made bore no fruit whatever. No sooner had the invader entered the country than it lay at his mercy, save only the walled cities into which the people had crowded. In the range of the mountains stretching across Upper Galilee were three places of great strength, Gabara, Gischala, and Jotapata. The last named had been very strongly fortified by Josephus himself, and here he intended to take up his own position.

"It is a pitiful sight truly," Joab remarked to John as they saw the long line of fugitives, men, women, and children, with such belongings as they could carry on their own backs and of their beasts of burden—"it is a pitiful sight, is it not?"

"It is a pitiful sight, Joab, and one that fills me with foreboding as well as with pity. What agonies may not these poor people be doomed to suffer when the Romans lay siege to Jotapata!"

"They can never take it," Joab said scornfully.

"I wish I could think so, Joab. When did the Romans ever lay siege to a place and fail to capture it? Once, twice, three times they may fail, but in the end they assuredly will take it."

"Look at its position. See how wild is the country through which they will have to march."

"They have made roads over all the world, Joab; they will make very short work of the difficulties here. It may take the Romans weeks or months to besiege each of these strong places, but they will assuredly carry them in the end, and then better a thousand times that the men had in the first place slain the women and rushed to die on the Roman swords."

"It seems to me, John," Joab said stiffly, "that you are overbold in thus criticising the plans of our general."

"It may be so," John said recklessly, "but methinks when we are all risking our lives, each man may have a right to his opinions. I am ready, like the rest, to die when the time comes, but that does not prevent me having my opinions; besides, it seems to me that there is no heresy in questioning the plans of our general. I love Josephus, and would willingly give my life for him. He has shown himself a wise ruler, firm to carry out wht is right and to suppress all evil-doers; but, after all, he has not served in war. He is full of resources, and will, I doubt not, devise every means to check the Romans; but even so, he may not be able to cope in war with such generals as theirs, who have won their experience all over the world. Nor may the general's plan of defense which he had adopted be the best suited for the occasion."

"Would you have us fight the Romans in the open?" Joab said scornfully. "What has been done in the south? See how our people marched out from Jerusalem under John the Essene, Niger of Paræa, and Silas the Babylonian to attack Ascalon, held by but one cohort of Roman foot and one troop of horse. What happened? Antoninus, the Roman commander, charged the army without fear, rode through and through them, broke them up into fragments, and slew till night-time, when then thousand men, with John and Silas, lay dead. Not satisfied with this defeat, in a short time Niger advanced again against Ascalon, when Antoninus sallied out again and slew eight thousand of them. Thus eighteen thousand men were killed by one weak cohort of foot and a troop of horse, and yet you say we ought not to hide behind our walls, but to meet them in the open!"

"I would not meet them in the open where the Roman cavalry could charge, at any rate not until our people have learned discipline. I would harass them and attack them in defiles, as Cestius was attacked; harassing them night and day, giving them no peace or rest, never allowing them to meet us in the plains, but moving rapidly hither and thither among the mountains, leaving the women in the cities, which should offer no resistance so the Romans would have no point to strike at, until at length, when we have gained confidence and discipline and order, we should be able to take bolder measures gradually and fight them hand to hand."

"Maybe you are right, lad," Joab said thoughtfully. "I like not being cooped up in a stronghold myself, and methinks that a mountain warfare such as you speak of would suit the genius of the people; we are light-limbed and active, inured to fatigue, for we are a nation of cultivators, brave assuredly and ready to give our lives. They say that in the fight near Ascalon not a Jew fled. Fight they could not, they were powerless against the rush of the heavy Roman horse, but they died as they stood, destroyed but not defeated. Gabara and Gischala and Jotapata may fall; but, lad, it will be only after a defense so desperate that the haughty Roman may well hesitate; for if such be the resistance of these little mountain towns, what will not be the task of conquering Jerusalem garrisoned by the whole nation."

"That is true," John said, "and if our death here be for the safety of Jerusalem we shall not have died in vain. But I doubt whether such men as those who have power in Jerusalem will agree to any terms, however favorable, that may be offered. It may be that it is God's will that it should be so. Two days ago, as I journeyed hither after going down to Sepphoris with a message from the general to some of the principal inhabitants there, I met an old man travelling with his wife and family. I asked him whether he was on his way hither, but he said 'No,' he was going across Jordan and through Manasseh and ever Mount Hermon into Trachonitis. He said that he was a follower of that Christ who was put to death in Jerusalem some thirty-five years since, and whom many people still believe was the Messiah. He says that he foretold the destruction of Jerusalem by the Romans, and warned his followers not to stay in the walled cities, but to fly to the deserts when the time came."

"The Messiah was to save Israel," Jacob said scornfully. "Christ could not save even himself."

"I know not," John said simply, "I have heard of him from others, and my father heard him preach several times near the lake. He says that he is a man of wondrous power, and that he preached a new doctrine. He says that he did not talk about himself or claim to be the Messiah; but that he simply told the people to be kind and good to each other, and to love God and do his will. My father said that he thought he was a good and holy man, and full of the Spirit of God. He did works of great power too, but bore himself meekly, like any other man. My father always regarded him as a prophet, and said that he grieved when he heard that he had been put to death at Jerusalem. If he were a prophet, what he said about the destruction of Jerusalem should have weight with us."

"All who head him agreed that he was a good man," Jacob assented. "I have never known one of those who heard him say otherwise, and maybe he was a prophet. Certainly he called upon the people to repent and turn from their sins, and had they done as he taught them these evils might not have fallen upon us, and God would doubtless have been ready to aid his people as of old. However, it is too late to think about it now. We want all our thoughts for the matter we have in hand. We have done all that we can to put this town into a state of defense, and, methinks, if the Romans ever penetrate through these mountains and forests they will see that they have a task which will tax all their powers before they take Jotapata."

The position of the town was indeed immensely strong. It stood on the summit of a lofty mass of rock, which, on three sides, fell abruptly down into the deep and almost impassable ravines which surrounded it.

On the north side alone, where the ridges sloped more gradually down, it could be approached. The town extended part of the way down this declivity, and at its foot Josephus had built a strong wall. On all sides were lofty mountains covered with thick forests, and the town could not be seen by an enemy until they were close at hand.

As soon as Vespasian had arrived at Ptolemais (on the site of which city stands the modern Acre) he was met by a deputation from Sepphoris. That city had only been prevented from declaring for the Romans by the exertions of Josephus, and the knowledge that all Galilee would follow him to attack it should it revolt. But as soon as Vespasian arrived at Ptolemais, which was scarce twenty miles away, they sent deputies with their submission to him, begging that a force might be sent to defend them against any attack by the Jews.

Vespasian received them with courtesy, and sent Placidus with a thousand horse and six thousand foot to the city. The infantry took up their quarters in the town, but the horsemen made raids over the plains, burning the villages, slaying all the men capable of bearing arms, and carrying off the rest of the population as slaves.

The day after the conversation between Joab and John a man brought the news to Jotapata that Placidus was marching against it. Josephus at once ordered the fighting men to assemble, and, marching out, placed them in ambuscade in the mountains on the road by which the Romans would approach.

As soon as the latter had fairly entered the pass the Jews sprang to their feet and hurled their javelins and shot their arrows among them. The Romans in vain endeavored to reach their assailants, and numbers were wounded as they tried to climb the heights, but few were killed for they were so completely covered by their armor and shields that the Jewish missiles thrown from a distance seldom inflicted mortal wounds. They were, however, unable to make their way further, and Placidus was obligated to retire to Sepphoris, having failed signally in gaining the credit he had hoped for from the capture of the strongest of the Jewish strongholds in upper Galilee.

The Jews, on their part, were greatly inspirited by the success of their first encounter with the Romans, and returned rejoicing to their stronghold. All being ready at Jotapata, Josephus, with a considerable number of the fighting men, proceeded to Garis, not far from Sepphoris, where the army had assembled. But no sooner had the news arrived that the great army of Vespasian was in movement that they dispersed in all directions, and Josephus was left with a mere handful of followers, with who he fled to Tiberias.

Thence he wrote earnest letters to Jerusalem, saying that unless a strong army was fitted out and put in the field it was useless to attempt to fight the Romans, and that it would be wiser to come to terms with them than to maintain a useless resistance which would bring destruction upon the nation. He remained a short time only at Tiberias, and thence hurried up with his followers to Jotapata, which he reached on the 14th of May.

Vespasian marched first to Gadara, which was undefended, the fighting men having all gone to Jotapata; but although no resistance was offered, Vespasian put all the males to the sword and burned the town and all the villages in the neighborhood, and then advanced against Jotapata.

For four days the pioneers of the Roman army had labored incessantly cutting a road through the forests, filling up ravines, and clearing away obstacles, and on the fifth day the road was constructed close up to Jotapata.

On the 14th of May Placidus and Ebutius were sent forward by Vespasian with a thousand horse to surround the town and cut off all possibility of escape. On the following day Vespasian himself, with his whole army, arrived there. The defenders of Jotapata could scarcely believe their eyes when they saw the long heavy column, with all its baggage and siege engines, marching along a straight and level road, where they had believed that it would be next to impossible for even the infantry of the enemy to make their way. If this marvel had been accomplished in five days, what hope was there that the city would be able to withstand this force which had so readily triumphed over the defenses of nature!

Chapter Five

THE SIEGE OF JOTAPATA

"Well, Joab, what do you think now?" John said as he stood on the wall with his older companion watching the seemingly endless column of the enemy. "It seems to me that we are caught here like rats in a trap, and that we should have done better a thousand times in maintaining our freedom of movement among the mountains. It is one thing to cut a road, it would be another to clear off all the forests to shelter us the Romans could never have overtaken us. Here there is nothing to do but die."

"That is so, John. I own that the counsel you urged would have been wiser than this. Here are all the best fighting men in Galilee shut up without hope of succor or of mercy. Well, lad, we can at least teach the Romans the lesson that the Jews know how to die, and the capture of this mountain town will cost them as much as they reckoned would suffice for the conquest of the whole country. Jotapata may save Jerusalem yet."

John was no coward and was prepared to fight to the last; but he was young, and the love of life was strong within. He thought of his old father and mother, who had no children but him; of his pretty Mary, far away now, he hoped, on the slopes of Mount Hermon; and of the grief that his death would cause them; and he resolved that although he would do his duty he would strain every nerve to preserve the life so dear to them.

He had no other duties to perform other than those common to all able to bear arms. When the Romans attacked, his place would be near Josephus, or were a sally ordered he would issue out with the general, but until then his time was his own. There was no mission to be performed now, no fear of plots against the life of the general, therefore he was free to wander where he liked. Save the newly erected wall across the neck of rock below the town there were no defenses, for it was deemed impossible for man to climb the cliffs that fell sheer down at ever other point. John strolled quietly round the town, stopping now and then to look over the low wall that bordered the precipice, erected solely to prevent children from falling over. The depth was very great, and it seemed to him that there could be no escape anywhere save on that side which was now blocked by the wall, and which would, ere long, be trebly blocked by the Romans.

The town was crowded. At ordinary times it might contain three or four thousand inhabitants; now, over twenty-five thousand had gathered there. Of these more than half were men, but many had brought their wives and children with them. Every vacant foot of ground was taken up. The inhabitants shared their homes with the strangers, but the accommodation was altogether insufficient, and the greater part of the new-comers had erected little tents and shelters of cloths or blankets.

In the upper part of the town there were at present comparatively few people about, for the greater part had gone to the slope, whence they watched with terror and dismay the great Roman column as it poured down in an unbroken line hour after hour. The news of the destruction which had fallen on Gadara had been brought in by fugitives, and all knew that although no resistance had been offered there, every male had been put to death and the women taken captives.

There was naught then to be gained by surrender, even had any one dared to propose it. As for victory over such a host as that which was marching to the assault, none could hope for it. For hold out as they might, and repel every assault on the wall, there was an enemy within which would conquer them. For Jotapata possessed no wells. The water had daily to be fetched by the women from the stream in the ravine, and although stores of grain had been collected sufficient to last for many months, the supply of water stored up in cisterns would scarce suffice to supply the multitudes gathered on the rock for a fortnight.

Death, then, certain and inevitable, awaited them; and yet an occasional wail from some woman as she pressed her children to her breast alone told of the despair which reigned in every heart. The great portion looked out silent and as if stupefied. They had relied absolutely on the mountains and forests to block the progress of the invader. They had thought that at the worst they would have had to deal with a few companies of infantry only. Thus the sight of the sixty thousand by the camp swelled to nigh a hundred thousand by the camp-followers and artificers, complete with its cavalry and machines of war, seemed like some terrible nightmare.

After making the circuit of the rock, and wandering for some time among the impromptu camps in the streets, John returned to a group of boys whom he had noticed learning against the low wall with a carelessness as to the danger of a fall over the precipice which proved that they must be natives of the place.

"If there be any possible way of descending these precipices," he said to himself, "it will be the boys who will know of it. Where a goat could climb these boys, born among the mountains, would try to follow, if only to excel each other in daring and to risk breaking their necks." Thus thinking he walked up to the group, who were from twelve to fifteen years old.

"I suppose you belong to the town?" he began.

There was a general assent from the five boys, who looked with considerable respect at John, who, although but two years the senior of the eldest among them, wore a man's garb and carried sword and buckler.

"I am one of the body-guard of the governor," John went on, "and I dare say you can tell me all sorts of things about this country that may be useful for him to know. It is quite certain that no one could climb up these rocks from below, and that there is no fear of the Romans making a surprise in that way?"

The boys looked at each other, but no one volunteered to give information.

"Come!" John went on; "I have only just left off being a boy myself, and I was always climbing into all sorts of places when I got a chance, and I have no doubt it's the same with you. When you have been down below there you have tried how far you can get up. Did you ever get up far, or did you ever hear of any one getting up far?"

"I expect I have been up as far as any one," the eldest of the boys said. "I went up after a young kid that had strayed away from its mother. I got up a long way—halfway up, I should say; but I couldn't get any further. I was barefooted too. I am sure no one with armor on could have got up anything like so far. I don't believe he could get up fifty feet."

"And have any of you ever tried to get down from above?"

They shook their heads.

"Jonas the son of James did once," one of the smaller boys said. "He had a pet hawk he had tamed, and it flew away and perched a good way down, and he clambered down to fetch it. He had a rope tied round him, and some of the others held it in case he should slip. I know he went down a good way, and he got the hawk, and his father beat him for doing it, too."

"Is he here now?" John asked.

"Yes, he is here," the boy said. "That's his father's house, the one close to the edge of the rock. I don't know whether you will find him there now. He ain't indoors more than he can help. His own mother's dead, and his father's got another wife, and they don't get on well together."

"Well, I will have a chat with him one of these days. And you are all quite sure that there is no possible path up from below?"

"I won't say there isn't any possible path," the eldest boy said; "but I feel quite sure there is not. I have looked hundreds of times when I have been down below, and I feel pretty sure that if there had been any place where a goat could have got up I should have noticed it. But you see the rock goes down almost straight in most places. Anyhow, I have never heard of any one who ever got up, and if any one had done it, it would have been talked about for years and years."

"No doubt it would," John agreed. "So I shall tell the governor that he need not be in the least uneasy about an attack except in front."

So saying he nodded to the boys and walked away again.

In the evening the whole of the Roman army had arrived, and Vespasian drew up his troops on a hill less than a mile to the north of the city, and there encamped them.

The next morning a triple line of embankments was thrown up by the Romans around the foot of the hill, where alone escape or issue was possible, and this entirely cut off those within the town from any possibility of flight. The Jews looked on at these preparations as wild animals might regard a line of hunters surrounding them. But the dull despair of the previous day had now been succeeded by a fierce rage. Hope there was none. They must die, doubtless; but they would die fighting fiercely to the last. Disdaining to be pent up within the walls, many of the fighting men encamped outside, and boldly went forward to meet the enemy.

Vespasian called up his slingers and archers, and these poured their missiles upon the Jews, while he himself with his heavy infantry began to mount the slope toward the part of the wall which appeared the weakest. Josephus at once summoned the fighting men in the town, and sallying at their head through the gate rushed down and flung himself upon the Romans. Both sides fought bravely; the Romans strong in their discipline, their skill with their weapons, and their defensive armor; the Jews fighting with the valor of despair, heightened by the thought of their wives and children in the town above.

The Romans were pushed down the hill, and the fight continued at its foot until darkness came, when both parties drew off. The number of killed on either side was small, for the bucklers and helmets defended the vital points. The Romans had thirteen killed and very many wounded, the Jews seventeen killed and six hundred wounded.

John had fought bravely by the side of Josephus. Joab and two others of the little band were killed; all the others were wounded more or less severely, for Josephus was always in front, and his chosen followers kept close to him. In the heat of the fight John felt his spirits rise higher than they had done since the troubles had begun. He had fought at first so recklessly that Josephus had checked him with the words:

"Steady, my brave lad. He fights best who fights most coolly. The more you guard yourself the more you will kill."

More than once when Josephus, whose commanding figure and evident leadership attracted the attention of the Roman soldiers, was surrounded and cut off, John with three or four others made their way through to him and brought him off. When it became dark both parties drew off; the Romans sullenly, for they felt it a disgrace to have been thus driven back by foes they despised; the Jews with shouts of triumph, for they had proved themselves a match for the first soldiers in the world, and the dread with which the glittering column had inspired them had passed away.

The following day the Jews again sallied out and attacked the Romans as they advanced, and for five days in succession the combat raged, the Jews fighting with desperate valor, the Romans with steady resolution. At the end of that time the Jews had been forced back behind their wall, and the Romans established themselves in front of it. Vespasian, seeing that the wall could not be carried by assault as he had expected, called a council of war, and it was determined to proceed by the regular process of siege, and to erect a bank against that part of the wall which offered the greatest facility for attack.

Accordingly the whole army, with the exception of the troops who guarded the banks of circumvallation, went into the mountains to get materials. Stone and timber in vast quantities were brought down, and when these were in readiness the work commenced. A sort of penthouse roofing, constructed of wattles covered with earth, was first raised to protect the workers from the missiles of the enemy upon the wall, and here the working parties labored securely, while the rest of the troops brought up earth, stone, and wood for their use.

The Jews did their best to interfere with the work, hurling down huge stones upon the penthouse, sometimes breaking down the supports of the roof and causing gaps, through which they poured a storm of arrows and javelins until the damage had been repaired. To protect his workmen Vespasian brought up his siege engines, of which he had a hundred and sixty, and from these vast quantities of missiles were discharged at the Jews upon the walls.

But they were not inactive. Sallying out in small parties, they fell with fury upon the working parties, who, having stripped off their heavy armor, were unable to resist their sudden onslaughts. Driving out and slaying all before them, the Jews so often applied fire to the wattles and timbers of the bank that Vespasian was obliged to make his work continuous along the whole extent of the wall, to keep out the assailants. But in spite of all the efforts of the Jews the embankment rose steadily, until it almost equaled the height of the wall, and the struggle now went on between the combatants on even terms, they being separated only by the short interval between the wall and bank. Josephus found that in such a conflict the Romans, with their crowd of archers and slingers and their formidable machines, had all the advantage, and that it was absolutely necessary to raise the walls still higher.

He called together a number of the principal men and pointed out the necessity for this. They agreed with him, but urged that it was impossible for men to work exposed to such a storm of missiles. Josephus replied that he had thought of that. A number of strong posts were prepared, and at night these were fixed securely standing on the wall. Along the top of these a strong rope was stretched, and on this were hung, touching each other, the hides of newly killed oxen. These formed a complete screen, hiding the workers from the sight of those on the embankment.

The hides, when struck with the stones from the balistæ, gave way and deadened the force of the missiles, while the arrows and javelins glanced off from the slippery surface. Behind this shelter the garrison worked night and day, raising the posts and screens as their work proceeded, until they had heightened the wall no less than thirty-five feet, with a number of towers on its summit and a strong battlement facing the Romans.

The besiegers were much discouraged at their want of success, and enraged at finding the efforts of so large an army completely baffled by a small town which they had expected to carry at the first assault, while the Jews proportionately rejoiced. Becoming more and more confident they continually sallied out in small parties through the gateway or by ladders from the walls, attacked the Romans upon their embankment, or set fire to it. And it was the desperation with which these men fought, even more than their success in defending the wall, that discouraged the Romans, for the Jews were utterly careless of their lives, and were well content to die when they saw that they had achieved their object of setting fire to the Roman works.

Vespasian at length determined to turn the siege into a blockade, and to starve out the town which he could not capture. He accordingly contented himself by posting a strong force to defend the embankment, and withdrew the main body of the army to their encampment. He had been informed of the shortness of supply of water, and had anticipated that in a very short time thirst would compel the inhabitants to yield.

John had taken his full share in the fighting, and had frequently earned the warm commendation of Josephus.

His spirits had risen with the conflict, but he could not shut his eyes to the fact that sooner or later the Romans must become masters of the place. One evening, therefore, when he had done his share of duty on the walls, he went up to the house which had been pointed out to him as that in which lived the boy who had descended the face of the rocks for some distance.

At a short distance from the door a lad of some fifteen years old, with no covering but a piece of ragged sackcloth round the loins, was crouched up in a corner seemingly asleep. At the sound of John's footsteps he opened his eyes in a quick watchful way that showed that he had not been really asleep.

"Are you Jonas the son of James?" John asked.

"Yes I am," the boy said, rising to his feet. "What do you want with me?"

"I want to have a talk with you," John said. "I am one of the governor's body-guard, and I think perhaps you may be able to give us some useful information."

"Well, come away from here," the boy said, "else we shall be having her," and he nodded toward the house, "coming out with a stick."

"You have rather a hard time of it from what I hear," John began when they stopped at the wall a short distance away from the house.

"I have that," the boy said. "I look like it, don't I?"

"You do," John agreed, looking at the boy's thin half-starved figure; "and yet there is plenty to eat in the town."

"There may be," the boy said; "anyhow I don't get my share. Father is away fighting on the wall, and so she's worse than ever. She is always beating me, and I dare not go back now. I told her this morning the sooner the Romans came in the better I should be pleased. They could only kill me, and there would be an end of it; but they would send her to Rome for a slave, and then she would see how she liked being cuffed and beaten all day."

"And you are hungry now?" John asked.

"I am pretty near always hungry," the boy said.

"Well, come along with me then. I have got a little room to myself, and you shall have as much to eat as you like."

The room John occupied had formerly been a loft over a stable in the rear of the house in which Josephus now lodged, and it was reached by a ladder from the outside. He had shared it at first with two of his comrades, but these had both fallen during the siege. After seeing the boy up into it, John went to the house and procured him an abundant meal, and took it with a small horn of water back to his quarters.

"Here's plenty for you to eat, Jonas, but not much to drink. We are all on short allowance, same as the rest of the people, and I am afraid that won't last long."

There was a twinkle of amusement in the boy's face, but without a word he set to work at the food, eating ravenously all that John had brought him. The latter was surprised to see that he did not touch the water, for he thought that if his stepmother deprived him of food, of which there was abundance, she would all the more deprive him of water, of which the ration to each person was so scanty.

"Now," John said, "you had better throw away that bit of sackcloth and take this garment. It belonged to a comrade of mine who has been killed."

"There's not much of it," the boy said. "If you don't mind my tearing it in half, I will take it."

"Do as you like with it," John replied; and the boy tore the long strip of cotton in two and wrapped half of it round his loins.

"Now," he said, "what do you want to ask me?"

"They tell me, Jonas, that you are a first-rate climber and can go anywhere?"

The boy nodded.

"I can get about, I can. I have been tending goats pretty well ever since I could walk, and where they can go I can."

"I want to know, in the first place whether there is any possible way by which one can get up and down from this place, except by the road through the wall?"

The boy was silent.

"Now look here, Jonas," John went on, feeling sure that the lad could tell something if he would; "if you could point out a way down the governor would be very pleased, and as long as the siege lasts you can live here with me and have as much food as you want, and not go near that stepmother of yours at all."

"And nobody will beat me for telling you?" the boy asked.

"Certainly not, Jonas."

"It wouldn't take you beyond the Romans. They have got guards all round."

"No, but it might enable us to get down to the water," John urged, the sight of the unemptied horn causing the thought to flash through his mind that the boy had been in the habit of going down and getting water.

"Well, I will tell you," the boy said. "I don't like to tell, because I don't think there's any one here knows it but me. I found it out and I never said a word about it, because I was able to slip away when I liked, and no one knows anything about it. But it doesn't make much difference now, because the Romans are going to kill us all. So I will tell you. At the end of the rock you have to climb down about fifty feet. It's very steep there, and it's as much as you can do to get down; but when you have got down that far, you get to the head of a sort of dried-up water-course, and it ain't very difficult to go down there, and that way you can get right down to the stream. It doesn't look from below as if you could do it, and the Romans haven't put any guards on the stream just there. I know because I go down every morning as soon as it gets light. I never tried to get through the Roman sentries, but I expect one could if one tried. But I don't see how you are to bring water up there, if that's what you want. I tell you it is as much as you can do to get up and down, and you want both your hands and your feet; but I could go down and bring up a little water for you in a skin hanging round my neck, if you like."

"I'm afraid that wouldn't be much good, Jonas," John said; "but it might be very useful to send messengers out that way."

"Yes," the boy said; "but you see I have always intended, when the Romans took the place, to make off that way. If other people go it's pretty sure to be found out before long, and then the Romans will keep watch; but it don't much matter. I know another place where you and I could lie hidden any time, if we had got enough to eat and drink. I will show you, but mind you must promise not to tell any one else. There's no room for more than two, and I don't mean to tell you unless you promise."

"I will promise, Jonas. I promise you faithfully not to tell any one."

"Well, the way down ain't far from the other one. I will show it you one of these days. I went down there once to get a hawk I had taken from the nest and tamed. I went down first with a rope tied round me, but I found I could have done it without that; but I didn't tell any of the others, as I wanted to keep the place to myself. You climb down about fifty feet, and then you get on a sort of ledge about three feet wide and six or seven feet long. You can't see it from above, because it's a hollow, as if a bit of rock has fallen out. Of course, if you stood up you might be seen by some one below, or on the hill opposite, but it's so high it is not likely any one would notice you. Anyhow, if you lie down there no one would see you. I have been down there often and often since. When she gets too bad to bear I go down there and take a sleep, or lie there and laugh when I think how she is hunting about for me to carry down the pails to the stream for water."

"I will say nothing about it, Jonas, you may be quite sure. That place may save both our lives, but the other path I will tell Josephus about. He may find it of great use."

Josephus was indeed greatly pleased when he heard that a way existed by which he could send out messages. Two or three active men were chosen for the work, but they would not venture to descend the steep precipice by which Jonas made his way down to the top of the water-course, but were lowered by ropes to that point. Before starting they were sown up in skins, so that if a Roman sentry caught sight of them making their way down the water-course on their hands and feet he would take them for dogs or some other animals. Once at the bottom they lay still till night, and then crawled through the line of sentries.

In this way Josephus was able to send out dispatches to his friends outside and to Jerusalem, imploring them to send an army at once to harass the rear of the Romans, and to afford an opportunity for the garrison of Jotapata to cut their way out. Messages came back by return, and for three weeks communications were thus kept up, until one of the messengers slipped while descending the ravine, and as he rolled down attracted the attention of the Romans, who after that placed a strong guard at the foot of the water-course.

Until this discovery was made Jonas had gone down regularly every morning and drank his fill, and had brought up a small skin of water to John, who had divided it among the children who he saw most in want of it, for the pressure of thirst was now heavy. The Romans, from rising ground at a distance, had noticed the women going daily with jugs to the cistern, whence the water was doled out, and the besiegers directed their missiles to that point, and my were killed daily while fetching water.

A dull despair now seized the Jews. So long as they were fighting they had had little time to think of their situation; but now that they enemy no longer attacked, and there was nothing to do but to sit down and suffer, the hopelessness of their position stared them in the face; but there was no thought of surrender. They knew too well the fate that awaited them at the hands of the Romans. They were therefore seized with rage and indignation when they heard that Josephus and some principal men were thinking of making an endeavor to escape. John, who had hitherto regarded his leader with a passionate devotion, although he thought that he had been wrong in making to the fortified towns instead of fighting among the mountains, shared in the general indignation at the proposed desertion.

"It is he who has brought us all here," he said to Jonas, who had attached himself to him with dog-like fidelity, "and now he proposes to go away and leave every one here to be massacred! I cannot believe it."

The news was, however, well founded; for when the inhabitants crowded down to the house, the women weeping and wailing, the men sullen and fierce, to beg Josephus to abandon his intention, the governor attempted to argue that it was for the public good that he should leave them. He might, he said, hurry to Jerusalem and bring an army to the rescue. The people, however, were in no way convinced.

"If you go," they said, "the Romans will speedily capture the city. We are ready to die all together, to share one common fate, but do not leave us."

As Josephus saw that if he did not accede to the prayers of the women the men would interfere by force to prevent his carrying out his intentions, he told them he would remain with them, and tranquility was at once restored. The men, however, came again and again to him asking to be led out to attack the Romans.

"Let us die fighting," was the cry; "let us die among our foes, and not with the agonies of thirst."

"We must make them come up to attack us again," Josephus said. "We shall fight to far greater advantage so, than if we sallied out to attack them in their own intrenchments, when we should be shot down by their archers and slingers before ever we should reach them."

"But how are we to make them attack us? We want nothing better."

"I will think it over," Josephus said, "and tell you in the morning."

In the morning, to the surprise of the men, they were ordered to dip large numbers of garments into the precious supply of water, and to hang them on the walls.

Loud were the outcries from the women as they saw the scanty store of water upon which their lives depended so wasted; but the orders were obeyed, and the Romans were astonished at seeing the long line of dripping garments on the wall.

The stratagem had its effect. Vespasian thought that the news he had received that the place was ill supplied with water must be erroneous, and ordered the troops again to take their station on the walls and renew the attack. Great was the exultation among the Jews when they saw movement among the troops, and Josephus, ordering the fighting men together, said that now was their opportunity. There was no hope of safety in passive resistance, therefore they had best sally out, and if they must die, leave at least a glorious example to posterity.

The proposal was joyfully received, and he placed himself at their head. The gates were suddenly opened, and they poured out to attack. So furious was their onslaught that the Romans were driven from the embankment. The Jews pursued them, crossed the lines of circumvallation, and attacked the Romans in their camp, tearing up the hides and penthouses behind which the Romans defended themselves, and setting fire to the lines in many places.

The fight raged all day; the Jews then retired to the city, only to sally out again the following morning. For three days the attacks were continued, the Jews driving in the Romans each day, and retiring when Vespasian brought up heavy columns who were unable, from the weight of their armor, to follow their lightly armed assailants.

Vespasian then ordered the regular troops to remain in camp, the assaults being repelled by the archers and slingers. Finding that the courage of the Jews was unabated, and that his troops were losing heavily in this irregular fighting, he determined to renew the siege at all hazards and bring the matter to a close. The heavy-armed troops were ordered to be in readiness, and to advance against the walls with the battering-ram.

This was pushed forward by a great number of men, being covered as it advanced with a great shield constructed of wattles and hides. As it was brought forward, the archers and slingers covered its advance by a shower of missiles against the defenders of the wall, while all the war machines poured in their terrible shower. The Jews, unable to show themselves above the battlements, or to oppose the advance of the terrible machine, crouched in shelter until the battering-ram was placed in position.

Then the ropes by which it swung from the framework overhead was seized by a number of soldiers, and the first blow was delivered at the wall. It quivered beneath the terrible shock, and a cry of dismay arose from the defenders. Again and again the heavy ram struck in the same place. The wall tottered beneath the blows, and would soon have fallen had not Josephus ordered a number of sacks to be filled with straw and let down by ropes from the walls, so as to deaden the blows of the ram.

For a time the Romans ceased work, and then fastening scythes to the ends of long poles cut the ropes. The Jews were unable to show themselves above the walls, or to interfere with the men at work. In a few minutes the sacks were cut down, and the ram recommenced its work of destruction.

Chapter Six

THE FALL OF THE CITY

Two Roman soldiers, seeing the wall of Jotapata tremble beneath the blows of the battering-ram, whose iron head pounded to powder the stones against which it struck, redoubled their efforts, when suddenly, from three sally ports which they had prepared, the Jews burst out, carrying their weapons in their right hands and blazing torches in their left. As on previous occasions, their onslaught was irresistible. They swept the Romans before them, and set fire to the engines, the wattles, and the palisades, and even to the woodwork of the embankment.

The timber had by this time dried, and as bitumen and pitch had been used as cement in the construction of the works, the flames spread with great rapidity, and the work of many days was destroyed in an hour. All the engines and breastworks of the Fifth and Tenth Legions were entirely consumed. Just as the attack began, Eleazar the son of Sameas, a Galilean, with an immense stone from the wall, struck the iron head of the battering-ram and knocked it off. He then leaped down from the wall, seized the iron head, and carried it back into the city.

He was pierced by five arrows; still he pressed on and regained the walls, and held up the iron head in the sight of all, and then fell down dead. Such was the spirit with which the Jews were animated; and the Roman soldiers, trained as they were to conflict among many peoples, were yet astounded by the valor displayed by the race that they had considered as unwarlike peasants. But the Romans were not discouraged;

heavy masses of troops were brought up, the Jews were driven within their walls, and toward evening the ram was again in position.

While Vespasian was directing the attack he was struck by a javelin in the heel. The Romans ceased from the attack and crowded round their general; but as soon as they ascertained that his wound was not serious they returned to the attack with redoubled fury. All that night the contest raged unceasingly. The Roman engines swept the walls with missiles. The towers came crashing down under the blows of the huge stones, while the javelins, arrows, and the stones from the slings created terrible havoc among the defenders of the wall. But as fast as these fell fresh combatants took their places, and they continued hurling down stones and blazing brands upon the freshly erected wattles round the battering-ram.

The Romans had the advantage in this strife; for, while the fires on the walls, at which the Jews lighted their brands and boiled the pitch and sulphur in which these were dipped, enable them to aim accurately, they themselves worked in deep shadow at the foot of the wall. The night was a terrible one; the bolts, stones, and arrows which passed over the wall spread ruin and death over the town. The din was unceasing. The thundering noise of the great stones; the dull, deep sound as the ram struck the wall; the fierce shouts of the combatants as they fought hand to hand—for the corpses were in places piled so thick that the assailants could mount upon them to the top of the walls—the shrieks of the women and the screams of the children, combined in one terrible and confused noise which was echoed back and multiplied by the surrounding mountains.

Morning was just breaking when the shaken wall gave way and fell with a crash. Vespasian called off his weary troops and allowed them a short time for refreshment then he prepared to storm the breach. He brought up first a number of his lowest horsemen dismounted and clad in complete armor. They were provided with long pikes, and were to charge forward the instant the machines for mounting the breach were fixed. Behind these were the best of his infantry, while in their rear were the archers and slingers. Other parties with scaling ladders were to attack the uninjured part of the wall, and to drave off the attention of the besiegers. The rest of the horse extended all over the hills round the town so that none might make their escape.

Josephus prepared to receive the attack. He placed the old, infirm, and wounded to repel the attack on the uninjured parts of the walls. He then chose the five strongest and bravest men, and with them took his place to form the front line of the defenders of the breach. He told them to kneel down and cover their heads with their bucklers until the enemy's archers had emptied their quivers, and when the Romans had fixed the machines for mounting, they were to leap down among the enemy and fight to the last, remembering that there was now no hope of safety, naught but to revenge the fate which was impending over them, their wives and children.

As the Romans mounted to the assault a terrible cry broke out from the women. They saw the Romans still manning the lines which cut off all escape, and they believed that the end was at hand. Josephus, fearing that their cries would dispirit the men, ordered them all to be locked up in their houses, and then calmly awaited the assault. The trumpet of the legion sounded, and the whole Roman host set up a terrible shout, while at the same moment the air was darkened by the arrows of their bowmen. Kneeling beneath their bucklers the Jews remained calm and immovable, and then, before the Romans had time to set foot upon the breach, with a yell of fury they rushed upon them and threw themselves into the midst of their assailants. For a time the Romans could make no way against the desperate courage of the Jews, but as fast as the leading files fell fresh troops took their places, while the Jews, who were vastly reduced by their losses, had no fresh men to take the place of those who died. At last the solid phalanx of the Romans drove back the defenders and entered the breach.

But as they did so, from the walls above and from the breach in front vessels filled with boiling oil were hurled down upon them. The Roman ranks were broken, and the men in agony rolled on the ground unable to escape the burning fluid which penetrated through the joints of their armor. Those who turned to fly were pierced by the javelins of the Jews, for the Romans carried no defensive armor on their back, which were never supposed to be turned toward an enemy.

Fresh troops poured up the breach to take the place of their agonized comrades; but the Jews threw down upon the planks vessels filled with a sort of vegetable slime. Unable to retain their footing upon the slippery surface the Romans fell upon each other in heaps. Those rolling down carried others with them, and a terrible confusion ensued, the Jews never ceasing to pour their missiles upon them. When evening came Vespasian called off his men. He saw that to overcome the desperate resistance of the defenders fresh steps must be taken before the assault was repeated, and he, accordingly, gave orders that the embankment should be raise much higher than before, and that upon it three towers, each fifty feet high and strongly girded with iron, should be built.

This great work was carried out in spite of the efforts of the besieged. In the towers Vespasian placed his javelin men, archers, and light machines, and as these now looked down upon the wall they were enabled to keep up such a fire upon it that the Jews could no longer maintain their footing, but contented themselves with lying behind it and making desperate sallies whenever they saw any parties of Romans approaching the breach.

In the meantime a terrible calamity had befallen the neighboring town of Japha. Emboldened by the vigorous defense of Jotapata it had closed its gate to the Romans. Vespasian sent Trajan with thousand foot and a thousand horse against it. The city was strongly situated and surrounded by a double wall. Instead of waiting to be attacked the people sallied out and fell upon the Romans. They were, however, beaten back, and the Romans, pressing on their heels, entered with them through the gates of the outside walls. The defenders of the gates through the inner walls, fearing that these too would be carried by the mob, closed them and all those who had sallied out were butchered by the Romans.

Trajan, seeing that the garrison must now be weak, sent to Vespasian and asked him to send his son to complete the victory. Titus soon arrived with a thousand foot and five hundred horse, and at once assaulted the inner walls. The defense was feeble. The Romans affected their entry, but inside the town a desperate conflict took place, the inhabitants defending every street with the energy of despair, while the women aided their efforts by hurling down stones and missiles from the roofs. The battle lasted six hours, when all who could bear arms were slain; the rest of the male population were put to death, and the women taken as slaves.

In all, fifteen thousand were killed, two thousand one hundred and thirty taken prisoners. In another direction a heavy blow had also been struck by the Romans. The Samaritans had not openly joined the revolt, but had gathered in great force on Mount Gerizim. Cerealis was sent by Vespasian with three thousand infantry and six hundred horse against them. He surrounded the foot of the mountain, and abstained from an assault until the Samaritans were weakened by thirst, many dying from want of water. Cerealis then mounted the hill, and sent to them to throw down their arms. On their refusal he charged them from all sides, and put every soul—in number eleven thousand six hundred—to the sword.

The situation of the defenders of Jotapata was now pitiable; indeed scarce a man but had received wounds, more or less severe, in the desperate combats. All were utterly worn out with fatigue, for they were under arms day and night in readiness to repel the expected attack. Numbers of the women and children had died of thirst and terror. Save the armed men lying in groups near the foot of the wall in readiness to repel an assault, scarce a soul was to be seen in the lately crowded streets. The houses were now ample to contain the vastly diminished number. Here the women and children crouched in utter prostration. The power of suffering was almost gone; few cared how soon the end came.

The siege had now continued for forty-seven days, and the Roman army, strong in numbers, in discipline, and in arms, and commanded by one of the best generals, had yet failed to capture the little town which they had expected to take within a few hours of their appearance before it, and so fierce was the valor of the besieged that Vespasian did not venture to order his legions forward to renew the assault. But now a deserter informed him that the garrison was greatly exhausted, that the men on guard could not keep awake, and that the breach could be carried at night by a sudden assault.

Vespasian prepared for the assault, which was to take place at daybreak. A thick mist enveloped the town, and the sleeping sentries were not aroused by the silent steps of the approaching Romans. Titus was the first to enter the breach, followed by a small number of troops. These killed the sleeping guards, and the main body of the Romans then poured in. before the Jews were conscious of their danger the whole Roman army was upon them.

Then the slaughter commenced. Many of the Jews killed each other rather than fall into the hands of the Romans, many threw themselves over the precipices, numbers took refuge in the deep caverns under the city. That day all in the streets or houses were killed; the next, the Romans searched the caverns and underground passages, slaughtering all the men and boys, and sparing none but infants and women.

During the siege and capture forty thousand men fell. Only twelve hundred women and children were spared. So complete was the surprise, and so unresistingly did the Jews submit to slaughter, that only one Roman was killed. This was Antoninus, a centurion. He came upon a Jew in a deep cavern, and told him he would spare his life if he would surrender. The Jew asked him to give him hand as a pledge of his faith, and to help him out of the cave. Antoninus did so, and the Jews at once ran him through with a spear.

John was asleep when the Romans entered. He was aroused by Jonas rushing into the room. The boy was at all times restless, and suffered less than most of those within the walls, for there was an abundance of grain up to the end of the siege, and until the Romans had discovered the way down to the water he had not suffered in any way from thirst. He was considered too young to take part in the actual fighting, but had labored with the rest in repairing the defenses, carrying food to the men on the walls, and carrying away the dead and wounded.

"Get up, John!" he exclaimed. "In the mist I have just run upon a mass of Roman soldiers ranged in order. The town is taken. Quick, before they scatter and begin to slay!"

John caught up his sword and ran out. Just as he did so a terrible shout was heard, followed by shrieks and cries. The work of butchery had begun.

John's plans had been made for some time. At night Jonas had frequently descended to the ledge, taking with him food and jars of water he brought up from below, and once or twice John had descended, Jonas fastened a rope round his body and lowering it gradually, for, active as he was, John could not get down without such assistance. Indeed, to any one who looked casually over the top the descent appeared absolutely impossible.

At the top of their speed the lads ran to the spot at which the descent had to be made. The rope was hidden close at hand. John slipped the noose at the end over his shoulders, Jonas slipped the rope once around a stunted tree which grew close by, and allowed it to go out gradually. As soon as the strain upon it ceased, and he knew John was upon the ledge, he loosened the rope and dropped the end over, and then began himself to descend, his bare feet and hands clinging to every inequality, however ever slight, in the rock. He presently stood by the side of John. The latter had coiled up the rope and laid it by him, and had then thrown himself down and was sobbing bitterly. Jonas sat down quietly beside him till he had recovered his composure.

"It is no use fretting," he said philosophically, "there's no one you care about particularly up there, and I'm sure there's no one I care about; only I should like to have peeped in and have seen her face when the Romans burst open that door. I don't suppose she was very sorry, though, for it will be better to be a Roman slave than to be going through what they have been for the last month."

"It was horrible!" John said, "horrible! However, Jonas, let us thank God for having thus preserved our lives when all besides are in such terrible danger of death."

For a time the two lads sat silent. John was the first to speak.

"I am thankful," he said, "that owing to our being down the face of the rock the sound is carried away above our heads and we can hear but little of what is going on there. It seems a confusion of sounds, and comes to us rather as an echo from the hills yonder than directly from above."

Sometimes, indeed, thrilling screams and shouts were heard, but for the most part the sounds were so blended together that they could not be distinguished one from another. As soon as the mist cleared off the lads lay down as far back from the ledge as they could get.

"We must not lift up a head to-day," John said; "the guards below and on the hills will have their eyes fixed on the rock on the lookout for fugitives, and until night-time we must not venture to sit up. Fortunately that outer edge of the shelf is a good deal higher than it is back here, and I don't think that even those on the mountain opposite could see us as we lie."

"I should think a good many may escape like us," Jonas said presently; "there are numbers of caverns and passages from which they have dug the stone for the building of the houses. A lot of the people are sure to hide away there."

"I dare say they will," John agree; "but I fear the Romans will hunt them all out."

"How long do you think we shall have to stay here, John?"

"Till the Romans go, whether it is one week or two; but I do not think they will stay here many days. The town is so full of dead that in this hot weather it will be unbearable before long. At any rate we shall be able to pass a good deal of time in sleep. We have not had much of it lately. Till last night I have not been in a house at night for over a fortnight. But I felt last night as if I must have a sleep whatever came of it. I suppose the guards at the breach must have felt the same, or the Romans could never have got in with the alarm being given."

For a few minutes John lay thinking of the terrible scenes that must be passing on the rock above, then his drowsiness overcame him and he was soon fast asleep. It was dark when he woke; as he moved, Jonas spoke.

"Are you awake, John? Because if you are, let us have something to eat. I have been awake the last four hours, and I have been wishing you would stir."

"There was no occasion to wait for my waking, Jonas; there is the grain and the water close at hand, and no cooking is required."

"I wasn't going to eat till you woke, if it had been all night," Jonas said; "still I am glad you are awake; they are quiet now up above, and I have heard the Roman trumpets sounding. I expect that most of them have marched back to their camp."

The next day passed like the first. Occasionally cries of agony were heard; sometimes bodies hurled from the top of the rock but a short distance from where they were lying.

The next two days passed more quietly, but upon that following, a murmur, as a multitude of men working, was heard. From time to time there were heavy crashes as masses of stones, hurled down the precipice, struck against its face as they fell, and then bounded far out beyond the stream at its foot. All these sounds were echoed back by the surrounding hills until it seemed as if a storm was raging far away in the heart of the mountains.

"They are destroying the town," John said, in answer to his companion's question as to the cause of the uproar. "That is the best thing possible for us. Had it remained standing they might have left a garrison here to prevent our people reoccupying it. If they destroy it, it's a sign that they intend to march away altogether."

Several times Jonas wished to climb up at night to ascertain what was going on, but John would not hear of it.

"There is nothing to find out, Jonas. We know what they did at Gadara, where they slew all the males and carried off all the women, although no resistance was offered. We may be sure that there will be no more mercy shown at Jotapata, which has affronted the Roman power by keeping their great army at bay for nearly seven weeks, and whose capture has cost them thousands of men. We know what has happened—they have slain every soul, save a few young women who were worth money as slaves. Now they are leveling the town to its foundations. The place that defied them will cease to exist. And yet they talk of Roman magnanimity! Would we had five thousand fighting men hidden here with us; we would climb then, Jonas, and fall upon them in the night and take mighty vengeance for the woes they have inflicted. But, being alone, we will remain here till we have reason to believe that the last Roman has left. Did one of them catch sight of you your fate would be sealed. They have no boys among them, and the slightest glimpse of your figure would be enough to tell them that you are a Jew who had been in hiding, and in their fear that one man should escape their vengeance they would hunt you down as a pack of wolves might hunt down a solitary lamb."

"They could never get down here, John."

"Not by the way you came; but they would lower a cage full of armed men from above, and slay us without pity."

"But if I were found out, John, I would not lead them here. I would throw myself over the precipice rather than that risk should come to you!"

"But I don't want you to throw yourself over the precipice, Jonas, I want to keep you with me; in the first place, because we are great friends now; in the second, because if you are killed I might as well throw myself over at once, for I do not think I could ever climb up this rock without your assistance."

"It is much easier going up than coming down, John."

"That may be and indeed I have no doubt it is so, but I would rather not put the matter to the test. No; we have provision and water here enough to last us for ten days, and until they are consumed it were best not to stir from here."

Four days later, however, they heard the sound of the Roman trumpets, and on raising their head carefully a few inches saw that the guards on the opposite hills had all been withdrawn. Having now less fear of being seen, they raised their heads still further and looked up the valley to the great camp on the hillside, where at night they had seen the fires of Romans blazing high.

"They are going!" Jonas exclaimed joyously. "Look at the sun sparkling on the long lines of arms and armor. Not a sound is to be heard above—the work is done. They are about to march away."

"Do not let us expose ourselves further," John said; "it may be that they have left a few watchers to see if any who have eluded their search may show themselves believing that they have gone. I have no doubt they are going, and by tomorrow it may be safe for us to move."

All day they heard the sound of trumpets, for the great host took a long time getting into motion, but gradually the sound grew fainter and fainter as the rear-guard of the army took the road which they had cut through the mountains eight weeks before.

That night when darkness fell, and the two lads sat up on their ledge and looked round, not a light was to be seen and not a sound broke the silence of the night.

"At daybreak tomorrow, Jonas, as soon as it becomes light enough for you to see your way, you shall go up and look round; they may have left a guard behind, but I should hardly think so. After the wholesale slaughter at Gadara and here the hatred of the Romans will be so intense that, confident as they are in their arms and discipline, they would hardly venture to leave a small body of men in the heart of these mountains."

As soon as it was daylight Jonas prepared to climb up to the plateau above. He took with him the rope, arranging that if he found that the place was absolutely deserted he would lower one end to John and fasten the other to the tree above, and that he would then aid John as much as his strength would permit in making his way up the rock.

John watched his companion making his way up, and observed exactly where he placed his feet and hands until he was out of sight; then he waited. In about a quarter of an hour the end of the rope fell in front of him. He fastened it securely under his arms, and then, taking off his sandals, began the ascent. It was not so difficult as it had looked, and the steady strain which Jonas kept on the rope from above aided him and gave him confidence. In three or four minutes he gained the top of the rock.

"There is not a soul to be seen," Jonas said; "the town has gone, and the people, and the Romans. All is desolation!"

The scene was indeed changed since John had last looked upon it. Not a wall in the so lately busy little town had been left standing. The whole area was covered three or four feet deep with a chaos of stones, mortar, and beams, forming a great grave, below which lay the bodies of forty thousand of the defenders of the place. The wall so bravely defended had disappeared, and the embankment whose erection had cost the Romans so much labor and bloodshed had been destroyed by fire. A dead silence hung over the place, and the air was tainted with a terrible odor of corruption.

The desolation and solitude of the scene overpowered John, and he sad down on a fragment of masonry and wept unrestrainedly for some time. He roused himself at last as Jonas touched him.

"I shall go down again and get what grain there is left," the boy said. "There is no chance of finding any thing to eat within a day's march of here. The Roman horse will have destroyed every village within a wide circuit."

"But I cannot let you go down again, Jonas; the danger is too great."

"But I have been up and down lots of times," Jonas said.

"That may be, Jonas; but you might be dashed to pieces this time."

"Well, if you like I will fasten the rope round me; then if I should slip I shall be safe."

John consented with some reluctance, but he was so nervous and shaken that he walked some distance away, and did not turn round until he heard Jonas' footsteps again approaching him.

"Now we can start," the boy said. "We have got grain here enough for three days, and tonight we will crush it and cook it. I have had enough of eating raw grain for a long time to come."

The boy's cheerfulness restored the tone of John's nerves, and making their way with some difficulty over the chaos of stone and timber until they arrived at the pile of charred timber which marked the spot where the Roman embankment had stood, they stepped out briskly, descended the hill, crossed the deserted lines of circumvallation, and then began to ascend the mountains, which had for some distance been stripped of their timber for the purposes of the siege. In another hour's walking they reached the forest, and pressed on until the afternoon. Not that there was any need for speed now, but John felt a longing to place as wide a gap as possible between himself and the great charnel ground which alone marked the spot where Jotapata had stood.

At length Jonas urged the necessity for a halt for rest and food. They chose a spot at the foot of a great tree, and then set to work to collect a store of firewood. John took out the box of tinder, which in those days every one carried about with him and a fire was soon lighted. Jonas then looked for two large flat stones, and set to work to grind some grain.

The halting place had been chosen from the vicinity of a little spring which rose a few yards distant. With this the pounded grain was moistened, and after kneading it up Jonas rolled it in balls and placed them in the hot ashes of the fires. In half an hour they were cooked, and the meal was eaten with something like cheerfulness. Another day's walking brought them to a little village nestled in the forest. Here they were kindly received, though the people scarce believed them when they said that they were survivors of the garrison of Jotapata. The news of the capture of the town and the destruction of its defenders had already spread through the country, and John now learned for the first time the fate which had befallen Japha and the Samaritans on Mount Gerizim, events which filled him with consternation.

The folly of the tactics which had been pursued of cooping all the fighting men up in the walled cities, to be destroyed one after the other by the Romans, was more than ever apparent. He had never from the first been very hopeful of the result of the struggle, but it seemed now as if it could end in nothing but the total destruction of the Jewish race of Palestine. John stayed for two days in the little mountain village, and then, with a store of provisions sufficient to last him some days, pursued his way, following the lines of the Anti-Libanus until that range of hills joined the range of Mount Hermon north of the sources of the Jordan.

He had stopped for a day at Dan, high up among the hills. Here the people had no fear of Roman vengeance, for the insurrection had not extended so far north, and the Roman garrison of Cæsarea Philippi overawed the plains near the upper waters of the Jordan. Determined, however, to run no unnecessary risks, John and his companion pursued their way on the lower slopes of the hills, until, after six days' walking, they arrived at Neve.

Here they learned where the farm of John's kinsman was situated, and made their way thither. As they came up to the house a woman came out, gazed intently at John and, with a scream of terror ran back into the house. It was one of Martha's maids. John stood irresolute, fearing that his sudden appearance might startle the other inmates, when suddenly Mary appeared at the door, looking pale but resolute. She too gazed fixedly at John, and her lips moved, but no sound came from them.

"Don't you know me, Mary?" John said.

The girl gave a scream of joy and threw herself into his arms. A moment later Martha, followed by Miriam and the other servants, came out.

"It is no spirit, mother, it is John himself," Mary exclaimed, and the next moment John was clasped in his mother's arms.

It was no surprising that the first who saw John had thought that he was a spirit. The news had already been received that the whole of the garrison of Jotapata had been put to the sword, and John's appearance was changed so greatly within the last three months that he would scarcely have been known. Fatigue, anxiety, and the loss of blood from several wounds which he had received in the course of the siege had so pulled him down that he was but a shadow of his former self. His clothes were in rags. He had washed them at the village where he had first stopped, for before that they had been stiffened with blood, and even now, stained and ragged as they were, they gave him the appearance of a mendicant. Jonas had held back a little while the first joyful greeting was going on, but John soon turned to him.

"Mother," he said, "this must be as another son to you, for, next to the protection of God, it is to him I owe my life." Martha welcomed the young stranger affectionately.

"Before you tell us aught that has befallen you, John, go and change your garments and wash, while we prepare a meal for you, the clothes of your uncle's son Silas, who is about your age, will fit you, and those of his younger brother will do for your friend."

"Was the news of my father good?" John asked.

"Yes, the Lord be praised, he was well when we heard of him a week since."

The travelers were at once conducted to a room and supplied with water and clean garments. By the time they had changed and returned to the general room John's uncle and cousin had been fetched in from the farm, and he received another hearty welcome.

It almost seemed to him, as he sat down to a comfortable meal with Mary and his mother waiting upon him, that the events of the past two months had been a hideous dream, and that he had never left his comfortable home on the shore of the Lake of Galilee. As to Jonas, unaccustomed to kind treatment or to luxury of any kind, he was too confused to utter a word. When the meal was over John was asked to tell his news, and he related all the stirring incidents of the siege, and the manner in which he and his companion had effected his escape.

"We are, no doubt," he concluded, "the sole male survivors of the siege."

"Not so, my son," Martha said. "There is a report that Josephus has survived the siege, and that he is a prisoner in the hands of the Romans."

"It may be that they have spared him to grace Vespasian's triumph at Rome," John said. "It is their custom, I believe, to carry the generals they may take in war to Rome to be slain there."

It was not until some time afterward that John learned the particulars of the capture of Josephus. When he saw that all was lost, Josephus had leaped down the shaft of a dry well, from the bottom of which a long cavern led off, entirely concealed from the sight of those above. Here he found forty of the leading citizens, who had laid in a store of food sufficient to last for many days. Josephus, at least, who gives his account of all these circumstances, says that he quite unexpectedly found these forty citizens in hiding there; but this is improbable in the extreme, and there can be little doubt that he had long before prepared this refuge with them when he found that the people would not allow them to attempt to make their escape from the city.

At night Josephus came up from the well and tried to make his escape, but finding the Romans everywhere vigilant, he returned to the place of concealment. On the third day a women, who was aware of the hiding-place, informed the Romans of it, probably in return for a promise of freedom, for the Romans were searching high and low for Josephus, who could not, they were convinced, have escaped through their lines. Vespasian immediately sent two tribunes, Paulinus and Gallicanus, to induce him to surrender by promise of his life.

Josephus refused to come out, and Vespasian sent another tribune, Nicanor, a personal friend of Josephus, to assure him of his safety if he would surrender. In the account Josephus gives of the transaction he says that at this moment he suddenly remembered a dream in which it was revealed to him that all these calamities should fall upon the Jews, that he himself should be saved, and that Vespasian should become emperor, and that therefore if he passed over to the Romans he would do so not as a renegade, but in obedience to the voice of God.

It was certainly a happy coincidence that the dream should have occurred to him at this moment. He at once announced his readiness to surrender, but his forty companions did not see the matter in the same light. The moment Josephus left them the Roman soldiers would throw combustibles down the well and suffocate them if they did not come out and submit to slaughter.

They urged upon Josephus that he was their leader; that they had all followed his orders and cast in their lot with his; and that it would be treacherous and base in the extreme for him now to save his life by going over to the Romans, when all the inferior people had slain themselves or had submitted to slaughter rather than beg their lives of the Romans. Josephus argued with them at length, but they were not convinced, and drawing their swords, threatened to kill him if he tried to leave them. They would all die together, they said. Josephus then proposed that, in order to avoid the sin of suicide, they should draw lots as to which should kill each other. To this they assented; and they continued to draw lots as to which should slay the other until only Josephus and one other remained alive.

This is the story Josephus tells. He was, of course, endeavoring to put his own case in the best light, and to endeavor to prove that he was not, as the Jews universally regarded him, a traitor to his country. It need hardly be said that the story is improbably in the extreme, and that had any one of the forty men survived and written the history he would probably have told a very different tale. The conduct of Josephus from the first outbreak of the trouble showed that he was entirely adverse to the rising against the Romans. He himself, having been to Rome, had seen her power and might, and had been received with great favor by Poppæa, the wife of Nero, and had made many friends there.

He has, therefore, at the outset opposed as far as he was able, without going so far as to throw suspicion on his patriotism, the rebellion against the Romans. During the events in Galilee he had shown himself anxious to keep in favor with the Romans. He had rebuked those who had attacked the soldiers traveling as an escort with a large amount of treasure belonging to King Agrippa, and would have sent back the spoils taken had not the people risen against it. He affected great indignation at the plunder of Agrippa's palace at Tiberias, and, gathering all he could of the spoils, had handed them over to the care of the chief of Agrippa's friends there.

He had protected the two officers of Agrippa whom Jews would have killed, had released and sent them back to the king; and when John of Gischala wished to carry off large quantities of grain stored by the Romans in Upper Galilee, Josephus refused to allow him to do so, saying that it should be kept for its owners. It is almost certain that Josephus must in some way have entered into communication with the Romans; for how otherwise could he, with the principal inhabitants, have proposed to make their escape when every avenue was closed? Josephus was a man of great talent and energy, full of resources, and of great personal bravery—at least if his own account of his conduct during the siege is to be believed. But no on can read his labored excuses for his own conduct without feeling sure that he had all along been in correspondence with the Romans, and that he had beforehand been assured that his life should be spared.

He had from the first despaired of successful resistance to the Romans; and his conduct in throwing himself, at the last moment, into a town about to be besieged, and, as he must have known, captured—for the want of water alone rendered its fall a mere question of time—when his presence and leadership were so urgently required among the people to whose command he had been appointed, seems to prove that he wished to fall into their hands. It would not be just to brand Josephus as a traitor. He had done his best to induce the Galileans to form themselves into an army and to defend the province; and it was only when that army dispersed at the approach of the Romans that he went to Jotapata. It was his leadership that enabled that city to continue its heroic defense. It cannot therefore be said that Josephus in any way betrayed the trust confided to him by the council at Jerusalem. But the conclusion can hardly be avoided, that from the first, foreseeing that utter ruin and destruction would fall upon the Jews, he had set himself to work to prepare a way of pardon and escape for himself, and that he thought a position of honor among the Romans vastly preferable to an unknown grave among the mountains of Galilee.

Upon being taken out of the well Josephus was taken to Vespasian, and in the presence only of the general, his son Titus, and two other officers, announced that he was endowed with prophetic powers, and that he was commissioned by God to tell Vespasian that he would become emperor, and that he would be succeeded by his son Titus. The prophecy was one that required no more penetration than for any person in the present day to predict that the most rising man in a great political party would one day become prime minister. The emperor was hated, and it was morally certain that his fall would not long be delayed; and in that case the most popular general in the Roman army would almost certainly be chosen to succeed him.

Vespasian himself was not greatly affected by the prophesy. But Josephus declared that he had all along predicted the success of the Romans, the fall of the town after forty-six days' siege, and his own safety; and as some of the female captives were brought up, and, on Josephus appealing to them whether this was not so, naturally replied in the affirmative, Josephus says that Vespasian was then satisfied to his prisoner's divine mission, and thenceforth treated him with great honor.

It is much more easy to believe that an agreement already existed between Vespasian and Josephus, and that the latter only got up this story to enable him to maintain that he was not a traitor to his country, but acting in accordance with the orders of God. Certain it is that no similar act of clemency was show by Vespasian to any other Jew, that no other thought of pity or mercy entered his mind during the campaign, that he spared no man who fell alive into his hands, and that no more ruthless and wholesale extermination than that which he inflicted upon the people of Palestine was ever carried out by the most barbarous of conquerors.

To this day the memory of Josephus is hated among the Jews.

Chapter Seven

THE MASSACRE ON THE LAKE

John remained for three weeks at his uncle's. A messenger with the news of his safe arrival there had been sent off to his father, who came up to see him three days later. The formal act of betrothal between John and his cousin took place. Simon and Martha would have been willing that the full ceremony of marriage should take place, and the latter even urged this upon her son.

"You are now more than seventeen, John, and have taken your place among men, and may well take to yourself a wife. Mary is night fifteen, and many maidens marry earlier. You love each other. Why, then, should you not be married? It would cheer the old age of your father and myself to see our grandchildren growing up around us."

"Had the times been different, mother, I would gladly have had it so; but with the land torn by war, with our brethren being slaughtered everywhere, with Jerusalem and the Temple in danger, it is no time for marrying and giving in marriage. Besides, the law says that for a year after marriage a man shall not go to war or journey upon business, but shall remain at home quiet with his wife. I could not do that now. Did the news come tomorrow that the Romans were marching upon Jerusalem, assuredly I should do my duty and take up arms and go to the defense of the Holy City; and maybe Mary would be left a widow before the days of rejoicing for the marriage were over.

"No, mother; the life of no man who can yield a weapon is his own at present. The defense of the temple is the first and greatest of duties. If I fall there you will adopt Mary as your child and marry her to some one who will take my place and be a son to you. Mary will grieve for me, doubtless, for a time, but it will be the grief of a sister for a brother, not that of a wife for her husband; and in time she will marry the man to whom you shall give her and will be happy. Even for myself I would rather that it were so left. I shall feel more free from cares and responsibilities; and though, if you and my father lay your orders upon me, I shall of course obey them, I pray you that in this matter you will suffer me to have my way."

Martha talked the matter over with her husband, and they agreed that John's wishes should be carried out, and that the marriage should be postponed until the troubles were over. Neither of them believed that John would fall in the struggle. They regarded his escape from Jotapata as well-nigh miraculous, and felt assured that God, having specially protected him through such great danger, would continue to do so to the end.

Contrary to expectation, Vespasian had not followed up his success at Jotapata by a march against Jerusalem. His army had suffered very heavy losses in the siege, and the desperate valor which the defenders of the town had shown had doubtless impressed upon his mind the formidable nature of the task he had undertaken. If a little mountain town had cost him so dearly, what would not be the loss which would be entailed by the capture of a city like Jerusalem, with its position of vast natural strength—its solid and massive fortifications, and defended as it would be by the whole strength of the Jewish nation fighting with the fury of religious fanaticism and despair!

His army, strong as it was, would doubtless capture the city, but at such a cost that it might be crippled for further action, and Vespasian was keeping on eye upon Rome, and wished to have his army complete and in perfect order in readiness for anything that might occur there. Therefore, after the fall of Jotapata he marched first to Cæsarea, and after a short halt there passed north to Cæsarea Philippi, where the climate, cooled by the breezes from the mountains, was pleasant and healthful, and here he gave the army twenty days to rest and recover from their wounds and fatigues. He then marched south again to Scythopolis, or Behtsan, lying just within the borders of Samaria and not far from Jordan. Here Titus with a detached force joined him, and they prepared to reduce the cities near the lake.

Simon had by this time returned home accompanied by John and Jonas. Simon tried to persuade his son to remain with his mother, but John had entreated that he might accompany him.

"The war may last for a long time, father, and the land must be tilled, else why should you yourself return home? We are in the province of King Agrippa, and after what has befallen Jotapata and Japha it is not likely that the people of Hippos or of other towns will venture to show disaffection—therefore there is no reason why the Romans should carry fire and sword through Agrippa's country east of Jordan. It is well that my mother and Mary should not return, for if evil days should come they could not save themselves by rapid flight; besides we risk but death, and death were a thousand times better than slavery among the Romans. If we find that they are approaching and are wasting the land, we can fly. The boats are close by, and we can take to the lake and land where we will and make our way back here."

"And you will not seek, John, when the Romans approach to enter Tiberias or Gamala, or any other cities that may hold out against the Romans?

"No, father. I have had my share of defending a walled city, and save for Jerusalem I will fight no more in cities. All these places must fall sooner or later if the Romans sit down before them. I will not be cooped up again. If any leader arises and draws together a band in the mountains to harass and attack the Romans I will join him, for it has always seemed to me that in that way only can we fight successfully against them; but if not, I will aid you in the labors of the farm until the Romans march against Jerusalem."

Simon yielded to his son's wishes, for the events of the last year had aged him much and he felt the need of assistance on the farm. The men who had worked for him has, save Isaac and one or two of the older men, gone away to Jerusalem or to Gamala, or one or other of the fortified towns. The time for the harvest was at hand and there would be few to gather it in. Martha would fain have accompanied them, but Simon would not hear of this.

"You are in a safe refuge here, wife, and rather than that you should leave it, I would abandon our farm altogether. If you come, Mary and the women must come also, and even for us men the danger would be greater than were we alone."

Mary so tried her power of persuasion, but Simon was not to be moved, and the three set off together, for Jonas as a matter of course accompanied John wherever he went. The three weeks' kindness, rest, and good feeding had done wonders for him. The wild reckless expression which John had noticed when he had first met him had well-nigh disappeared, his bones had become better covered and his cheeks filled out, and comfortably clothed as he now was few would have recognized in him the wild goatherd of Jotapata.

Simon was mounted on a donkey, the others walked.

"It is well that I am off again," Jonas said; "another month there and I should have got fat and lazy, and should have grown like the dwellers on the plains."

"There will be plenty of work for you on the farm, Jonas," Simon said; "you need not be afraid of growing fat and lazy there."

"I don't think I am fond of work," Jonas said thoughtfully, "not of steady work, but I will work hard now, Simon; you have all been so good to me that I would work till I dropped for you. I wouldn't have worked before, not if they had beaten me ever so much, because they were always unkind to me; and why should on work for those who do nothing for you but beat and ill-use you?"

"You should always do your duty, Jonas," Simon said. "If others do not do their duty to you, so much the worse for them; but that is no excuse for your not doing your duty as far as you can."

Jonas, being a little behind Simon, made a little face expressive of his disagreement with this option, but he said nothing. They followed the course of the river Hieromax down to Capitolias, where they slept that night in the house of some friends of Simon, and on the following evening arrived at the farm. John received a hearty greeting from Isaac and the other men, and several of the fishermen, when they heard of his return, came in to see him.

For the next fortnight, John and Jonas worked from daylight to dark, and by the end of that time the greater part of the corn was gathered in the granary; a portion was stored away in a deep pit, straw being laid over it when the hole was nearly full, and earth being thrown in level to the surface, so that should the Romans come and sack the granary there should still remain a store which would carry them on until the next harvest. Then the news came from across the lake that the Romans were breaking up their camp at Scythopolis and were moving toward Tiberias.

No resistance was expected to be offered there. The greater part of the inhabitants had all along been well affected to the Romans, and had only been compelled by a small faction in the city and by the fear of the country people of Galilee to join in the insurrection. It was, too, the richest city in the dominions of King Agrippa, for although these lay for the most part east of Jordan the towns of Tiberias and Tarichea were included in them. Tiberias was, in fact, his chief city.

Here he had his richest palace, and the city, which greatly benefited by being the seat of his government, was Roman rather than Jewish in its hopes and feelings. So confident was Vespasian that no resistance would be offered, that when he arrived within half a mile of the town he sent forward an officer with fifty horse to exhort the people to open their gates.

When he got near the town the officer dismounted and went forward to speak, when a party of the war faction, headed by Jesus the son of Shaphat, charged out upon him. The officer, having had no orders to fight the Jews, fled on foot with five of his men who had also dismounted. Their assailants seized the horses and carried them in triumph into the city. The senate of Tiberias at once issued out from the city and hurried to the camp of Vespasian, and implored him not to visit the crime of a small body of desperate men upon a whole city, whose inhabitants had always been favorably disposed toward Rome. Agrippa added his entreaties to theirs, and Vespasian, who had just given orders for the troops to advance to storm and sack the city, recalled them. The insurgents under Jesus fled to Tarichea, and the gates being opened the Romans entered Tiberias, Vespasian issuing strict orders against plundering and the ill-treatment of the inhabitants.

At Tarichea were assembled not only the insurgents from Tiberias, but fighting men from all the towns on the lake and from the country on the east. The city had been carefully fortified by Josephus, and as the inhabitants had a very large number of vessels in the port, they relied upon these for escape in case the town should be reduced to extremities. No sooner did the Romans appear before their walls and begin to lay out their siege works than the Tiberians and others under the command of Jesus sallied out and dispersed the workmen.

When the Roman troops advanced in regular order some of the Jews retired into the city; others made for their boats, which were ranged along on the shore, and in these putting out a little distance, they cast anchor and opened fire with their missiles upon the Romans.

In the mean time a large number of Jews had just arrived from the further side of Jordan. Vespasian sent Titus with six hundred chosen horse to disperse them. The number of Jews was so large that Titus sent for further succor, and was re-enforced by Trajan with four hundred horse, while Antonius Silo with two thousand archers was sent by Vespasian to the side of a hill opposite the city to open fire thence upon the defenders of the walls and thus prevent them from harassing the Roman horsemen as they advanced.

The Jews resisted the first charge of the cavalry, but they could not long withstand the long spears and the weight and impetus of the horses, and fled in disorder toward the town. The cavalry pursued and tried to cut them off from it, but although great numbers were slaughtered, the rest by pure weight of numbers broke through and reached the city. A great dissension arose within the walls. The inhabitants of the town, dismayed by the defeat inflicted by a small number of Romans upon the multitude in the field, were unwilling to draw upon themselves the terrible fate which had befallen the towns which had resisted the Romans, and therefore clamored for instant surrender. The strangers, great numbers of whom were mountaineers from Paræa, Ammonitis, and Hermon, who knew little of what had been passing in Galilee, where for resistance, and a fray arose in the town.

The noise of the tumult reached Titus, who called upon his men to seize the moment while the enemy were engaged in civil discord to attack. Then leading his men he dashed on horseback into the lake, passed round the end of the wall, and entered the city. Consternation seized the besieged; the inhabitants attempted no resistance, still hoping that their peaceful character would save them from ill-treatment, and many allowed themselves to be slaughtered unresistingly. Jesus and his followers, however, fought gallantly, striving, but in vain, to make their way down to the ships in the port. Jesus himself and many of his men were killed. Titus opened the gates and sent word to his father that the city was captured, and the Roman army at once entered.

Vespasian placed a number of his troops in the large vessels in the port, and sent them off to attack those who had first fled to the boats. These were for the most part fishermen from the various towns on the lake. The cavalry were sent all round the lake to cut off and slay those who sought to gain the land. The battle, or rather the slaughter, went on for some time. The fishermen in their light boats could do nothing against the soldiers in the large vessels. These slew them with arrows or javelins from a distance, or ran them down, and killed them as they struggled in the water. Many of the boats were run ashore, but the occupants were slain there by the soldiers on the lookout for them. Altogether six thousand perished in the slaughter.

In the meantime Vespasian had set up his tribunal in Tarichea. The inhabitants of the town were separated from the strangers. Vespasian himself was, as Josephus said, unwilling to shed more blood, as he had promised when he entered the city to spare the lives of all, but he yielded to the arguments of those who said that the strangers were mountain robbers, the foes of every man.

Accordingly they were ordered to leave the city by the road to Tiberias. As soon as they had left the town the troops surrounded them, headed by Vespasian in person. Twelve hundred of the aged and helpless he ordered to be slain at once; six thousand of the most able-bodied he went to Nero, to be employed on the canal he was digging across the isthmus of Corinth; thirty thousand four hundred were sold as slaves; and a large number were bestowed upon Agrippa, who also sold them as slaves. This act, after the formal promise of pardon, disgraces the memory of Vespasian even more than the wholesale massacres of the garrisons of the towns which resisted to the last.

The news of this act of wholesale vengeance spread such terror through the land that the whole of the cities of Galilee at once opened their gates, and sent deputations to Vespasian to offer their submission and ask for pardon. Gamala, Gischala, and Itabyrium, a town on Mount Tabor which had been strongly fortified by Josephus, alone held out. Itabyrium lay some ten miles to the west of Tiberias.

Standing back among the trees at a short distance from the lake, Simon, John, and the workers on the farm watched with horror the slaughter of the fishermen on the lake. None of their neighbors were among those who had gone out to aid in the defense of Tarichea, for Simon had gone among them to dissuade them from launching their boats and joining the flotilla as it proceeded down the lake in the morning. He urged upon them that if they took part in the affair they would only bring down vengeance upon themselves and their families.

"There is no lack of men," he said, "in Tiberias and Tarichea. Such aid as you can give would be useless, and whether the cities fall at once, or whether they resist, the vengeance of the Romans will fall upon you. In a few hours their horsemen can ride round the shores of the lake and cut off all who are absent from returning to their homes, and give the villages to fire and sword. Those who can point to their boats drawn up at the side of the lake will be able to give proof to the Romans that they had not taken part against them. So far we have escaped the horrors of war on this side of Jordan. If the strong cities of Galilee cannot resist the Roman arms, what hope should we have on this side, where the population is comparatively scanty, and where there are few strong places? Do not let us provoke the Romans, my friends. If they go up against Jerusalem, let those who will go and die in defense of the Temple, but it would be worse than folly to provoke the wrath of the Romans by thrusting yourselves into the quarrel here."

Warmly did the fishermen congratulate themselves when they saw the combat proceeding on the lake, and when a strong body of Roman horse rode along the shore, leaving parties at regular intervals to cut off those who might try and land. A body of twenty were posted down by the boats, and two came into the village and demanded food for the party. Simon, when he saw them coming, ordered all the able-bodied men to retire and remain in the olive groves on the slopes at a distance from the lake until the Romans had gone, while he and Isaac and some other old men went down and met the soldiers.

"Are any of the people of this place out there on the lake?" the officer in command of the twenty men asked, as Simon and his party, bringing bread, fruit, and wine, came down to the water-side.

"No, sir," Simon replied; "we have but eight boats belonging to the village, and they are all there. We are peaceable people, who till the soil and fish the lake, and take no part in the doings of the great towns. We are subjects of King Agrippa, and have no cause for discontent with him."

"A great many other people have no cause for discontent, old man," the officer said, "but they have, nevertheless, risen in rebellion. However, as your boats are here, and your people seem to have taken no part in this matter, I have naught to say against you, especially as your wine is good, and you have brought down plenty of it."

Simon and his companions withdrew, and, with aching hearts, watched from a distance the massacre upon the lake. The fury, however, pronounced among the men in the towns and villages on the shore at the sight of the numerous corpses washed ashore was so great that many of the young men left their avocations and started for Gamala, which, relying upon the strength of its position, which was even stronger than that of Jotapata, was resolved to resist to the last.

Several of the young men of the village, and many from the villages near, were determined to take this course, maddened by the slaughter of many friends and relations. John himself was as furious as any, especially when the news came of the violation of faith at Tarichea, and of the selling of nigh forty thousand men into slavery.

"Father," he said that evening, "I had thought to stay quietly with you until the Romans advanced against Jerusalem, but I find I cannot do so. The massacre at Jotapata was bad enough, but the slaughter of defenseless men on the lake is worse. I pray you let me go."

"Would you go into Gamala and die there, John?" Simon asked. "Better to die at the Temple than to throw away your life here."

"I do not intend to go into Gamala, father, nor to throw away my life, though I care little for it, except for the sake of you and my mother and Mary; but I would do something, and I would save the sons of our neighbors and others from the fate that assuredly awaits them if they enter Gamala. They know not, as I do, how surely the walls will go down before the Roman engines; but even did they know it, so determined are they to fight these slayers of our countrymen that they will still go. What I propose to do is to carry out what I have always believed to be the true way of fighting the Romans. I will collect a band, and take to the mountains, and harass them whenever we may find opportunity. I know the young men from our village will follow me if I will lead them, and they will be able to get their friends along the shore to do the like. In that way the danger will not be so great, for in the mountains the Romans would have no chance of overtaking us, while, if we are successful, many will gather round us, and we may do good service."

"I will not stay you, John, if you feel that the Lord has called upon you to go; and, indeed, you may save, as you say, the lives of many of our neighbors, by persuading them to take to the hills with you, instead of shutting themselves up in Gamala. Go down then to the village and talk to them, and see what they say to your plan."

John had little doubt as to his proposal being accepted by the younger men of the village. The fact that he had been chosen as one of the bodyguard of Josephus had at once given him importance in the eyes of his neighbors, and that he should have passed through the siege of Jotapata, and had escaped, had caused them to regard him not only as a valiant fighter, but as one under the special protection of God. Since his return scarce an evening had passed without parties coming from one or other of the villages along the shore to hear from his lips the story of the siege. As soon, then, as he went down to the fishing village, and told the young men who had determined to leave for Gamala that he thought badly of such action, but that he intended to raise a band and take to the mountains and harass the Romans, they eagerly agreed to follow him, and to obey his orders. There were eight of them, and John at once made them take an oath of obedience and fellowship, swearing in all things to obey his orders, to be true to each other to death, to be ready to give their lives when called upon for the destruction of the Romans, and never, if they fell into the hands of the enemy, to betray the secrets of the band, whatever might be the tortures to which they were exposed.

John could have obtained more than eight men in the village, but he would only take quite young men.

"I want only men who can undergo fatigue and watching, who can climb mountains, and run as fast as the Roman horse can gallop; besides, for work like this it is necessary that there should be one leader, and that he should be promptly obeyed. If I take older men, they will naturally wish to have a voice in the ordering of things, I have seen enough of military matters to know that, for prompt decision and swift execution, one head, and one head only, is necessary. Besides, we may find difficulties in the way of getting food, and at first I wish for only a small band. If success attends us, we shall increase rapidly. Twenty will be quite enough to begin with."

As soon as the eight young men, of whom all but two were under twenty years old, had taken the oath, they started at once to the villages round.

"Do each of you gather in two, but no more," John said; "and let them be those whom you know to be strong and active. Do not bring more, and if four of you bring but one so much the better. If you find many more eager to join, you can tell them that we will send for them when the time comes to increase our numbers, and pray them to abide here and not to go into Gamala. Let each bring his arms and a bag of meal, and meet me tomorrow evening at sundown on the Hieromax River, three miles below Capitolias, that will be opposite to Abila, which lies on the mountain side. Let all travel singly, for the Roman horse may be about. However, as we shall be walking east, while Gamala lies to the west of south, they will not take us, should we come upon them, for men going thither to aid in the defense of the town."

The young men started at once on their missions, full of confidence in John, and feeling certain that under his leadership they should soon come to blows with the Romans, being also in their hearts well satisfied that their warfare would be in the open country, and they should not be called upon to fight pent up in walls from which there was no escape. Having seen his followers off, John returned home and told Simon the progress he has made. The old man sighed.

"I do not seek to keep you, John, for your duty to your country stands now in the first rank of all, and it may be that the Lord preserved you at Jotapata because he intends you to do great deeds for him here. I do not say spare yourself or avoid danger for our sakes; I only say do no throw away your life by rashness. Remember that, young as you are, you are a leader, and be prudent as well as brave. After Gamala has fallen, as fall I fear it will, and the Romans have moved away from these parts, as they will then do, for there is no resistance to them on this side of Jordan save at that town. I shall bring your mother and Mary back again, and you will find us waiting here to welcome you if you return. If not, my son, I shall mourn for you as Jacob mourned for Joseph, and more, seeing that you are the only prop of my old age; but I shall have the consolation of knowing that you died for your country."

"You will find in Mary a daughter, father; and you must find a husband for her who will take my place. But it may be that if the Romans march not direct upon Jerusalem—and they say that Vespasian has arranged that two of the legions shall winter on the seacoast at Cæsarea and the third at Scythopolis—it is probable that he will not move against Jerusalem till the spring. In that case I may be often here during the winter. For I will not go down to Jerusalem until the last thing, for there all is turmoil and disturbance, and until the time comes when they must lay aside their private feuds and unite to repel the invader, I will not go down."

Father and son talked until later in the night. In the morning John made his preparations for departure. He had told Jonas of his intentions. The boy listened silently, only saying, "Where you go, John, I am ready to go with you; it makes no difference to me;" and afterward went down to the lake side, where he filled his pouch with smooth pebbles, each of which he selected with great care; for when herding his goats among the mountains, Jonas had been always practicing with a sling, and many a cony had fallen before his unerring aim. All the lads in the mountains were accustomed to the use of the sling, but none in Jotapata had approached Jonas in their skill with this weapon.

In the morning John prepared to start. He and Jonas each carried a small sack, supported by a strap passing over the shoulders, and containing some eight pounds of meal and a gourd of water. Jonas carried no weapon save a long knife hidden under his garment, and his sling and pouch of stones. John carried a sword and buckler and a horn. Before they started John knelt before his father and received his blessing, and Simon, as he bade him adieu, gave him a small bag of money.

"You will need to buy things in the mountains, lad, and I would not that you should be driven, like the robber bands, to take food by force. It is true that they who go not to war should support those who risk their lives for their country; but there are many aged men who, like myself, cannot fight, there are many women whose husbands are away in Gamala or Jerusalem, and these may not be able to afford to assist others.

Therefore it is well that you should have means of paying for what you require, otherwise the curse of the widow and fatherless may fall upon you. And now, farewell, my son! May God have you in his keeping, and send you home safe to your mother and me!"

Chapter Eight

AMONG THE MOUNTAINS

Jonas was in high spirits as they started from the farm. He was leaving no friends behind, and so long as he had John with him he was perfectly contented. He was delighted to be on the move again, for although he had worked steadily in getting in the harvest, regular labor was distasteful to him; and accustomed as he had been to wander for weeks free and unchecked with his goats among the mountains, the regular life and order of the farm were irksome to him. John, on the other hand, was silent, replying briefly to the boy's questions. He felt the danger of the enterprise upon which he had embarked, and his responsibility as leader, and the thought of the grief which his father and mother would feel did aught befall him, weighted on his mind. Presently, however, he aroused himself.

"Now, Jonas, you must keep a sharp lookout round, for if we see any Roman soldiers in the distance I must hide my sword and buckler before they discover us, and you must stow away your sling and pouch; then we will walk quietly on. If they question us, we are going to stay with friends at Capitolias, and as there will be nothing suspicious about us, they will not interfere with us. After they have passed on, we will go back to our arms. We are not traveling in the direction of Gamala, and they will have no reason to doubt our story."

The did not, however, meet any of the parties of the Roman horse who were scouring the country, carrying off grain and cattle for the use of the army, and they arrived in the afternoon on the bank of the Hieromax. Upon the other side of the river rose the steep slopes of Mount Galaad, high up on whose side was perched the little town of Abila.

"Here we can wait, Jonas. We are nearly opposite the town. The others will doubtless soon be here."

It was not long before the band made their appearance, coming along in twos and threes as they had met on the river bank. By sunset the last had arrived, and John found that each of his first recruits had brought two others. He looked with satisfaction at the band. The greater part of them had been fishermen, all were strong and active, and John saw that his order that young men only should be taken had been obeyed, for not one of them was over the age of twenty-three, and, as he had laid it down as an absolute rule, all were unmarried. All were, like himself, armed with sword and buckler, and several had brought with them bags with javelin heads, to be fitted to staves later on. All their faces bore a look of determination, and at the same time of gladness.

The massacre on the lake had excited the inhabitants of the shore to fury, and even those who had hitherto held back from the national cause were now eager to fight against the Romans; but many shrank from going to Gamala, which was indeed already as full of fighting men as it could hold, and John's proposal to form a band for warfare in the mountains had exactly suited the more adventurous spirits.

All present were known to John personally. Many of them were sons of friends of Simon, and the others he had met at village gatherings, or when fishing on the lake. There were warm greetings as each accession to the party arrived, and each member of the band felt his spirits rise higher at finding that so many of those he knew personally were to be his comrades in the enterprise. When the last come had arrived John said:

"We will now be moving forward. We had best get well up the mountain before night falls; it matters not much where we camp tonight; tomorrow we can choose a good spot for our headquarters."

It being now the height of the dry season the river was low, and they had no difficulty in wading across. Then they struck up the hill to the right of Abila until they had fairly entered the forests which clothed the lower slopes of the mountains. Then John gave the word for a halt.

Dead wood was soon collected and a fire made. Cakes of meal were baked in the ashes, and after these had been eaten the party lay round the fire, and a few minutes later John rose to his feet.

"You all know the reason for which we are gathered together here. We all long for vengeance on the oppressors of our country, the murderers of our kinsmen and friends, the men who carry off our women to shame and slavery in Rome. We are all ready to die for our country and our God; but we would fain die doing as much harm to the Romans as we can, fighting like freemen in the open, instead of rats slaughtered in a cage. That is why, instead of going into Gamala, we have gathered here.

"I am the youngest among you; but I have so far assumed the leadership because, in the first place, I have been much with Josephus, who, although he may now most unworthily have gone over to the Romans to save his life, was yet a wise governor and a great leader. From him I have learned much of the Romans. In the second place, I have seen more of their warfare than any of you, having passed through the terrible siege of Jotapata.

"Lastly, I believe that God, having saved me almost alone of all the host that defended the town, has intended me as an instrument for his service. Therefore have I taken upon myself the command, in the first place, of this band; but, at the same time, if you think that I am too young, and would rather place another at your head, I will stand aside and release from their oath those who have already sworn. I am not self-seeking. I crave no the leadership over you, and will obey whomsoever you may choose for your chief. But to whomsoever is the leader prompt obedience must be given, for there must, even in a band like this, be order and discipline. We work for the common good, but we must yield to the direction of one will and one hand. Now what say you? I will walk away to leave you free to consult one with another, and will abide by your decision whatever it be. Only, the decision once made must be adhered to. There must be no after-grumbling, no hesitation or drawing back. You must have absolute confidence and give absolute obedience to him whom you choose. For only so can we hope to succeed in our enterprises."

John had gone but a short way among the trees when he was called back again. All had come prepared to follow him. His father had always been a man of weight and position among the villagers on the shore, and democratic as were the Jewish institutions, there was yet a certain respect paid to those of position above their fellows. John's experience, and especially his escape from Jotapata, seemed specially to mark him as one destined to play an important part. And his quiet, resolute bearing now—the feeling that he knew what was to be done and how to do it, that he was, in fact, the natural leader—came home to all, and it was with sincerity that they assured him that they accepted him as their leader.

"Very well," John said quietly. "Then let those who have not already taken the oath stand up and do so."

This was done, and John then said:

"Now I will tell you more of my plans, although these of course cannot be in any way settled until we see how things turn out. It is by watching for opportunities and seizing the right moment only that we can hope for success. We are all ready to give our lives for our country, but we do not wish to throw them away. We want each of us to do as much as possible. We want to live so as to share in the defense of the Temple; therefore we have to combine prudence with daring.

"As for an attack upon any strong body of Roman troops, it would be impossible unless they attempt to follow us among the mountains. One of our first duties will be to learn the country well, so that we may know where to defend ourselves should they come up after us; where from eminences we can cast down rocks upon them; where there are crags which we can climb, but up which their heavy-armed soldiers cannot follow us. This is our first task, for as yet they have not commenced to siege of Gamala. When they do so we must draw down near them and hide ourselves, mark the position of their camp, see how their tents are arranged, and where their sentries are placed.

"Then we can begin work; sometimes falling upon their guards, at other times creeping in past their sentries scattering through the camp, and at a given signal firing their tents with the brands from their fires, slaying those who first rush out, and then making off again to the hills. Then, too, they will be sending great numbers of men up the hills to cut timber and branches for their embankments, their breastworks, and the construction of the wattles to protect their machines. We shall be in hiding, and when a party of men separates from the rest we will fall upon these; we will harass their workers from a distance, always avoiding a regular combat, but hindering their work and wearing them out. Thus we may do better service to the defenders of Gamala than if we were within the walls.

"At present we have only swords, but we must get bows and arrows. It would not have been safe to have carried them across the plains, but we can procure them at Abila or Jabez Galaad. I fear that we shall not be able to interfere with the provisioning of the army, for upon the plains we shall have no chance with their cavalry; but here in these mountains, stretching away over Peræa into Arbis and Moab, we can laugh at pursuit by the Romans; and even Agrippa's light-armed Arabs will have difficulty in following us, and of them we need have little fear. At Jotapata we proved ourselves a match for the Romans, and their light-armed troops will not care to venture against me alone, as they will not know our numbers, and will fear being led into ambushes.

"There is one question which we have to consider, and this is food; as to flesh, we shall have it in abundance. There will be many flocks of goats belonging to those in Gamala straying among the mountains without an owner, therefore of goats' milk and flesh we can take abundance; but there will be a scarcity of grain. I have some money with me which we can purchase it in Abila and the villages. As for Jabez Galaad it is too close to Gamala, and the Romans will probably ascend the hill and destroy it, or place a guard there. At any rate, the money will be sufficient to purchase meal for us for some time, much longer probably than Gamala will be able to hold out, and when that has fallen it will be time to arrange about the future. Only let us take nothing without payment; let us not be like the robber bands which prey upon the people, until they long for the

Romans as masters.

"Only we must remember that while we desire now to do the Romans as much harm as possible, this is but the beginning of our work, and that we must save ourselves for the future. Gamala is but one town, and we shall have plenty of opportunities for striking at the enemy in the future. We have put our hands to the plow now, and so long as the war lasts we will not look back. It may be that our example may lead others to follow it, and in that case the Romans' difficulties will thicken every day.

"Were there scores of bands of determined men like us hanging around them, ready to attack small bodies whenever they venture away from their camps to gather in provisions and forage, and to harass them at night by constant alarms, we could wear them out; only we must always avoid a pitched battle. In irregular fighting we are as good as they; better, for we can move more quickly; but when it comes to fighting in order of battle we have no chance with them whatever. Their cavalry the other day outside Tarichea were like wolves among a flock of sheep. Nothing but disaster can come of fighting in the plain.

"Every people should fight in the way that suits them best, and an attempt to meet an enemy in their own way of fighting is sure to lead to disaster. Let the Romans keep the plain with his cavalry and his heavy infantry; let the Jew, light-footed and swift, keep to the hills. He is as much superior there as is the Roman in the plains. And now we must establish signals. One long note will mean, gather to me; two, fall back gradually; three, retire at once with all speed to the spot agreed upon before setting out in the morning.

"Two short notes will mean, advance and attack in the manner arranged; one short note oft repeated will tell you the Romans are advancing, sound your horns; for it were well that each provided himself with a cow's horn, so that the signals can be repeated. If we are scattered over a hillside among the trees, and the Romans hear horns sounded in many quarters, they will think there must be a large body of men assembled. This will make them slow and cautious in all their movements, will force many to stand prepared with their arms to guard those at work, and will altogether confuse and puzzle them. And now we will lie down and sleep; as soon as it is dawn we will be on foot again."

The next two days were spent in exploring that part of the mountains, examining the direction and extent of each valley and ravine, seeing where steep precipices afforded an opportunity for rolling down rocks upon an enemy passing along the valley or trying to storm the height, in searching for pools in dried water-courses, and in deciding upon a spot favorable for the camp.

They fixed upon a spot high up on the mountains, two miles east of Abila, as their headquarters. It was in a pass between two peaks, and gave them the option of descending either to the north or south, or of skirting along the mountains toward the sources of the Jabbok River, and thence crossing the Hermon range beyond the limits of Paræa. Jonas was sent the first thing to discover whether the Romans had taken possession of Jabez Galaad, which lay but five miles from Gamala, and on the southern side of the range of hills on whose western spur Gamala was built.

He returned in a short time saying that he had found the inhabitants in a state of great alarm, for that a Roman force could be seen coming up the road from the plain. Most of the fighting men of the town were in Gamala; the rest of the young women were leaving, so that only old people and children would be found in the town when the Romans arrived. Jonas also brought word that Vespasian's whole army was moving against Gamala. John had given Jonas money before he started to purchase bows and arrows. He had brought back bows for the whole party, and as many arrows as he could carry.

"I paid nothing for them," he said as he threw them down. "The man who sold them was praying those who were leaving the town to take them, for he thought that if the Romans found them in his house they would destroy it; but no one listened, all were too busy in carrying off such of their household goods as they could take to burden themselves further; so he gladly gave me as many as I could take. I carried off nearly all his bows, and I left him breaking up the rest of his store of arrows in order to burn them before the Romans arrived. A boy carrying a bag of arrow-heads came with me some little distance. I paid the man for them, and they are no hidden in the forest. You can fetch them when you will, but I could not carry more with me that I have got."

"You have done well, Jonas," John said as the men seized each a bow and divided the arrows among them; and then stood waiting, expecting orders from John to proceed at once to harass the Roman column as it ascended the hill.

"No," John said in answer to their looks, "we will not meddle with them to-day. Did we shoot at them they would suppose that we belonged to Jabez Galaad, and would in revenge destroy the town and all those they may find within it, and our first essay against them would bring destruction upon thousands of our countrymen."

The others saw the justness of his reasoning, and their faith in him as their leader was strengthened by his calmness and readiness of decision.

"Is the bag of arrow-heads heaven, Jonas?"

"It is for as much as the boy, who was about my age, could carry," Jonas replied.

"Then do you, Pineas, and you Simeon, go with Jonas to the place where the bag is hidden, and carry it to the place we have fixed upon for our camp. If on the way you come across a herd of goats, shoot two or three of them and take them with you, and get fires ready. The day is getting on, but he will go across the mountains and see where the Romans are pitching their camp, and by sunset we will be with you."

Making their way along the mountain the band came, after an hour's walk, to a point where they could obtain a view of Gamala.

The city stood on the western extremity of the hill, which, after sloping gradually down, rose suddenly in a sharp ridge like the hump of a camel, from which the town had its name, Gamala. On both sides this rock ended abruptly in a precipitous chasm, in which ran the two branches of the Hieromax, which met at the lower end of the ridge, and ran together into the end of the lake at Tarichea, three miles away.

Thus Gamala was only accessible from behind, where the ridge joined the mountains. Across this neck of land a deep fosse had been dug, so as to cut off all approach. The houses were crowded thickly on the steep slope of the ridge, which was so abrupt that the houses seemed to overhang one another. On the southern crag, which was of immense height, was the citadel of the town. There was a spring supplying abundance of water within the walls. Had it been defended by a garrison as brave and numerous as that of Jotapata it would have been well-nigh impregnable, but Cheres and Joseph, who commanded, had none of the genius of Josephus, although they were brave and determined. The city was crowded with fugitives from all parts, and had already, for seven months, resisted a besieging force which Agrippa had sent against it.

It was impossible to blockade the whole circuit of the town, but Vespasian took possession of all the neighboring heights and established his camp, with that of the Fifteenth Legion, on the hill facing the city to the east. The Fifth Legion threw up works opposite the center of the city, while the Tenth set to work to fill up ditches and ravines in order to facilitate the approaches. Agrippa approached the wall to persuade the inhabitants to surrender, but was struck in the right elbow by a stone from a sling and forced to retire.

This insult to the native king, who came in the character of an ambassador, enraged the Romans, and they set about the operations for the siege with great vigor. In spite of the efforts of the Jews the fosse which protected the wall on the east was speedily filled up, and the Romans then began, as at Jotapata, to raise an embankment facing the wall.

The day after the Romans had established their camp John and his followers advanced along the mountain until they could look down upon it, and for a long time watched the Romans at work, and learned all the details of the camp.

"You must fix them in your minds," John said, "in order that even on a dark night you may be able to make your way about it without difficulty, so that you may be able, after striking a blow, to fly directly to the mountain, for any who get confused and miss their way will assuredly be killed. You see the enemy have placed a strong guard half-way up the hillside in order to protect themselves from surprise; but it will be possible, by moving down to the streams and then mounting again, to reach the camp without passing through them. And by the same way we must make our retreat, for if we succeed in setting the camp on fire the flames will enable the guard on this mountain to see us approaching them. I had hoped that we might be able to penetrate unobserved to the tent of Vespasian, and to slay him and some of his generals; but by the bustle that we see round that tower on the hillside, and by the strong force of cavalry picketed round it, it is evident that he has taken up his quarters there, and, indeed, from the top of the tower he can look down upon the town and on all that is passing there, and issue his directions to his troops accordingly, so we must give up that idea. Another time we may be more fortunate. But, see, a great number of troops are ascending the hill toward us, doubtless to cut timber for their works. As soon as they are at work we will attack them."

The party retired into the forest, and as soon as they heard the sound of the Roman axes they crept quietly forward, moving noiselessly with their sandaled feet among the trees. When within a short distance of the Romans John ordered them to halt, and crept forward with Jonas to reconnoiter. There was little fear of their being heard, for several hundred men were at work felling trees, a line of sentries at ten paces apart standing under arms to prevent a surprise. The Romans were working too thickly to permit of any successful action by so small a party, and John saw that the idea of attack must be abandoned, and that he must confine himself for the present to harass the sentries.

Rejoining his men he told them what he had discovered, and bade them scatter along the line, and, crawling up under the protection of the trees, to approach as near as they could to the line of sentries, and then to shoot at them or at the workmen, many of whom, having thrown off their heavy armor to enable them the better to work, offered more favorable marks for the arrows than the sentries, whose faces only were exposed. They were on no account to come to close quarters with the Romans. If the latter advanced they were instantly to retire, approaching again as soon as the Romans recommenced their work; and so to continue until he blew the signal for them to draw off altogether. They were not to begin until they heard his signal for attack.

After allowing some little time to elapse for the men to get into position, John blew his horn. A moment, and cries and shouts were heard along the whole Roman line. The sound of chopping instantly ceased, and the Roman trumpets blew to arms. John had advanced sufficiently near to see the Roman workmen before he gave the signal. Jonas was a little in advance of him, and as the horn sounded he saw him step up from behind a tree, whirl his sling round his head and discharge a stone, and almost simultaneously a Roman sentinel, some forty paces away, fell with a crash upon the ground.

The Roman soldiers who had retained their armor ran instantly forward to support their sentries. The others hastily buckled on their breastplates, caught up their bucklers and helmets, and joined their comrades. Arrows continued to fall among them from their invisible foes, and although most of these fell harmless from their armor, several soldiers fell in addition to the seven or eight who had been killed by the first volley. The centurion on command soon saw that the number of assailants was small, but, afraid of being drawn into an ambush, he hesitated to give orders for an advance, but dispatched a messenger instantly to camp, contenting himself with throwing out strong parties a hundred yards in advance of his line. These now became the objects of attack, while arrows ceased to fall among the main body of the troops.

John moved round the flank till he gained a position whence he could observe the camp. The trumpets above had been heard there, and the troops had already taken up their position under arms. As he looked on he saw the messenger run up to a party of mounted officers. A minute later a trumpet sounded, and a strong body of Arabian archers advanced at a run up the slope. John at once withdrew to his first position, and sounded the order for instant retreat, and then hurrying back half a mile, sounded the note for his followers to assemble at the spot where he was standing.

In a few minutes all had joined him. They were in high spirits at the success of this first skirmish, and wondered why they had been so suddenly called off when the Romans had shown no signs of advancing against them.

"There are fully a thousand Arab archers in the forest by this time," John said. "They are as fleet of foot as we are, and it would be madness to remain. We have stopped their work for a time, and have killed many without a scratch to ourselves. That is well enough for to-day; tomorrow we will beat them up again."

At daybreak two of the party were sent forward to the edge of the wood to see with what force the Romans went out to work. They brought back the report that they were accompanied by a strong body of archers, and that as soon as they reached the forest the archers were scattered in front of them for a long distance, and that it would be impossible to approach them unobserved. On the previous afternoon John had dispatched Jonas to Abila, and he had returned with a number of cow horns. Round the fires in the evening the men set to work to pierce the points with heated arrowheads, and had converted them into instruments capable of giving a deep, prolonged sound. On the return of the scouts John set his men in motion.

"We cannot fight them to-day, but we can hinder their work. We will scatter through the forest, and as we approach them each is to sound his horn, and continue to do so from time to time. The Romans will think that a great force is advancing against them."

This was done with the effect John had anticipated. Hearing the sound of the horns all over the mountain side, the Romans concluded that a great force was advancing to attack them, and the archers were at once recalled.

The troops all stood to arms, and for several hours remained waiting an attack. Then after strong bodies of heavy-armed troops, preceded by the archers skirmishing before them, had pushed some distance into the forests without meeting with an enemy, the work recommenced, a considerable number still standing to their arms as protectors of the rest. Although a certain amount of time had been gained for the city by the interruption of the work of bringing in timber, John had undertaken these sham attacks rather with the purpose of accustoming his band to work together and to give them confidence, than with the view of troubling the Romans. In this he was perfectly successful. The band when they reached their camp that evening were in high spirits.

They had for two days puzzled and baffled a large Roman force, and inflicted some loss upon them, and forced them to desist from their work. They were pleased with themselves and their leader, and had lost much of the dread of the Romans which the capture of Jotapata, Japha, and Tarichea, and the tales of their cruelty and ferocity, had excited among the whole population. A reverse at the commencement of their work would have been fatal, and John had felt that however earnest the men were in their determination to die fighting for their country, the loss of a few of their number at the outset would have so dispirited the rest that the probability was that the band would disperse, or would at any rate be unwilling to undertake any desperate operation. But in their present mood they were ready for any enterprise upon which he might lead them, and he accordingly told them that he should abstain next day from a continuance of his attacks upon the working party, but that at night he would carry out the design of setting fire to their camp.

Accordingly the following day the Romans pursued their work unmolested, although they still continued the precaution of keeping a force of archers and parties of heavy-armed troops in advance of those working in the wood. John did not move till the afternoon, and then, descending the hill to the right, he skirted along in the lower forest until within two miles of Gamala; here he halted until nightfall. While waiting for the hour of action he gave final instructions to his men and assigned them to the order in which they should ascend from the river toward the rear of the camp. When they approached the spot where they would probably find Roman sentries posted they were to advance singly, crawling along upon the ground.

Those who first went through were to keep straight on until they reached the further end of the camp, stopping as near as they could judge fifty paces apart. They were then to wait for half an hour so as to be sure that all would have gained their allotted positions. Then when they saw a certain star sink below the horizon (a method of calculating time to which all were accustomed) they were to creep forward into the Roman camp, and each to make his way as noiselessly as possible until he came within a few paces of one of the smoldering fires of the Romans and to wait until they heard a single note from John's horn. Each was at once to spring forward, seize a lighted brand and fire the nearest tent, and then to crawl away, cutting, as they went, the ropes of the tent, so as to bring them down and create as much confusion as possible. Then, either by crawling, or, if discovered, by leaping to their feet and making a sudden rush, all were to make their way down to the river again, to follow its banks for half a mile, and then wait in a body for an hour. At the end of that time they were to make their way back to their camp in the mountains, certain by that time that all who were alive would have rejoined them. Should he himself not be with the party they were at once to proceed to the election of another leader.

At about ten o'clock they again moved forward, and descending to the river followed its banks until they arrived at the spot they had fixed on; then in single file they began to climb the hill. John placed himself in the middle of the line in order to have a central position when the attack began. As soon as they reached the top of the slope they lay down and one by one crawled forward into the darkness, two or three minutes being allowed to elapse between the departure of each man. They could hear the call of the Roman sentries as they answered each other every half-hour, and knew that they line was but a hundred yards or so in front of them.

The night was very dark, and no sudden shout proclaimed that those ahead had been noticed. When John's turn came to advance, Jonas was to follow next behind him. All had left their bows, arrows, bucklers, and swords behind them, and carried only their knives, for they had not come to fight, and the knives were required only for cutting the tent-ropes, or, in case of discovery, to enable them to take a life or two before they fell fighting. Each had sworn to kill himself if he found escape impossible, in order to escape a death by torture if he fell alive into the hands of the Romans.

John, on approaching the line of sentries, was guided by sound only in trying to avoid them. He could not see their figures, but could hear the sound of their footsteps and the clash of their arms as they tramped a few yards backward and forward. He was, like his comrades, stripped to the waist, having only on a short garment reaching half-way down the knee, as it was upon speed and activity that his life would depend.

Without interruption he crawled through the lines of sentries, and continued his course until he was, as near as he could tell, opposite the center of the long line of tents; then he lay quiet watching the setting of the star. No sound was heard from the camp in front, although from down the hillside beyond it came a confused noise, as if a host of men at work, and the glare of many fires reddened the skies, for there five thousand men were at work raising the embankment against the doomed city, while the archers and slingers maintained a never-ceasing conflict of missiles with the defenders on the walls.

The star seemed to John as if it hung on its course, so long was it in sinking to the horizon. But at last it sank, and John, crawling noiselessly forward, made his way into the Roman camp.

It was arranged with wide and regular streets laid out with mechanical accuracy. Here and there, in front of a tent of a commanding officer, sentries paced to and fro, the sound of their footsteps and the clash of their arms each time they turned giving warning of their positions. In the center of the streets the fires, round which the soldiers had shortly before been gathered, still glowed and flickered; for although the days were hot the cold at night rendered fires desirable, and there was an abundance of fuel to be obtained from the hills.

John crawled along with the greatest care. He had no fear of being seen, but had he come roughly against a tent-rope he might have brought out some wakeful occupant of the tent to see who was moving.

He continued his course until he found himself opposite a fire in which some of the brands were burning brightly, while there was no sentry on guard within a distance of fifty yards. So far everything had gone well; neither in passing through the lines of the sentries nor in making their way into the camp had any of the band been observed. It was certain now that some at least would succeed in setting fire to the tents before they were discovered, and the wind, which was blowing briskly from the mountains, would speedily spread the flames, and a heavy blow would be inflicted upon the enemy.

Chapter Nine

THE STORMING OF GAMALA

At last John made sure all his followers must have taken up a favorable position. Rising to his feet he sounded a short note on his horn, then sprang forward and seized one of the blazing brands and applied it to a tent. The canvas, dried by the scorching sun, lit in an instant, and as the flame leaped up John ran further among the tents, lighted another, and leaving the brand down. But this time, although not twenty seconds had elapsed since he had given the signal, a sudden uproar had succeeded the stillness which had reigned in the camp. The sentries had started on their posts as they hear the note of the horn, but had stood a moment irresolute, not knowing what it meant. Then, as the first flash of flame shot up, a simultaneous shout had arisen from every man on guard, rising louder and louder as the first flame was flowed almost instantly by a score of others in different parts of the camp.

It was but a few seconds later that the first trumpeter who rushed from his tent blew the alarm. Before its notes ceased it was answered all over the camp, and with a start the sleeping soldiers sprang up, caught up their arms, and rushed out of their tents. Startled as they were with the suddenness of the awaking and the sight of the blazing tents, there was none of that confusion that would have occurred among troops less inured to warfare. Each man did his duty; and buckling on their arms as best they might, stumbling over the tent-rows in the darkness, amazed by the sound of the fall of tents here and there, expecting every moment to be attacked by their unseen foe, the troops made their way speedily to the wide streets and there fell in together in military array and waited for orders. These were not long in coming.

As soon as the generals reached the spot they told off a number of men to endeavor to extinguish the flames, sent other parties to scour the camp and search for the enemy, while the rest in solid order awaited any attack that might be made upon them. But short as was the time that had elapsed since the first alarm, it had sufficed to give the flames such hold and power that they were beyond control.

With extraordinary rapidity the fire had leaped from tent to tent, and threatened to overwhelm the whole camp. The soldiers tried in vain to arrest the progress of the flames, rushing among the blazing tents, cutting the ropes to bring them to the ground, and trying to beat out the masses of fire as they fell. Many were terribly burned in their endeavors, but in vain, and the officers soon called them off and set them to work pulling down the tents which the fire had not yet reached, but even this was useless; the flakes of fire, driven before the wind, fell on the heaps of dried canvas, and the flames spread almost as rapidly as they had done when the tents were standing.

Nor were the parties in search of the incendiaries more successful. John had lain quiet where he threw himself down for a minute or two, by which time the tents had emptied of their occupants; then pausing only occasionally to circle a tent and cut away its ropes, he made his way to the edge of the camp. By this time the sheet of flame had extended well nigh across the camp, extending high above it and lighting it almost as if by day. But between him and the fire lay still a dark mass of tents, for the wind was blowing in the opposite direction, and light as it was elsewhere, in the black shadow of the tents it was still dark in the extreme.

John made his way along until he came to the end of the next street, and then paused. Already three or four active figures had run past him at the top of their speed, and he wished to be the last to retreat. He stayed till he heard the tramp of troops coming down, driven out by the spreading flames, and then sprang across the end of the road, and dashed along at full speed, still keeping close the line of tents.

A shout which rose from the leading files of the Roman column showed that he was seen. As he neared the end of the next opening the Roman soldiers were pouring out, and he turned in among the tents again. Through these he made his way, dashing across the open spaces, and once rushing through the midst of a Roman column, through which he passed before the troops had time to strike at or seize him.

At last he reached the extremity of the camp; the slope down to the river was but fifty yards away, and once over the brow he would be in darkness and safe from pursuit. But already the Romans had drawn up a column of men along the edge of the plateau to cut off any who might try to pass. John paused among the last row of the tents, hesitating what course to adopt. He could not make directly up the mountain, for the space between it and the camp was now covered by the Roman cavalry, the greater portion of their infantry being still engaged in trying to save at least some portion of the camp.

Suddenly he heard a footstep among the tents close behind him. He drew back into the tent by which he was standing and peered cautiously out. A Roman soldier came hastily along and entered the next tent, doubtless to fetch some article of value which he had left behind him as he rushed out on the first alarm.

A sudden idea flashed across John's brain: he waited till the soldier came out, followed him with silent steps, and then sprang upon him at a bound, hurling him to the ground and burying his knife again and again in his body.

Not a cry had escaped the Roman. The instant he was sure he was dead John rose to his feet, placed the helmet of the fallen man on his head, secured the breastplate by a single buckle round his neck, took up his buckler and sword, and then emerging from one of the tents ran toward the Roman line, making for one of the narrow openings between the different companies. Several others were also hurrying to take their places in the ranks, therefore no special attention was paid to John until he was within a few yards of the opening. Then a centurion at the end of the line said sternly:

"You will be punished tomorrow for not being in your place. What is your name?" for as John was between him and the sheet of flame rising from the camp, the Roman was unable to see his face. Instead of halting, as he expected, John sprang past him, throwing down his helmet and buckler dashed through the space between the companies.

"Seize him! Cut him down!" the centurion shouted; but John was already descending the slope. As he ran he swung the loosely buckled breastplate round on his back, as it was well he did so, for a moment later a Roman javelin rang against it, the force of the blow almost throwing him on his face. But in a moment he continued his course. He was in total darkness now; and though the javelins were flying around him, they were thrown at random. But the descent had now become so steep he was obliged to pause in his course, and to make his way cautiously.

He undid the buckle and left the breastplate behind him, threw down the sword, and climbed down until he stood by the side of the river. He could hear shouts above him, and knew that the Romans were searching the hillside, hoping that he had been killed or wounded by their darts. But he had no fear of pursuit. He swam the river, for he struck upon a deep spot, and then at full speed ran along on the bank, knowing that some of the Roman cavalry were encamped upon the plain and would soon be on the spot. However, all was quiet, and he met no one until he arrived opposite the place where it had been arranged that the party should meet. Then he waded across.

"Is that you, John?" a voice exclaimed.

"It is I, Jonas. Thank God you have got back safely! How many are with you?"

There was a loud cry of satisfaction; and as he made his way up the bank a number of his followers crowded round him, all in the highest state of delight at his return. Jonas threw his arms round his neck, crying with joy.

"I thought you must have fallen, John. I have been here ten minutes; most of the others were here before me, only three have arrived since, and for the last five minutes none have come."

"I fear no more will come," John said; "the Romans have cut off all retreat. How many are missing?"

"We were nineteen here before you came," one of the men replied.

"Then there are six missing," John said. "We will not give them up. Some may have made their way straight up the mountain, fearing to be seen as they passed the ends of the open spaces; some may have made their way down the opposite slope to the other arm of the river. But even if all are killed we need not repine. They have died as they wished—taking vengeance upon the Romans. It has been a glorious success. More than half the Roman camp is assuredly destroyed, and they must have lost a prodigious quantity of stores of all kinds. Who are missing?"

He heard the names of those absent.

"I trust we may see some of them yet," he said; "but if not, Jonas, tomorrow shall carry to their friends the news of their death. They will be wept; but their parents will be proud that their sons have died in striking so heavy a blow upon our oppressors. They will live in the memory of their villages as men who died doing a great deed; and women will say, Had all done their duty as they did the Romans would never have enslaved our nation. We will wait another half-hour here; but I fear that no more will join us, for the Romans are drawn up all along the line where alone a descent could be made in the valley."

"Then how did you escape, John," Jonas asked, "and how is it that you were not here before? Several of those who were in the line beyond you have returned."

"I waited till I hoped that all had passed," John said. "Each one who ran past the open spaces added to the danger, for the Romans beyond could not but notice them as they passed the spaces lighted by the flames, and it was my duty as leader to be the last to go."

"Six of those who were beyond you have joined us," one of the men said. "The other six are those that are missing."

"That is what I feared," John answered. "I felt sure that those behind me would have got safely away before the Romans recovered from their first confusion. The danger was of course greater in proportion to the distance from the edge of the slope."

"But how did you get through, John, since you say that all escape was cut off?"

John related how he had slain the Roman solder and escaped with his armor, and the recital raised him still higher in the estimation of his followers; for the modern feeling that it is right to kill even the bitterest enemy only in fair fight was wholly unknown in those days, when, as was done by the Romans at Jotapata, men would cut the throat of a sleeping foe with no more compunction than if they were slaughtering a fowl.

Perceiving by John's narration that there was no chance of any of their comrades getting through to join them now, the party struck off into the hills, and after three hours' march reached their encampment. They gave a shout of joy as they approached it, for a fire was burning brightly, and they knew that some of their comrades must have reached the spot before them. Four men rose as they approached, and joyful greetings were exchanged. Their stories were soon told. As soon as they heard by the shouts of the Romans on the hillside, and of the outer sentries, that they were discovered as they passed the spaces lit up by flames, they had turned back. Two of them had made their way up a deep water-course past the roman guard on the hill, the attention of the soldiers being fixed upon the camp. The other two had climbed down the precipitous rocks on the other side of the hill.

"It was terrible work in the darkness," one of them said. "I fell once and thought I had broken my leg; but fortunately, I had caught on a ledge, and was able to go on after a time. I think two of our party must have perished there; for twice as I was descending I heard a sudden cry and then a sound as of a body falling from rock to rock."

"Better so than to have fallen into the hands of the Romans," John said, "and to have been forced to slay themselves by their own hands, as we agreed to do. Well, my friends, we have done a glorious deed. We have begun well. Let us trust that we may strike many more such blows against our tyrants. Now, let us thank God that he has fought by our hands, and that he has brought so many of us back from so great a danger! Simeon, you are the oldest of the party; do you lift up your voice for us all."

The party all stood listening reverently while Simeon said a prayer of thanksgiving. Then one of them broke out into one of the psalms of triumph, and all joined at once. When this was done they gathered round the fire, prepared their cakes of meal, and put meat on long skewers on the flames. Having eaten, they talked for hours, each in turn giving his account of his share in the adventure.

They then talked of their missing friends, those from the same village telling what they knew of them, and what relations they had left behind. At last, just as morning was breaking, they retired into the little bowers of boughs that had been erected to keep off the cold, which was at this elevation sharp at nights. They were soon fast asleep.

The first thing the next morning Jonas set off to explore the foot of the precipices on the south side of the Roman camp, and to search for the bodies of their two missing comrades. He found one terribly crushed; of the other he could find no sign whatsoever. On his returning to the mountain camp one of the young men was sent off to bear to the relative of the man whose body had been found the certain news of his death, and to inquire of the friends of the other whether he had any relations living near the mountains to whom he might have made his way if hurt or disabled by his fall. The messenger returned on the following day with the news that their missing comrade had already arrived at his home. His fall had not been a very deep one, and when he recovered consciousness, some hours before daybreak, he found that one of his legs was useless and an arm broken.

Thinking that in the morning the Romans might search the foot of the precipices, he dragged himself with the greatest difficulty a few hundred yards and there concealed himself among some bushes. A man came along in search of an ass that had strayed; he called to him, and on the man hearing that he was one of the party who had caused the great fire in the Roman camp, the sight of whose flames had caused such exultation in the heart of every Jew in the plains around, he hurried away, and fetched another with a donkey. Upon this the injured man was lifted and carried down to the lake, passing on the way several parties of Roman soldiers, to whom the idea did not occur that the sick man was one of the party who had inflicted such a terrible blow upon them on the previous night. Once by the side of the lake there was no difficulty in getting him on board a boat, in which he was carried to his native village.

The Romans were furious at the blow which had been struck them. More than half their camp and camp equipage had been destroyed, a great part of the baggage of the officers and soldiers had been burned, and each man had to deplore losses of his own as well as the destruction of the public property. But more than this they felt the blow to their pride. There was not a soldier but felt humiliated at the thought that a number of the enemy—for from the fire breaking out simultaneously, it was certain at least a score of men must have been engaged in the matter—should penetrate unseen into the midst of their camp; and worse still, that after effecting all this damage all should have succeeded in making their escape—for, so far as they know, the whole of the Jews got safely away.

But not for a moment did they relax their siege operations. The troops engaged upon the embankment were relieved at the usual hour, and half a legion went up into the mountains as usual to procure timber, while four thousand archers, divided into parties two hundred strong, extended themselves all over the hills and searched the forest for miles for some sign of their enemy, who were, they were now convinced, comparatively few in numbers.

The news of the daring attack on the Roman camp spread far and wide among the towns and villages of the plains, and aroused the drooping spirits of the people, who had begun to think that it would be worse than useless to offer any opposition to the Roman power. Whence came the party which had accomplished the deed or who was its leader none knew, and the inhabitants of the villages near Hippos, who alone could have enlightened them, were careful to maintain an absolute silence, for they knew that if by any chance a rumor reached the Romans of the locality from which their assailants had come they would have carried fire and sword among all the villages by the lake. Titus was away, being absent on a mission in Syria, and Vespasian himself went among the troops exhorting them not to be downcast at the disaster that had befallen them, for that the bravest men were subject to sudden misfortunes of this kind, and exhorted them to push on the siege with all the more vigor in order that they might the sooner remove the camping-grounds where they would not be exposed to such attacks by a lurking foe.

The soldiers replied with cheers, and the next day, the embankment being completed, they opened so terrible a fire from their war engines upon the defenders of the walls that these were forced to retire into the city. The Romans at once pushed forward their battering-rams to the walls, and setting to work with the greatest vigor speedily made three breaches, through which they rushed with exulting shouts. The Jews ran down to oppose them and a desperate conflict took place in the narrow streets; but the Romans, pouring in in great numbers through the breaches, pressing them step by step up the steep hill. The Jews, animated by despair, again turned, not withstand the assault, and were driven down the steep lanes and paths with great slaughter.

But those who fled were stopped by the crowd of their own men pressing up the hill from below, and the Roman soldiers, jammed, as it were, between the Jews above and their own countrymen below, took refuge in the houses in great numbers. But these were not constructed to bear the weight of so many men in heavy armor. The floors fell in, and as many of the Romans climbed up on the flat roofs these also fell, bringing the walls down with them. Standing, as they did, almost one above the other, each house that fell brought down the one below it, and thus the ruin spread as one house of cards brings down another until the whole of the town standing on the steep declivity on its eastern side was a mass of ruins.

The confusion was tremendous. The dust of the falling houses so thickened the air that men could not see a yard in front of them. Hundreds of Roman soldiers were buried among the ruins. Some were killed at once; others, jammed between fallen timbers, strove in vain to extricate themselves, and shouted to their comrades to come to their assistance, but these, enveloped in darkness, ignorant of the ground, half-suffocated with dust, were powerless to aid them.

In the confusion Romans fell by the swords of Romans. Many who could not extricate themselves slew themselves with their own swords; while the exulting Jews, seeing in this terrible disaster a miracle affected in their favor, crowded down from above, slaying with their swords, hurling masses of stone down on the foe, killing those unable to retreat, and adding to the confusion and terror with their yells of triumph, which rose high above the confused shouts of the Romans.

Vespasian himself, who had entered the town with his soldiers and had pushed forward with them up the hill, was nearly involved in the common destruction; but as the houses came crashing down around him he shouted loudly to the soldiers near to gather round him, and to lock their shields together to form a testudo. Recognizing the voice of their beloved general, the soldiers near rallied round him, and, sheltered beneath their closely packed shields, resisted the storm of darts and stones from above, and gradually and in good order made their way down over the ruins and issued safely from the walls.

The loss of the Romans was great. The soldiers were greatly dispirited by their defeat, and especially by the thought that they had deserted their general in their retreat. Vespasian, however, was wise enough to see that this was no time for rebuke, and he accordingly addressed them in language of approbation. He said that their repulse was in no way due to want of valor on their part, but to an accident such as none could foresee, and which had been brought about to some extent by their too impetuous ardor, which led them to fight rather with the desperate fury of the Jews than with the steady discipline that distinguished Roman soldiers.

The defenders of the city were full of exultation at their success, and setting to work with ardor, soon repaired the breaches and strengthened the walls. But all knew that in spite of their momentary success their position was desperate, for their provisions were almost exhausted. The stores which had been laid up were very large, but the siege had lasted for many months before the arrival of the Romans, and the number of the people assembled within the walls far exceeded the usual population.

The Romans, on their part, increased the height of their embankment and prepared for a second assault.

In the mean time Itabyrium had fallen. The hill of Tabor was inaccessible except on the north side, and the level area on the top was surrounded by a strong wall. Placidus had been sent with six hundred horse against the place, but the hill was so steep and difficult that he hesitated to attack it. Each party pretended to be anxious to treat, each intending to take advantage of the other. Placidus invited the garrison to descend the hill and discuss terms with him. The Itabyrians accepted the invitation with the design of assailing the Romans unawares. Placidus, who was on his guard, feigned a retreat. The Itabyrians boldly pursued on to the plain, when the Roman horse, wheeling round, dashed among them, inflicting terrible slaughter and cutting off their retreat toward the city. Those who escaped the slaughter fled to Jerusalem. The town, weakened by the loss of so many fighting men, and being much distressed by want of water, again opened negotiations, and surrendered upon the promise that the lives of all within it should be spared.

Hunger was now doing its work among the people of Gamala. The inhabitants suffered terribly, for the provisions were all taken for the use of the fighting men, and the rest had to subsist as best they could on any little hoards they might have hidden away, or on garbage of all kinds. Numbers made their escape through the sewers and passages which led into the ravines, where the Romans had placed no guards. Still the assaults of the Romans were bravely repelled, until on the night of the 22d of September two soldiers of the Fifteenth Legion contrived to creep unobserved to the foot of one of the highest towers of the wall and began silently to undermine its foundations. Before morning broke they had got in so far that they could not be perceived from the walls. Still they worked in, leaving a few stones in their place to support the tower until the last moment. Then they struck these away and ran for their lives. The tower fell with a terrible crash, with the guards upon it.

In their terror the defenders of the walls leaped up and fled in all directions, and many were killed by the Romans' darts, among them Josephus, one of their two leaders; while Chares, who was lying in the height of a fever, expired from the excitement of the calamity. The confusion in the town was terrible. Deprived of their two leaders, and with the town open to assault, none knew what was to be done. All expected instant destruction, and the air was filled with the screams and wailings of the women; but the Romans, mindful of their last repulse, did not at once advance to the assault. But in the afternoon Titus, who had now returned taking two hundred horse and a force of infantry, crossed the breach and entered the town.

Some of the defenders rushed to meet him, others catching up their children, ran with their wives to the citadel. The defenders fought bravely, but were driven steadily up the hill by the Romans, who were now reinforced by the whole strength of the army led by Vespasian. Quarter was neither asked nor given. The defenders contested every foot of the hill, until the last defender of Gamala outside the citadel had fallen.

Then Vespasian led his men against the citadel itself. It stood on a rugged rock of great height offering tremendous difficulties to the assailants. The Jews stood upon the summit rolling down great stones and darts upon the Romans as they strove to ascend. But the very heavens seemed to fight against the unfortunate Jews, for a terrific tempest suddenly broke upon the city. So furious was the wind that the Jews could no longer stand on the edge of the crag, or oppose the progress of the enemy; while the Romans, sheltered from the wind by the rock itself, were able to press upward. The platform once gained, they rushed upon the Jews, slaying all they met, men, women, and children.

Vast numbers of the Jews in their despair threw themselves headlong, with their wives and children, over the precipices, and when the butchery was complete five thousand bodies were found at the foot of the rocks; four thousand lay dead on the platform above. Of all those in Gamala when the Romans entered, two women alone escaped. They were the sisters of Philip, a general in Agrippa's army. They managed to conceal themselves until the carnage was over and the fury of the Romans had subsided, and then showed themselves and proclaimed who they were.

Gischala now alone of the cities of Galilee defied the Roman arms. The people themselves were for the most part tillers of the soil, and were anxious to make their submission; but John, the rival and bitter enemy of Josephus, with the robber band he had collected, was master of the town, and refused to allow any talk of submission. The city had none of the natural strength of Jotapata and Gamala, and Vespasian sent Titus against it with a thousand horse, while he ordered the Tenth Legion to take up its winter quarters of Scythopolis, and himself moved with the other two legions to Cæsarea. Titus, on his arrival before Gischala, saw that the city could be easily taken by assault, but desirous of avoiding any more shedding of blood, and learning that the inhabitants were desirous of surrendering, he sent an officer before it to offer terms of capitulation.

The troops of John of Gischala manned the walls; and when the summons of Titus was proclaimed, John answered that the garrison accepted willingly the generous terms that were offered, but that the day being the Sabbath, nothing could be concluded without an infringement of the law until the next day. Titus at once granted the delay and drew off his troops to a neighboring town. In the night John of Gischala marched away with all his armed men, followed by many of the inhabitants with their wives and children, fearing to remain in the city exposed to the anger of Titus, when he found he had been duped.

The women and Children soon began to drop behind; but the men pressed on, leaving the helpless and despairing women behind them.

In the morning when Titus appeared before the town it opened its gates to him at once, the people hailing him as their deliverer from the oppression they had so long suffered at the hands of John and his bands of ruffians. Titus entered Gischala amid the acclamations of the people, and behaved with great moderation, injuring no one and contenting himself with throwing down a portion of the walls, and warning the inhabitants that if they again rose in rebellion the same mercy would not be extended to them. He had at once dispatched a troop of horse in pursuit of the fugitives. They overtook them and slew six thousand of the men, and brought three thousand women and children back into the city. John himself with the strongest of his band were not overtaken, but made their way to Jerusalem.

The fame of the successful exploit of the destruction of the Roman camp brought large numbers of young men flocking to the hills as soon as the Romans retired from Gamala, all eager to join the band, and John could have recruited his numbers to any extent; but now that all Galilee had fallen, and the Romans retired to their winter quarters, he did not see that there was anything to be done until spring. It would be madness to attack either of the great Roman camps at Scythopolis or Cæsarea; and although doubtless the garrisons left in Tiberias, Tarichea, and other towns, might have been driven out, this would only have brought upon those cities the anger of the Romans, and involved them in ruin and destruction.

Still less would it have been of any advantage to go down at present to Judea. That province was suffering woes as great as the Romans could inflict upon it, from the action of the factions. Under the pretense of punishing all who were supposed to be favorable to making terms with Rome, bands of armed men pervaded the whole country, plundering and slaying the wretched inhabitants.

Law and order were at an end. Those in Jerusalem who claimed for themselves the chief authority in the country had done nothing to assist their countrymen in the north in their struggle with the Romans. Not a man had been dispatched to Galilee. The leaders were occupied in their own desperate feuds, and battles took place in the streets of the city. The peaceful inhabitants were plundered and ill-treated, and the condition of those within the walls was as terrible, as was that of those without. Anarchy, plunder, and carnage extended throughout Judea, and while the destruction of Jerusalem was threatened by the Roman army in the north, the Jews made no preparation whatever for its defense, but spent their whole time and energy in civil strife. When, therefore, the numerous band who had now gathered round him urged him to lead them down to Jerusalem, John refused to do so. Getting upon an elevated spot where his voice could be heard by them all, he said:

"My friends, you have heard as well as I what is taking place in Jerusalem and the country round it. Did we go down there what good could we do? We should be drawn into the strife on one side or another, and the swords which should be kept for the defense of the Temple against the Romans would be stained with Jewish blood. Moreover, we should aid to consume the food stored away in the granaries. Nor can we through the winter attempt any enterprise against the Romans here. The woes of Galilee are over. Tens of thousands have fallen, but those that survive can go about their business and till their fields in peace. Were we to renew the war here we should bring upon them a fresh outburst of the Roman vengeance.

"Therefore, there is naught for us to do now; but in the spring, when the Romans get into motion against Jerusalem, we will march to its defense. We have naught to do with the evil deeds that are being performed there; we have but to do our duty; and the first duty of every Jew is to die, if need be, in the defense of the Temple. Therefore let us now disperse to our homes. When the first news comes that the Romans are stirring, those of you who are disposed to follow me and obey my orders can assemble here.

"But let only such come; let the rest make their way singly to Jerusalem. I am resolved to have only such with me who will follow me as one man. You know how the factious rage in the city. A compact body of men true to themselves and their leader, can maintain themselves aloof from the strife and make themselves respected by both parties; but single men must take sides with one faction or another, or be ill-treated by both. We are wanted at him; the fields are lying untilled for want of hands; therefore let us lay aside our arms until the spring, and do our duty to our families until we are called upon to aid in the defense of the Temple. When the hour comes I shall be ready to lead if you are ready to follow."

John's address received general approval, and the gathering dispersed, all vowing that they would assemble in the spring and follow John wherever he chose to lead them, for he was already regarded with an almost superstitious admiration in the country around. His deliverance at Jotapata, and the success that he alone of the Jewish leaders had gained over the Romans, marked him in their eyes as one specially chosen by God to lead them to victory, and in a few hours the hills above Gamala was deserted, and John and his followers were all on their way toward their homes.

Chapter Ten

CAPTIVES

John was received with great joy by his father, who had already heard the story brought by the injured member of the band from Gamala, and was filled with pride that his son should so have distinguished himself. He at once agreed to John's proposal that he should start on the following day to fetch the women from Neve, as there was no longer any fear of trouble from the Romans. Galilee was completely subdued, whatever events might take place in Judea, those in the north would be unaffected by them.

The day after his return, then, John set out with Jonas for Neve. John charged his companion on no account to say anything of their doings at the siege of Gamala; and as communication was difficult, and they had heard from Simon since John had left him, his friends at Neve were not aware that he had been absent from the farm. Martha and Mary were delighted to see him, to hear that all was well at home. They had been greatly alarmed at the news of the slaughter of the fishermen on the lake, fearing that John might have gone across to Tarichea with some of his friends in the village. Their fears on this head, however, abated as time passed on and they did not hear from Simon, who, they felt assured, would have brought the news to Martha had aught happened to their son.

They had mourned over the siege and massacre of Gamala, and had been filled with joy when the news had arrived three days before that the Roman army had marched away to take up its quarters for the winter, and they had looked for the summons which John brought for their return home.

"And does your father think, John, that there will be trouble again in the spring? Shall we have to leave home again as soon as the winter is past?"

"He hopes not, mother. Gamala was the only town on this side of the Jordan that resisted the Roman authority, and as all the territories of Agrippa are now peaceful there is no reason why the Romans should enter these again; and, indeed, all Galilee has now surrendered. As Vespasian moved toward the sea deputies came to him from every town and village, and I think now that there will be no more trouble there."

"It has been terrible enough, my son. What tens of thousands of men have perished, what destruction has been wrought? We have been mourning for months now for the woes which have fallen upon our people."

"It has been most terrible, mother, and yet it might have been worse. Nigh a hundred and fifty thousand have fallen at Gadara, Jotapata, Japha, Tarichea, and Gamala, besides those who were slain in the villages that had been sacked and destroyed. Still, considering all things, it might have been worse; and were it all over now, did no more dangers threaten our nation, we might even rejoice that no greater evils have befallen us for our revolt against Rome; but what has been done is but a preparation for the siege of Jerusalem. However, do not let us begin to mourn over the future; the storm has for the present passed away from us, and whatever misfortunes have befallen our countrymen we have happily escaped. The farm stands uninjured, and no harm has come to any of us."

"And all the villagers have escaped, John? Did none of our neighbors go out in their boats to Tarichea? We feared, when we heard of the sea-flight, that some must have fallen."

"No, mother. Fortunately they listened to the counsels of my father, who implored them not to put out on the lake, for that did they do so they would bring misfortune and ruin upon themselves."

"And have you heard, John," Mary asked, "anything of the champion who they say has arisen? We have heard all sorts of tales of him—how he harassed the Romans before Gamala and with his followers burned their camp one night and well-nigh destroyed them, and how when he goes into the fight the Roman javelins drop off without harming him, and how when he strikes the Romans fall before his blows like wheat before a sickle."

John burst into a laugh.

"I wonder, Mary, that the reports didn't say also that he could fly through the air when he chose, could render himself invisible to the enemy, and could by a wave his hand destroy them as the hosts of Sennacherib were destroyed. The Romans were harassed somewhat at Gamala by John and his followers, who crept into their camp at night and set it on fire, and had a few skirmishes with their working parties; but when you have said that you have said all that there is to say about it."

"That is not like you, John," Mary said indignantly, for the tales that had circulated through the province had fired her imagination. "Every one is talking of what he has done. He alone of all our leaders has checked the Romans, and has shown wisdom as well as valor in fighting. I should have thought you would have been one of the first to praise him. Every one is talking about him, and since we heard of what he has been doing mother and I pray for him daily as we pray for you and your father; and now you want to make out he has done nothing."

"I do not want to make out that he has done nothing, Mary, for doubtless the Lord has been with him, and has enabled him to give some trouble to the Romans; but I was laughing at the fables you have heard about him, and at the reports which had converted his skirmishes with the Romans into all sorts of marvelous action."

"I believe they were marvelous actions," Mary said; "why should what people say be all wrong? We believe in him, don't we, mother."

"Yes, Mary. It is true that the tales we have heard may be, as John says, exaggerated, but assuredly this new champion of our people must be a man of wisdom and valor, and I see not why, as God raised up champions for Israel in the old time, he should not do so now when our need is so great."

"There is no reason, mother," John said more quietly, "but I fear that the champion of Israel is not yet forthcoming. We have heard of the doings of this John, and, as I said, he has merely had some skirmishes with the Romans, his band being too small to admit of any regular fighting. He interrupted their work and gave them some trouble, and his men, creeping down into the camp, set it on fire, and so caused them a good deal of loss; but more than this cannot be said of him."

"At any rate," Mary said disdainfully, "he has done more than your Josephus, John, for he brought ruin on all who took his advice and went into the cities he had fortified. It may please you to make little of what this champion has done; others do not think so. Everywhere he is talked of and praised—the old men are talking of him, the Jewish maidens are singing songs in his honor; I heard them yesterday gathered round a well near Neve. His father must rejoice and his mother be proud of him, if they are alive. What do they say down by the lake, Jonas, of this captain? Are not the tales we have heard believed there?"

"I have heard nothing about the Roman javelins not harming him," Jonas said, "but he certainly got safely out of the hands of the Romans when they had well-night taken him, and all say that he is brave and prudent, and men have great confidence and trust in him."

"Ridiculous, Jonas!" John exclaimed angrily, and Mary and his mother looked at him in surprise.

"Truly, John," his mother said, "what Mary said is just. This is not like you. I should have thought you would have been one of the first to admire this new leader, seeing that he is fighting in the way I have heard you advocate as being that in which the Romans should be fought, instead of the Jews being shut up in the cities."

"Quite so, mother! No doubt he is adopting the proper way of fighting, and therefore has naturally had some success. I am only saying that he has done nothing wonderful, but has given the Romans some trouble by refusing to fight and by merely trying to harass them. If there were a thousand men who would gather small bands together and harass the Romans night and day in the same manner, they would render it well-night impossible for them to make any progress. As it was, he merely aided in delaying the fall of Gamala by a day or two. And now let us talk of something else. Our father has succeeded in getting in the principal part of the harvest, but I fear that this year you will be short of fruit. We have had no time to gather in the figs, and they have fallen from the trees, and although we have made enough wine for our own use, there will be but little to sell."

"It matters not at all," Martha said. "God has been very merciful toward us, and so that we have but bread to eat and water to drink until next harvest we shall have nothing to repine about when ruin and destruction have fallen upon so many."

That evening, when Mary and Martha had retired to their apartments, the former, who had been very silent all the evening, said:

"I cannot understand, mother, why John speaks so coldly of the doings of this brave leader, and why he was almost angry at our praises of him; it seems altogether unlike him."

"It is unlike him, Mary; but you must never be surprised at men; they do not like to hear each other praised; and though I should have thought, from what I know of my son, that he was above the feeling of jealously, I cannot but think that he showed some signs of that feeling to-day."

"But it seems absurd, mother. I can understand John being jealous of any one his own age who surpassed him in any exercises, though I never saw him so; for when in rowing on the lake, or in shooting with bows and arrows, or in other sports, some of our neighbors' sons have surpassed him he never seemed to mind at all, and it seems almost absurd to think that he could be jealous of a great leader who has done brave deeds for our people."

"It does seem so, Mary, and I wonder myself; but it has been ever one of our national faults to be jealous of our leaders. From the time the people vexed Moses and Aaron in the wilderness it has ever been the same. I grieve to see it in John, who has distinguished himself greatly for his age, and of whom we are proud; but no one is prefect, my child, and you must not trouble because you find that your betrothed husband is not free from all weaknesses."

"I don't expect him to be free from all weaknesses, mother; but this is one of the last weaknesses I should have expected to find in him, and it troubles me. When everything seemed so dark it was a pleasure to think that a hero, perhaps a deliverer, had arisen; and now John seems to say that he has done nothing."

"My dear child," Martha said, "something may have occurred to vex John on the way, and when men are put out they will often show it in the strangest manner. Probably John will another time speak as warmly in praise our new leader as you would yourself."

"Perhaps it may be so, mother," Mary assented. "I can hardly believe that John is jealous—it does seem so unlike himself."

"I would not speak on the subject again, Mary, if I were you, unless he himself brings it up. A wise woman keeps silence on subjects which may lead to disagreement. You will learn, when you have married, that this is the easiest and best way."

"I suppose so, mother," Mary said in a tone of disappointment; "but somehow it never seemed to me before that John and I could have any subject on which there would be disagreement."

"My dear Mary," Martha said, smiling, "John and you are both mortal; and although you may truly love each other, and will, I trust, be very happy as husband and wife, subjects will occur upon which you will differ; and then, as you know, the wisest plan is for the wife to be silent. It is the wife's duty always to give way to the husband."

Mary gave a little shrug of her shoulders, as if to intimate that she did not regard altogether favorably this view of a wife's duties; however, she said no more, but kissed Martha and retired to bed.

The next morning they started early, and journeyed to Capitolias, where they stayed at the house of some friends. In the evening the talk turned upon the new leader who had burned the Roman camp. When they did so John at once made some excuse and went out. He regretted now that he had not at once told his mother what he had been doing. He had intended, in the first place, to give her a little surprise, but had no idea of the exaggerated reports that had been spread about; and when Mary broke out into praise of the unknown leader, it seemed to him that it would have been absurd to say that he himself was the person of whom she had formed so fantastically exalted an opinion.

Not having said so at first, he did not see how he could say so afterward, and so left the matter as it stood until they should return home.

While John was out he heard news which caused him some uneasiness. It was said that parties of Roman horse from Scythopolis had been scouring the country, burning many villages under the pretext that some Roman soldiers had been killed by the peasants, slaughtering the people, and carrying off as slaves such young women and men as were likely to fetch good prices. He told his mother what he had heard, and asked her whether she did not think that it would be better to stay where they were for a time, or return to Neve. But Martha was anxious to be at home again; and the friend with whom they were stopping said that these reports were a week old, and that doubtless the Romans had returned to their camp. She determined, therefore, that she and Mary would continue their journey, but that the maids should remain with their friend at Capitolias until the Roman excursions ceased.

They accordingly set out in the morning as before, the two women riding, and John and Jonas walking by the side of the donkeys. Following the road by the side of the Hieromax, they kept on without meeting anything to cause alarm until they reached the angle of the stream where the road to Hippos branched off from that which followed the river down to Tarichea. They had gone but a short distance when they saw a cloud of dust rising along the road in front of them and the sparkle of arms in the sun.

"Turn aside, mother," John exclaimed. "Those must be the Romans ahead."

Turning aside they rode toward some gardens and orchards at no great distance, but before they reached them two Roman soldiers separated themselves from the rest and galloped after them.

"Fly, John!" Martha said hurriedly. "You and Jonas can escape."

"It would only insure evil to you if we did, mother. No; we will keep together."

The Roman soldiers rode up and roughly ordered the party to accompany them back to the main body, which consisted of fifty men. The leader, a young officer whose garments and armor showed that he belonged to a family of importance, rode forward a few paces to meet them.

"Some more of this accursed race of rebels!" he exclaimed.

"We are quiet travelers," John said, "journeying from Capitolias to Tarichea. We have harmed no one, my lord."

"You are all the same," the Roman replied, scowling upon them. "You speak fair one day, and stab us in the back the next. Pomponius," he continued, turning to the sergeant, "put these two lads with the rest. They ought to fetch a good price, for they are strong and active. As to the girl, I will make a present of her to the general to send to his wife in Rome. She is the prettiest Jewess I have seen since I entered the country. The old woman can go. She is of no use to any one."

Martha threw her arms round Mary and would have striven to resist with her feeble strength the carrying out of the order, when John said in Hebrew:

"Mother, you will ruin us all and lose your own life! Go home quietly, and trust me to save Mary."

The habit of submitting to her husband's will which Martha practiced all her life asserted itself. She embraced Mary passionately, and drew aside as the Roman soldiers approached, and then tottering away a short distance, sank weeping on the ground. Mary shed no tear, but, pale as death, walked by the side of the soldier, who led her to the rear of the cavalcade, where four of five other young women were standing in dejected attitudes. John and Jonas were similarly placed with some young men in the midst of the Roman soldiers. Their hands were tied behind them, and the troop resumed its way. They were traveling by the road along which the little party had just come. Whenever a house or small village was seen half of the troops galloped off. Flames were soon seen to rise, and parties of wretched captives were driven in. When about half-way to Capitolias the troop halted. The horses were turned into a field of ripe corn to feed; half the men sat down to a meal, while the remainder stood on guard over the captives. John had whispered to Jonas to work his hands so as to loosen his cords, if possible; and the lad, whose bones were very small, soon said that he could slip the ropes off without difficulty.

It was harder work for John; and indeed while on the march he did not venture to exert himself, fearing that the movements would be noticed by the guards. But when they halted he got into the middle of the group of captives and tried this best to loosen the cords. Jonas was close beside him.

"It is of no use, Jonas," he said. "The cords are cutting into my flesh, and they will not yield in the slightest."

"Let me try, John. Stand round close," Jonas said to the other captives in Hebrew. "I want to loosen my friend's knots. If he can get away he will bring rescue to you all."

The others moved so as to completely cover the movements of Jonas; and the lad, stooping down, applied his teeth to the knot in John's cords, and soon succeeded in loosening it.

"That will be enough, Jonas. I can draw my hand through now."

Jonas stood up again.

"When I make an effort to escape, Jonas, do you dash between the horsemen and run for it. In the confusion you will get a start, and they will not overtake you until you are across the river. Once on the hill you are safe. If you remain behind and I get away, as likely as not one of the soldiers would send a javelin through you, as being my companion."

After half an hour's halt, the Romans again mounted their horses and returned to retrace their steps.

Two Romans rode on either side of the captives, who were about fifty in number; and John gradually made his way to the front of the party between the two leading horsemen. The officer, talking to his sergeant, rode a few paces ahead in the middle of the road. Since the cords had been loosened John had continued to work his fingers until the circulation was restored. Suddenly he slipped his hands from their fastenings, gave three bounds forward, and vaulted on the back of the horse behind the officer. He had drawn the knife which had been hidden in his girdle, and he threw one arm round the officer, while he struck the knife deep into the horse's flank. The animal reared in the air, and then, at a second application of the knife, sprang forward at the top of his speed before the astonished Roman knew what had happened.

John held him in his arms like a vise, and, exerting all his strength, lifted him from the saddle and hurled him headlong to the ground, where he lay bleeding and insensible. John had now time to look around. Struck with astonishment at the sudden incident which had passed under their eyes, the Romans had at first instinctively reined in their horses. The sergeant had been the first to recover himself, and, shouting to the five leading soldiers on each side to follow him, had spurred in pursuit just as his officer was hurled to the ground. But John was already some fifty yards away, and felt sure that he could not be overtaken.

He had remarked the horse ridden by the officer while they were eating, and saw that it was of far higher blood and swifter pace than any of those ridden by the soldiers. His own weight, too, was far less than that of the heavy-armed men in pursuit of him; and with a shout of scornful defiance and a wave of his hand he continued his course. Before a mile had been passed he had left his pursuers far in the rear, and, seeing the hopelessness of the pursuit, they presently reined up and returned to the main body. Jonas had carried out John's instructions, and the instant the latter sprang on the officer he slipped under the belly of the horse next to him and ran at the top of his speed for the river.

It was but a hundred yards away, and he had gone three-quarters the distance before any of the soldiers, confused at the attack upon their officer, doubtful whether the whole of the captives were not about to fall upon them, and without orders how to act, set out in pursuit. Jonas plunged into the stream, dived to the other side, and then sprang forward again, just as three or four soldiers reached the bank he had left. Their javelins were hurled after him, but without effect, and with a shout of triumph he sprang up the hillside, and was soon safe from pursuit.

As soon as he saw that the Romans had turned back, John sprang from his horse, unstrapped the heavy armor which covered its chest and sides, and flung it away, and then mounting, resumed his course. At the first house he came to he borrowed a shepherd's horn, and as he approached the first village sounded his signal for the assembly.

Two or three young men ran out from their houses as he dashed up, for there was not a village in those parts from which some of the young men had not gone up to the mountains to join him after the fall of Gamala, and all were ready to follow him anywhere. He rapidly gave them orders to go to all the villages round, and instruct the young men to assemble with all speed possible at their old trysting-place near Jabez Galaad, and to spread the news, as they went, some from each village being sent as messengers to others. Then he pursued his way at full speed, and by sunset had issued his orders in some twenty villages. Being convinced that by night a sufficient number of men would have gathered in the mountain for his purpose, he rode back to the river, swam his horse across, and then leaving it to shift for itself, made his way up the mountains.

Some seventy or eighty men had already arrived at the appointed place, and fresh parties were coming in every minute. Jonas was already there, John having arranged with him to watch the movements of the Romans until the sun set, and then to bring word to the place of meeting as to their movements.

"Well, Jonas, what is your news?"

"The Romans have halted for the night at a spot about a mile this side of where we left them. They remained where they were until the party who had ridden after you returned, then they went slowly back, after having made a litter with their spears, on which four of them carried the officer you threw from his horse—what a crash he made! I heard the clang of his arms as I was running. They stopped near one of the villages they burned as we went past, and when I turned to make my way here their fires were burning, so there's no doubt they mean to halt there for the night."

"That is good news, indeed!" John said. "Before morning we will rouse them up in a way they little expect."

John's followers arrived eager for the fight, for the news of the devastations committed by this party of Romans had roused the whole district to fury. As a rule the Romans, except when actually on a campaign, abstained from all ill-treatment of the inhabitants, the orders against plundering and injuring the people being here, as in other countries held by the Roman arms, very stringent. In the present case there was no doubt that Roman soldiers had been killed, but these had brought their fate upon themselves by their ill-treatment and insult of the villagers; and no notice would have been taken of the slaying of men while acting in disobedience of orders, had it not been that they belonged to the company of Servilius Maro. He was a young noble, possessed of great influence in Rome, and of a ferocious and cruel disposition, and he had urged the general so strongly to allow him to go out to inflict punishment upon the country people that consent had reluctantly been given. But even at this time, although the Jews were not aware of it, a messenger was on his way to Scythopolis, as most serious reports as to his cruelty to peaceful inhabitants had come to the general's ears.

But that message Servilius was never to receive. By midnight upward of four hundred men had gathered at the rendezvous in the mountains. John divided the force into four bodies, and gave each their orders as to the part that they were to take, and then marched down the hill, crossed the river, and advanced toward the Roman bivouac.

When within a quarter of a mile of the fires the band broke up into sections, and proceeded to surround the enemy. When each company reached the position John had marked out for it the men began to crawl slowly forward toward the Romans. John sounded a note on his horn, and with a shout the whole band rushed to their feet and charged down upon the enemy. Before the latter could spring to their feet and mount their horses the Jews were among them.

John, with a picked band of twenty men, at once made his way to the center of the camp, where the captives, ignorant of the cause of this sudden alarm, stood huddled together, placing his men around them to prevent any Roman soldier injuring them, John joined in the fray. It was short. Taken by surprise, unable to get together and form in order of defense, the Roman soldiers were surrounded and cut down, each man fighting stubbornly to the last. One of the first to fall was their leader, who springing to his feet at the alarm, had rushed just as he was, without helmet or armor, among his soldiers, and was stabbed in a dozen places before he had time to draw his sword. The moment the conflict was over, and the last Roman had fallen, John ordered his men to disperse at once.

"Regain your homes before morning," he said; "there may be other parties of Romans out, and it is as well that none, even your friends, should see you return, and then the Romans will have no clew as to those who have taken part in this night's business. Take not any of their arms or spoils. We have fought for vengeance and to relieve our friends, not for plunder. It is well that the Romans should see that, when they hear of the disaster and march out to bury the dead."

The men were already crowding round the captives, relieving them from their bonds, and in many cases embracing and weeping on their necks, for among them were many friends and relations of the rescuing party.

John soon found Mary.

"Is this a miracle you have preformed, John?" the girl said. "Can it be true that our captors have been slain, and that we are free?"

"Yes, dear, we can continue our journey."

"But how has it happened, John—how has it all come about?"

"Jonas and I escaped, as I suppose you know, Mary."

"There was a great confusion and stir upon the road," Mary said, "but I did not know what had happened until we got here. Then some of the men said that two of the captives had escaped, and that one of them jumped on to the horse of the officer and overthrew him, and had ridden off. They said they were both young; and as I missed you both from among the party I thought it must have been you. But how did all these men come together?"

"I rode round the country, calling upon the young men in the villages to take up arms to rescue their friends who had been carried away captive into slavery, and to revenge the destruction which this band of ruffians had caused. There were plenty of brave men ready to undertake the task, and, as you can see, we have carried it out. And now, Mary, we had best be going. You see the others are dispersing fast, and it is as well to be as far from here by morning as possible. A troop of Roman horse may come along, journeying between Scythopolis and Capitolias, and if they came upon this camp they might scour all the country."

"I am ready, John. What a fate you have saved me from! I have seemed in a dream ever since the Romans met us this afternoon. I have tried to think of what my life was going to be, but could not. When we got here I tried to weep, but no tears would come. I have been sitting here as still and cold as if frozen, till I heard the notes of the horn. Oh, John, do you know John of Gamala was there?"

"How do you know, Mary?" John asked in surprise.

"One of the young men, we was a captive, was lying near, and he leaped to his feet when the horn sounded, and shouted, 'There is John of Gamala's horn; we are saved.' Did you know he was with you?"

"Yes, I knew he was," John said.

"You won't say anything against him again," Mary said. "Why did you not bring him here to us that we night thank him?"

"Certainly I will not say anything against him in future, Mary. And now let us be going. I am very anxious about my poor mother. We will follow the road to the spot where we left her. By the time we get there morning will be breaking. We will inquire for her at every village we pass through, for I am sure she cannot have gone far. The Romans did not take the asses, but even with them she could not have traveled far, and probably took shelter at the first place which she came to."

This proved to be the case. At the first village they arrived at, after passing the spot at which they had been taken captives they heard that late the evening before a woman had arrived in sore distress. She was leading two asses, which she seems too feeble to mount. She stated that her son and daughter, had been carried away by the Romans, and she had been received for the night in the principal house in the village.

Martha's delight when John and Mary entered the house where she had been sheltered was beyond words. She fell on their necks and kissed them, with broken sentences of thankfulness to God at their deliverance, and it was some time before she was sufficiently calm to hear how their escape had been effected by the night attack upon the Romans by the country people. She was scarcely surprised when she heard that John had effected his escape, and summoned the people to rise to rescue them.

"You told me to trust you to save Mary, John, and I have kept on saying your words over and over again to myself. It seemed to me as if I did not quite understand them, and yet there was comfort in them. I could not even think what you could do to help Mary, and yet it appeared as if you yourself must have some hope."

As soon as Martha was sufficiently recovered from her emotions to resume their journey the party again started. They made a détour to avoid Hippos, for, as John said, there might be inquiries as to every one who was noticed coming from the direction of the scene of the struggle. They made many halts by the way, for Martha was scarcely able to retain her seat on the donkey, and even Mary was greatly shaken by the event of her captivity and rescue. During the heat of the day they remained under the shade of some trees, and the sun was setting when they approached the farm. Simon and the men hurried out when the sound of the asses' feet was heard. Martha burst into tears as he assisted her to alight.

"What ails you, wife? I trust that no evil has befallen you by the way. Where are the maids? Why, Mary, my child, you look pale too!"

"No wonder, uncle, that aunt is shaken, and that I look pale. For John and I and Jonas were taken captives by the Romans, who carried us off to sell as slaves, leaving poor mother behind."

"And how then have you escaped, child?"

"John and Jonas got away from them, and raised all the country; for the Romans had done much harm killing and carrying away captives and burning. So when he called them the men took up arms and fell upon the Romans at night and slew them all, and rescued me and some fifty other captives who had fallen into their hands."

Simon asked no further questions for the time, but helped Martha into the house, and then handed her over to the care of Mary, and half an hour later she had recovered sufficiently to return to the room, and sit there holding Simon's hand in quiet happiness, and watching Mary as she resumed her accustomed tasks and assisted old Isaac in preparing supper.

"Everything looks just as it was, mother. I could hardly have believed things would have got on so well without me to look after them. And there are quantities of grapes on the vines still; they are too ripe for wine, but they will last us for eating for months, and that is ever so much better than making them into wine—."

She stopped, for Simon had taken his place at the head of the table, and offered up thanks in the name of the whole household for the mercies that had been vouchsafed to them, and especially that they were all once again assembled together in their house without there being one vacant place. Then the meal began. While it was eaten many questions were asked on both sides; Simon inquiring about his bother-in-law and his family and the life they had led at the farm, Martha asking after their neighbors, who had suffered and who had escaped without loss or harm. When Isaac and the men retired Jonas rose also to go, but Simon stopped him.

"Remain with us, Jonas. Your life has been strangely cast in that of John's, and I would that henceforth you take your place as one of the family. You saved his life at Jotapata, and you will henceforth be as an adopted son to me. Martha, I know that you will spare some of your affection for the lad who is a younger brother to John, and who would, I believe, nay, I feel sure, if need be, give his life for his friend."

Martha said a few kind words to Jonas, whose quiet and somewhat subdued manner, and whose evident affection for John, had greatly pleased her, and Mary gave him a little nod, which signified that she gladly accepted him as one of the family.

"And now, Martha," Simon said, "you have not yet told me how proud you must feel in the doings of our son. Our friends here are never weary of congratulating me, and truly I feel thankful that a son of mine should have done such deeds, and that the Lord should have chosen him as an instrument of his will."

"My dear father," John interrupted, "I have told you that there is nothing at all out of the way in what we have done. Jonas and the others did just as much as I did, and methinks that some of them make much more than is needful of our skirmishes, and praise me because in so doing they praise themselves, who did as much as I did."

"But I do not understand you, Simon," Martha said. "I know that John fought bravely at Jotapata, and that it was marvelous that he and Jonas escaped when so many fell. Is it that you are speaking of?"

"What! Has John said nothing about what he has been doing since?" Simon asked in surprise.

"No, father, I said nothing about it," John said before his mother could speak. "I thought, in the first place, that you would like to tell them, and, in the next, the people there had heard such magnified reports that I could not for very shame lay claim to be the hero they had pictured to themselves."

"But what has he done?" Martha asked more and more surprised; while Mary at his last words sprang to her feet and stood looking at him with and intent and eager face.

"He should have told you, Martha," Simon said. "It is no light thing that this son of ours has done. Young as he is the eyes of the people are upon him. For with a small band which he gathered here he harassed the enemy several days, and boldly entering their camp destroyed it by fire."

"Oh, John!" Mary said in a low voice; while Martha exclaimed:

"What! Is the John of whom we have heard so much, the young man of whom the people speak as their future leader, our boy? You cannot mean it, Simon!"

"There is no mistake about it, Martha. The lad came to me and said he thought that with a small band he could cause much trouble to the

Romans; so I told him he could go, not knowing whether he spoke from the restlessness of youth, or because it was the will of the Lord that he should go and fight for the country; indeed, it seemed to many that his marvelous escape from Jotapata showed that God had need of him. So I did not withstand him. There were many from the villages round who were ready to join themselves to him and follow him, for the fame of his escape had made him much talked of. So he went with twenty-four followers, and, of course, Jonas here; and truly he did, as all men say, great things. And though he saved not Gamala, as indeed could not have been done save by a miracle of God, with so small a band, he did much, and by the burning of their camp not only struck a heavy blow upon the Romans, but he inspired the people with hope. Before, it seemed that to resist the Romans was to bring certain destruction upon those who ventured it; now men see that with prudence, united with bravery, much may be done, and in the spring John will be followed by a great gathering of fighting men from all the country round."

Martha sat in speechless surprise looking at her son.

"My dear mother," John said, "what I told you before when you were praising the unknown John is equally true now that it is John your son. We acted with common sense, which so far no one seems to have exercise in our struggle with the Romans. We just kept out of their reach, and took good care never to come to actual blows with them. We constantly threatened them, and compelled them, who knew nothing of our members or strength, to cease working. As to the burning their camp, of course there was a certain amount of danger in it, but one cannot make war without danger. We crept through their sentries into the camp in the night and set it on fire, and then made our escape as best we could.

"As only one of our number was killed, and he from falling over a precipice and not by the sword of the Romans, you see the peril could not have been very great. It was just as I said, that because we did not throw away our lives, but were prudent and cautious, we succeeded. People have made a great fuss about it because it is the only success, however small, that we have gained over the Romans; but, as my father says, it has certainly had a good effect. It has excited a feeling of hopefulness, and in the spring many will take the field with the belief that after all the Romans are not invincible, and that those who fight against them are not merely throwing away their lives."

It was some time before Martha could realize that the hero of which she had heard so much was the quiet lad standing before her—her own son John.

"Simon," she said at last, "morning and night I have prayed God to protect him of whom we heard so much, little thinking that it was my own son I was praying for. To-night I will thank him that he has so blessed me. Assuredly God's hand is with him. The dangers he has run and the success that he has gained may, as he says, be magnified by report; nevertheless he has assuredly withstood the Romans, even as David went out against Goliath. To-morrow I will hear more of this; but I feel shaken with the journey and with this strange news. Come, Mary, let us to bed!" But Mary had already stolen away, without having said a single word after her first exclamation.

John was at work soon after daybreak next morning, for there was much to be done. The men were plowing up the stubble ready for the sowing, Jonas had gone off with Isaac to drive in some cattle from the hills, and John set to work to dig up a patch of garden ground near the house. He had not been long at work when he saw Mary approaching. She came along quietly and slowly, with a step altogether unlike her own.

"Why, Mary, is that you?" he said as she approached. "Why, Miriam herself could not walk slower. Are you ill this morning, child?" he asked with a change of voice as he saw how pale she was looking.

Mary did not speak until she came quite close, then she stopped and looked at him with eyes full of tears.

"Oh, John," she began, "what can I say?"

"Why, my dear Mary, what on earth is the matter with you?" he said, throwing down his spade and taking her hands in his.

"I am so unhappy, John."

"Unhappy!" John repeated. "What is making you unhappy, child?"

"It is so dreadful," she said, "to think that I, who ought to have known you so well, I, your betrothed wife, have been thinking that you were so mean as to be jealous, for I did think it was that, John, when you made light of the doings of that hero I had been thinking about so much, and would not allow that he had done anything particular. I thought that you were jealous, John; and now I know what you have done, and why you spoke so, I feel I am altogether unworthy of you."

"Well, Mary, I never thought you were a little goose before. What nonsense you are talking! It was only natural you should have thought I was jealous, and I should have been jealous if it had been any one else you were praising so much. It was my fault for not telling you at once. Concealments are always stupid; but I had thought that it would give you a pleasant surprise when you got home to hear about it; but instead of causing you pleasure I have caused you pain. I was not vexed in the slightest; I was rather amused when you answered me so curtly."

"I think it was cruel of you, John, to let me go on thinking badly of you, and showing yourself in so unworthy a light. That does not make it any the less wrong of me. I ought to have believed in you."

"You are making a mountain out of a molehill, Mary, and I won't hear any such nonsense. You heard an absurd story as to what some one had been doing, and you naturally made a hero of him. You were hurt by my speaking slightingly of this hero of yours, and naturally thought I was jealous at hearing such praises of another from my betrothed wife. It was all perfectly natural. I was not in the least offended with you, or put out in any way, except that I was vexed with myself for not telling at once that all these fables related to your Cousin John. Now, dry your eyes, and don't think any more about it. Go and pick two of the finest bunches of grapes you can find, and we will eat them together."

But it was some time before Mary recovered her brightness. The changes which the last few months had made almost depressed her. It was but a year ago that John and she had been boy and girl together; now he had become a man, had done great deeds, was looked upon by many as one chosen for the deliverance of the nation. Mary felt that she too had aged; but the change in her was as nothing to that of her old playfellow. It was but a year ago she had been gravely advising him, treating him sometimes as if she had been the elder. She would have treated him now, if he would have let her, with something of the deference and respect which a Jewish maiden would usually pay to a betrothed husband—one who was shortly to become her lord. But the first time he detected this manner John simply laughed at her and said:

"My dear Mary, do not let us have any nonsense of this sort. We have been always equals, you and I, friends and companions. You know just as well as I do that in all matters which we have had in common, you have always had quite as much sense as I, and on a great many matters more sense. Nothing has occurred since then to alter that. I have grown into a young man, you into a young woman; but we have advanced equally. On matters concerning warfare I have gained a deal of knowledge; in other matters, doubtless, you have gained knowledge. And if, dear, it is God's will that I pass through the troubles and dangers that lie before us, and we become man and wife, I trust that we shall always be the friends and comrades that we have been as boy and girl together. It is all very well, when young men and maidens have see nothing of each other until their parents bring them together as man and wife, for the bride to affect a deep respect, which I have not the least doubt she is generally far from feeling in her heart, for the man to whom she is given. Happily this has not been the way with us. We have learned to know each other well, and to know that in all things, I trust, we shall be companions and equals. I do hope, Mary, that there will be no change in our ways to few months we have to be together now.

"In the spring I go up to help defend Jerusalem, and it is no use hiding the fact from ourselves that there is but little chance of my returning. We know what has befallen those who have hitherto defended cities against the Romans, and what has happened to Jotapata and Gamala will probably happen at Jerusalem. But for this reason let us have no change; let us be as brother and sister to one another, as we have been all along. If God brings me back safe to you and you become my wife there will be plenty of time to settle exactly how much deference you shall pay me, but I shall expect that when the novelty of affecting the wifely obedience which is enjoined upon the females of our race is past you will be quite ready to take up that equality which is, after all, the rule of practice."

"I shall remember your words," Mary said saucily, "when the time comes. It may be you will regret your expressions about equality some day."

So during the winter Mary tried to be bright and cheerful, and Martha, whose heart was filled with anxiety as to the dangers and trials which lay before them—Jerusalem desperate enterprises—often wondered to herself when she heard the girl's merry laugh as she talked with John, and saw how completely she seemed to put aside everyone sort of anxiety; but she did not know how Mary often spent the entire night in weeping and prayer, and how hard was her struggle to keep up the brave appearance which was, she knew, a pleasure to John.

He was not much at home, being often absent for days together. Strangers came and went frequently. John had long conversations with them and sometimes went away with them and did not return for three or four days. No questions were asked by his parents as to these visitors or his absence. They knew that they had reference to what they considered his mission; and as when he returned home he evidently wished to lay aside all thought of other things and to devote himself to his life with them, they asked no questions as to what he was doing.

He spoke sometimes of things to Mary when they were together alone. She knew that numbers of young men were only waiting his signal to join him; that parties of them met him among the hills and were there organized into companies, each with officers of their own choice over them; and that, unknown to the Romans at Scythopolis, there were daily held throughout the country on both sides of the Jordan meetings where men practiced with their arms, improved their skill with the bow and arrow, and learned to obey the various signals of the bugle which John had now elaborated.

John was resolute in refusing to accept any men with wives and families. There were other leaders, he said, under whom these could fight; he was determined to have none but men who were ready to sacrifice their lives, and without the care of others dependent upon them.

He was ready to accept youths of fifteen as well as men of twenty-five, believing that, in point of courage, the one were equal to each other. But each candidate had to be introduced by others, who vouched for his activity, hardihood, and courage. One of his objects was to avoid increasing his band to too great dimensions. The number of those ready to go up to defend Jerusalem, and eager to enroll themselves as followers of this new leader, whose mission was now generally believed in in that part of the country, was very large; but John knew that a multitude would be unwieldy; that he would find it impossible to carry out the thousands of men tactics dependent for success upon celerity of movement; and, moreover, that did he arrive in Jerusalem with so great a following, he would once become an object of jealousy to the leaders of the factions there.

He therefore limited the number to four hundred men, urging upon all others who presented themselves or sent messages to him to form themselves similar bands, to choose leaders, and to act as independent bodies, hanging upon the rear of the Romans, harassing them with frequent night alarms, cutting off their convoys, attacking their working parties, and always avoiding encounters with strong bodies of the Romans by retreating into the hills. He said that although he would not receive more men into his own force than he thought could be easily handled, he should be glad to act in concert with the other leaders, so that at times the bands might all unite in a common enterprise, and especially that if they entered Jerusalem they might hold together, and thus be enabled to keep aloof from the parties of John of Gischala or Eleazar, who were contending for the mastery of the city.

His advice was taken, and several bands similar to his own were formed, but their leaders felt that they needed the prestige and authority which John had gained, and that their followers would not obey their orders with the faith which was inspired in the members of John's own band by their belief in his special mission. Their representations on this subject were so urgent that John, at their request, attended a meeting at which ten of these chiefs were present. It was held in a farm-house not far from the spot where Gamala had stood. John was embarrassed at the respect which these men, all of them several years older than himself, paid him; but he accepted the position quietly, for he felt that the belief that existed as to his having a special mission added greatly to his power of utility. He listened to their representations as to their want of authority, and to the rivalries and jealousies which already existed among those who had enrolled themselves. When they had finished he said:

"I have been thinking the matter well over. I am convinced that it is absolutely necessary that none of the commands shall exceed the numbers I have fixed upon, namely, four hundred men, divided into eight companies, each with a captain; but at the same time I do not see any reasons why all our corps should not be nominally under one leader. If, then, you think it will strengthen your position, I am ready to accept the general leadership and to appoint you each as commanders of your troops. Then you will hold my commissions, and I will support you in your commands with any authority I may have."

"At the same time you will understand that you will in reality act altogether independently of me, save and except when it seems to me that we can unite in any enterprise; if we enter Jerusalem we will then hold together for mutual protection from the factions; but even there you will each command independently, for did I assume a general command it would excite the jealousy of the leaders of the factions, and we should be forced to take part in the civil strife which is devastating the city."

A cordial consent to this proposition was given by the other leaders, who said that the knowledge that they were John's officers would add immensely to their authority, and would also raise the courage and devotion of their men, who would not believe that they were being led to victory unless they were acting under the orders of John himself.

"Remember," John said, "that if misfortune befalls us I have never laid claim to any divine commission. We are all agents of God, and it may be that he has specially chosen me as one of his instruments; but this I cannot say beyond the fact that so far I have been carried safely through great dangers and have been enabled to win successes over the Romans. But I do not set up as a specially appointed leader. I say this for two reasons: in the first place, that you should not think that I am claiming authority and command on ground which may not be justified; and in the second place, that if I should fall early in fighting, others should not be disheartened and believe that the Lord has deserted them.

"I am but a lad among you, and I recognize that it is God who has so strangely brought me into eminence, but having done that much he may now choose some other instrument. If this should be so, as may well be, one of you should obtain far greater success than may attend me, I shall be only too glad to lay aside this authority over the rest with which you are willing to invest me, and to follow him as cheerfully as you now propose to follow me."

The meeting soon afterward broke up, and the news that John of Gamala, as he was generally called from the success he had gained over the Romans before that town, had assumed the supreme command of the various bands which were being raised in Eastern Galilee and on the east of Jordan, spread rapidly and greatly increased the popular feeling of hope and confidence. Fresh bands were formed, the leaders all receiving their appointments from him. Before the spring arrived there were twenty bands formed and organized in readiness to march down toward Jerusalem as soon as the Roman legions got into motion.

Chapter Eleven

A TALE OF CIVIL STRIFE

Toward the spring, Simon and his family were surprised by a visit from the Rabbi Solomon Ben Manasseh. It was a year since they had last seen him, when he called to take leave of them on starting for Jerusalem. They scarcely recognized him as he entered, so old and broken did he look.

"The Lord be praised that I see you all safe and well!" he said as they assisted him to dismount from the donkey that he rode. "Ah, my friends, you are happy indeed in your quiet farm, free from all the distraction of this terrible time! Looking round here and seeing you just as I left you, save that the young people have grown somewhat, I could think that I left you but yesterday, and that I have been passing through a hideous nightmare. Look at me! My flesh has fallen away and my strength is gone. I can scarce stand upon my legs, and a young child could overthrow me. I have wept till my tears are dried up over the misfortune of Jerusalem, and yet no enemy has come within sight of her walls, or dug a trench against her. She is devoured by her own children. Ruin and desolation have come upon her."

The old man was assisted into the house and food and wine placed before him. Then he was led into the guest-chamber, and there slept for some hours. In the evening he had recovered somewhat of his strength, and joined the party at their meal. When it was concluded and the family were alone, he told them what had happened in Jerusalem during the past year. Vague rumors of dissension and civil war had reached them, but a jealous watch was set round the city, and none were suffered to leave, under the pretext that all who wished to go out were deserters who sought to join the Romans.

"I passed through with difficulty," the rabbi said, "after bribing John of Gischala with all my worldly means to grant me a pass through the guards, and even then should not have succeeded had he not known me in old times, when I looked upon him as one zealous for the defense of the country against the Romans, little thinking then that the days would come when he would grow into an oppressor of the people, tenfold as cruel and pitiless as the worst of the Roman tribunes.

"Last autumn, when, with the band of horsemen with steeds weary with hard riding he arrived before the gates of Jerusalem, saying that they had come to defend the city, thinking it was worth while to risk their lives in the defense of the country against the Romans, little thinking it not worth while to risk their lives in the defense of a mere mountain town like Gischala, the people poured out to meet him and do him honor. Terrible rumors of slaughter and massacre in Galilee had reached us, but none knew the exact truth. Moreover, John had been an enemy of Josephus, and since Josephus had gone over to the Romans his name is hated and accursed among the people, and thus they were favorably inclined toward John.

"I don't think any one was deceived by the story he told, for it was evident that John and his men had fled before the Romans. Still, the tidings he brought were reassuring, and he was gladly received in the city. He told us that the Romans had suffered very heavily at the sieges of Jotapata and Gamala, that they were greatly dispirited by the desperate resistance they had met with, that a number of the engines of war had been destroyed, and that they were in no condition to undertake the siege of a strong city like Jerusalem. But though all outwardly rejoiced, many in their hearts grieved at the news, for they thought that even an occupation by the Romans would be preferable to the suffering they were undergoing.

"For months bands of robbers, who called themselves Zealots, had ravaged the whole country, pillaging, burning, and slaying, under the pretense that those they assaulted were favorable to the cause of Rome. Thus gradually the country people all forsook their homes and fled to Jerusalem for refuge; and when the country was left a desert and no more plunder was to be gained, these robber bands gradually entered Jerusalem.

"As you know, the gates of the holy city were always open to all the Jewish people, and none thought of excluding the strangers who entered, believing that every armed man would add to the power of resistance when the Romans appeared before it. The robbers, who came singly or in small parties from all parts of the country, soon gathered themselves together in the city and established a sort of terror over the peaceable inhabitants. Men were robbed and murdered openly in the street; houses were broken open and pillaged; none dare walk in the street without the risk of insult or assault. Antipas, Levias, and Saphias, all of royal blood, were seized, thrown into prison, and there murdered; and many others of the principal people were slain. Then the robbers proceeded to further lengths.

"They took upon themselves to appoint a high-priest; selected a family which had no claim whatever to the distinction, and drawing lots among them, chose as high-priest one Phappias—a country priest, ignorant, boorish, and wholly unable to discharge the function of the office. Hitherto the people had submitted to the oppression of the Zealots, but this desecration of the holy office filled them with rage and indignation; and Ananus, the oldest of the chief priests, a man of piety and wisdom, was the head of the movement, and, calling the people together, exhorted them to resist the tyranny which oppressed them, and which was now desecrating the Temple; for the Zealots had taken refuge there and made the holy place their headquarters.

"The people seized their arms, but before they were ready for the attack the Zealots, learning what was going on, took the initiative and fell upon them. The people were less accustomed to arms than their foes, but they had the superiority of numbers, and fought with fury. At first the Zealots gained the advantage, but the people increased in numbers, those behind pressed those in front forward, and the Zealots were driven back into the Temple, and the Quadrangle of the Gentiles was taken.

"The Zealots fled into the inner court and closed the gates. Thither their wounded had already been carried, and the whole place was defiled with their blood. But Ananus, having the fear of God before his eyes, did not like to attack them there; and leaving six thousand chosen men on guard in the cloisters, and arranging that these should be regularly relieved, retired. Such was the state of things when John of Gischala arrived. He at once professed complete agreement with the party of Ananus, and was admitted into all their councils; but all the time, as we afterward learned, he was keeping up a secret correspondence with the Zealots, and betrayed to them all that took place at the council. There was some distrust of him, but in addition to the party that had entered the city with him, he had speedily gathered together many others; and, distracted as we already were with our troubles, none cared to add to the number of their enemies by openly distrusting John, who took many solemn oaths of fidelity to the cause of order.

"He at length volunteered to enter the inner Temple on a mission to the Zealots, and to persuade them to surrender and leave the city. But no sooner was he among them than he threw off the mask, and told the Zealots that the offers to allow them to depart in peace were blinds, and that they would at once be massacred if they surrendered. He therefore advised them to resist and to send for assistance without, recommending them especially to send to the Idumeans. Eleazar and Zacharias, the chiefs of the Zealots, felt sure that they above all would be sacrificed if they surrendered, and they embraced John's counsel and sent off swift-footed messengers to the Idumeans, urging them to come to their assistance.

"The Idumeans had, since their conquest by Hyrcanus, been incorporated with the Jews. They were a fierce and warlike people, of Arab descent; and immediately the messengers of the Zealots arrived they embraced the proposal, anticipating the acquisition of great plunder in Jerusalem. Marching with all speed, they appeared twenty thousand strong before the walls of Jerusalem.

"Although taken completely by surprise, for none knew that messengers had gone over to the Idumeans, the people manned the walls, and Jesus, a colleague of Ananus, addressed the Idumeans. He asked them to take one of three courses: either to unite with the people in punishing the notorious robbers and assassins who were desecrating the Temple, or to enter the city unarmed and arbitrate between the conflicting parties, or to depart and leave the city to settle its own difficulties. Simon, the leader of the Idumeans, answered that they came to take the part of the true patriots against men who were conspiring basely to sell the people into the hands of the Romans.

"At this answer Jesus left the wall, and we held debate upon the situation. Before the arrival of this new enemy we felt certain of overpowering the Zealots, and Ananus would ere long have been persuaded to lay aside his scruples and attack them, for as they were desecrating the sanctuary it would be better to shed their blood there, and, when these wicked men were slain, to offer up atonement and purify the Temple, as had been done before in the days of the Maccabees after the Temple had been defiled.

"We redoubled our guards round the Temple, so that none could issue out thence to communicate with the Idumeans. At night a terrible storm set in, with lightning, thunder, and rain, so that the very earth seemed to shake. A great awe fell upon all within and without the city. To all it seemed a sign of the wrath of God at the civil discords; but though doubtless it was the voice of the Almighty, it was rather a presage of further evils.

"Under shelter of the storm, which drove all the guards to take refuge, some of the Zealots cut asunder the bars of the gate and crept along the street to the wall. Then they sawed through the bars of the gate that faced the Idumeans, who were trembling with terror in the storm. Unseen by any one the Idumeans entered the gate, marched through the city, and approached the Temple. Then they fell upon our guards, while the Zealots attacked them from behind.

"Furious at the hours they had passed exposed into the tempest, ashamed of their fears, and naturally pitiless and cruel, the Idumeans gave no quarter, and a terrible carnage took place among the ten thousand men who had been placed in the outer court of the Temple. Some fought desperately, others threw themselves down from the wall into the city, and when morning dawned eighty-five hundred of our best fighting men had been slain.

"As soon as it was daylight the Idumeans broke into the city, pillaging and slaying. The high-priest, Ananus and Jesus, were among those who were slain, and in that terrible night were extinguished the last hopes of saving Jerusalem. Ananus was a man of the highest character. He had labored unceasingly to place the city in a posture of defense, believing, and rightly, that the stronger were its walls, and the more formidable the resistance it could offer, the better chance there was of obtaining favorable terms from the Romans.

"Ananus was the leader and hope of the peace party, which comprised all the respectable classes and all the older and wiser men in Jerusalem. His death left the conduct of affairs in the hands of the thoughtless, the rash, and the desperate. The massacre continued for days, the Idumeans hunting the citizens in the streets. Vast numbers were killed without question. The young men of the upper classes were dragged to prison and were there scourged and tortured to force them to join the Zealots; but not one would do so; all preferred death.

"Thus perished twelve thousand of the best and wisest in Jerusalem. Then the Zealots set up a tribunal, and by proclamation assembled seventy of the principal citizens remaining to form a court, and before it brought Zacharias, the son of Baruch, and upright, patriotic, and wealthy man. Him they charged with entering into correspondence with the Romans, but produced no shadow of evidence against him.

"Zacharias defended himself boldly, clearly establishing his own innocence, and denouncing the iniquities of his accusers. The seventy unanimously acquitted the prisoner, preferring to die with him to condemning an innocent man. The Zealots rushed forward with cries of rage and slew Zacharias, and with blows and insults turned the judges out of the Temple. The Idumeans at length began to weary of massacre and were sated with pillage, and declaring that they had been deceived by the Zealots, and that they believed no treason had been intended, they left the city, first opening the prisons and releasing two thousand persons confined there, who fled to Simon the son of Gioras, who was wasting the country toward Idumea.

"The Zealots after their departure redoubled their iniquities, and seemed as if they would leave none alive save the lowest of the people. Gorion, a great and distinguished man, was among the slain. Niger of Peræa who had been the leader in the attack on the Romans at Ascalon, a noble and true-hearted patriot, was also murdered. He died calling upon the Romans to come to avenge those who had been thus murdered, and denouncing famine, pestilence, and civil massacre, as well as war, against the accursed city.

"I had lain hidden with an obscure family, with whom I had lodged during these terrible times. So great was the terror and misery in the city that those who lived envied the dead. It was death to bury even a relative, and both within and without the city lay heaps of bodies decaying in the sun. Even among the Zealots themselves factions arose. John of Gischala headed one party, and that the more violent. Over these he ruled with absolute authority, and occupied one portion of the city. The other party acknowledged no special leader. Sometimes, then, the faction fought among themselves, but neither side ceased from plundering and murdering the inhabitants.

"Such, my friends, was the condition of Jerusalem when I left it, having, as I told you, purchased a permission from John of Gischala to pass through the guard at the gates.

"As I traveled here I learned that another danger threatens us. The sect called the Assassins, as you know, seized the strong fortress of Masada near the Dead Sea at the beginning of the troubles. Until lately they have been content to subsist on the plunder of the adjacent country, but on the night of the Passover they surprised Engaddi, dispersed all who resisted, and slew seven hundred women and children who could not escape. They carried off the contents of the granaries, and are now wasting the whole region.

"What hope can there be of success, my friends, when, with an enemy close to their gates, the Jews are slaying more of their fellow-countrymen than the Romans themselves? Did ever a country present so humiliating and terrible a spectacle? Were such atrocities ever perpetrated by men upon their brothers? And yet the madmen still believe that the Almighty will deliver them, will save from destruction that Temple which they have polluted, the altars that they have deluged with blood."

When the rabbi had finished his narration there was a long silence. Martha was in tears at the recital of the misery which was endured by the inhabitants of Jerusalem; Simon sat with his face covered with his hands; John had scarce moved since the rabbi had begun his story, but sat with a heavy frown on his face, looking straight before him; while Mary anxiously watched him to see the effect of the recital upon him. Simon was the first to speak.

"It is a tale of mourning, lamentation, and woe that you have told us, rabbi. Not even in the days of our captivity in Babylon were the Jewish people fallen so low. Let us to bed now. These things are too terrible to speak of until we have laid them before the Lord and asked his guidance. I wonder not now, rabbi that years seem to have rolled over your head since we last met."

The others rose. Mary, as she passed John, laid her hands on his shoulder with a caressing action, which was very rare to her, for she generally behaved to him as to a brother, holding any exhibition of greater affection un-maidenly until the days of betrothal were ended.

The action seemed to recall John from his gloomy thought, and he smiled down at her anxious face; then when the others went off to their apartments he went out into the night air and stood for hours nearly immovable with his eyes fixed on the stars. In the morning Mary joined him in the garden, as had come to be their custom, this being the only time in the day when they were alone together.

"Well, John?" she asked.

He understood her question.

"I have thought it over, Mary, in every way, but I cannot see that my duty is changed by what we heard last night. Affection for you and my parents would keep me here, and I wish that I could see that my duty could go hand in hand with my wishes. I have been sorely tempted to yield, to resign the struggle, to remain here in peace and quiet; but I should never be happy. I do not believe that I am, as so many think, specially called to be deliverer, though God has assuredly specially protected and aided me; but did I draw back now it would be a grievous discouragement to many. I have put my hand to the plow and cannot look back. God has permitted there miseries to fall upon Jerusalem, doubtless as a punishment for the sins of the people. It may be yet that his wrath will be abated, and that he will remember the mercies of old.

"He has suffered his temple to be profaned, but it may not be his purpose to allow it to be destroyed utterly. The evil doings, therefore, of evil men do not release us from our duty, and it has always been held the chief duty of all Jews to die, if need be, in defense of the Temple. Never so long as that stands can we say that the Lord has wholly turned his face from us, that he purposes another period of exile and captivity to befall his people. Therefore, Mary, I shall go on as I have intended, warring against the Romans and doing what I can to hinder their advance against Jerusalem. I think that the war may last longer than I had expected. Vespasian will have heard from those who, like the rabbi, have escaped Jerusalem, what is going on within the city, and knowing the great strength of its walls, and judging from what he saw at Jotapata and Gamala, how desperate would be its resistance were he to appear before it, he may well decide to leave it for the present, suffering the population to prey upon each other, to consume their provisions, and waste their strength till, when he marches against it, there will be no longer men left to man the walls."

"I thought you would decide so, John," Mary said quietly; "and much as I love you—for I do love you, John—I would rather part with you so, never to see you again, than that you should draw back now. I set you up on a pedestal before I knew that it was you who was my hero, and I would not have it said that he of whom such high hopes were cherished drew back from the enterprise he had taken up. Rather would I mourn for you all my life than that men should say of you, This is he of whom we said he is the deliverer, but who shrank from the dangers of battle and threw down his country's sword."

"Thank you, Mary. I am glad to hear you say so. I thought that I was right; but it was very hard so to decide. And now that you agree with me, my chief cause for hanging back is removed. Henceforth I shall trouble no more over it. My conscience tells me that I am right to go. You say go also; therefore now, whatever betides I shall not blame myself, but shall feel that I could not have taken any other course."

"I have faith, John, that you will come back to me when the troubles are over. I believe that whatever may happen in Jerusalem you will be spared to me. I think that it was either for the country or for me that your life was spared alone of all those that fought at Jotapata, and I mean to keep on thinking so. It will keep up my spirits while you are away, and will help me to cheer our mother."

"If the Romans do not move upon Jerusalem I may be able to be often at home. Our policy will be to strike a blow; and then, when the Romans gather in force, to scatter and disappear; so that I may often be home until the time comes when the enemy gather round Jerusalem. But at any rate, Mary, I shall try and believe that your hope is well founded, and that in the end I shall return alive to you. Certainly I shall not spare my life; for when one takes up the post of a leader of his fellows he must never hang back from danger, but must be always in the front. At the same time I shall never forget that you are thinking and praying for me, and will never throw away my life recklessly; and if the time comes when I see that all is lost, that fighting is no longer of avail, I will neither rush into the enemy's ranks to die, nor will I slay myself with my own weapons, but I will strive in every way to save my life for your sake, having done all that I could for our country and the Temple."

"That is all I ask, John. I am quite content to wait here until the day comes that you shall return; and then, though our cause be lost, our country ruined, and God's Temple destroyed, we can yet feel that God has been good and merciful to us, even if we be driven out of our home, and have to become exiles in a far land."

A week later the news came that the Romans were preparing to take the field. The young men of the village at once started as messengers through the country. At night a vast pile of brushwood was lighted on the hill above Gamala, and answering fires soon blazed out from other heights. At he signal men left their homes on the shores of Galilee, in the cities of the plains, in the mountains of Peræa and Batanæa. Captiolias, Gerisa and Pella, Sepphoris, Caphernaum and Tiberias, and even the towns and villages almost within sight of Cæsar's camp at Cæsarea, sent their contingents, and in twenty-four hours eight thousand armed men were gathered on the slopes of Mount Galaad.

Each man brought with him grain sufficient for a week's consumption, and all had, according to their means brought money, in accordance with instructions John and the other commanders had issued. For John held that although, as they were fighting for the country, they must, if necessary, live upon the country, yet that as far as possible they should abstain from taking food without payment, and so run the risk of being confounded with the bands who, under the cloak of patriotism, plundered and robbed the whole country.

The bands assembled, each under their leaders. It was easy to see that they had come from different localities. Tarichea and Tiberias had both sent two companies, and the aspect of these differed widely from that of the companies of peasants raised in the villages on the slopes of Hermon or among the mountains of Peræa; but all seemed animated by an equal feeling of devotion and of confidence in their young leader.

John, after carefully inspecting his own band, visited the camps of the other companies, and was everywhere received with acclamations. He addressed each company in turn, not only urging them to show bravery, for that every Jew had shown who had fought against the Romans, but pointing out that far more than this was required.

While they must be ready to give their lives when need be, they must be equally ready to shun the fight, to scatter and fly, when their leaders gave the orders. It was not by bravery that they could hope to overcome the Romans, but by harassing them night and day, by attacking their camps, cutting off their convoys, and giving them no rest. Above all, obedience was required.

"Look at the Roman soldiers," he said. "They have no wills of their own. They advance or retreat; they attack when they know that those who first attack must die; they support all hardships and fatigues; they accomplish marvels in the way of work; they give themselves up, in fact, to obey the orders given them, never questioning whether those orders are the best, but blindly obeying them; and so it must be here if we are to fight the Romans with a chance of success. The most useful man here—the man who will do best service to his country—is not he who is strongest or bravest, but he who is most prompt in his obedience of orders. The true hero is he who gives up his will and, if need be, his life, at the order of his leader. You have chosen your own officers, and I have confirmed the choice that you have made. It is for you now to give them your support and assistance. There will be hardships—these must be borne without complaint; there will be delays—these must be supported with patience; there will be combats and dangers—these must be met with confidence and courage, believing that God will give you success, and that although the issue of the strife is in his hands, each of you should do his best by his conduct and courage to gain success.

"We shall not act in one great body, for we could not find food in the villages for so large a number; moreover, to do so would be to give the Romans an opportunity of massing their forces against us, of surrounding and destroying us. On the great occasions and for a great object we may gather together and unite our forces. At other times, although acting upon a general plan and in concert with each other, each company will work independently. So we shall elude the Romans. When they strike at us, we shall be gone; when they try to enclose us, we shall disperse; when they pursue one body, others will fall upon them; when they think that we are in one part of the country, we will be striking a blow in another; when they fancy themselves in security, we will fall upon them. We will give them no rest or peace."

John's addresses were received with shouts of approval. By the great majority of those present he was now seen for the first time; but his appearance, the tone of authority with which he spoke, his air of confidence, and the manner in which he had evidently thought out the plans of action, and prepared for all contingencies, confirmed the reports which they had heard of him, and the conviction that he was a specially appointed leader was deepened and strengthened. How otherwise could one who was a mere youth speak with such firmness and authority!

The memories of the Jews were stored with legends of the prowess of Judas the Maccabean and his brothers and of other leaders who had from time to time arisen and enabled them to clear their country of oppressors, and they were thus prepared to accept willingly those who appeared to them especially sent as leaders, and the question of age and experience weighed but little with them. As none had been trained as soldiers, there were none who had to set aside superior claims.

Samuel had been chosen as a child, Saul was the youngest of his brethren, and David a lad when he slew the champion of the Philistines. Such being the case, the youth of John was no drawback in the eyes of his followers; and, indeed, the fact that, being still a youth, he had yet escaped from Jotapata, where all his elders had died, and that he had inflicted a heavy blow upon the Romans when all others who had opposed them had perished, seemed in itself a proof that he was under special protection.

John probably believed in himself less than did any man among his followers. Piously and devoutly brought up, he saw in the two escapes that he had had from death at the hands of the Romans signs of a special protection of God. But while he hoped that he might be able to do the Romans much harm, he had not any conviction that he was destined to deliver his country. He had none of the fervent enthusiasm of men who are convinced that they have a divine mission, and that miracles would be wrought in his favor.

He had seen the tremendous strength of the Roman army as it defiled from the mountains before Jotapata. He had learned the power of their war machines, and had evidence of their discipline, their bravery, and perseverance, and had no idea that such a force as that gathered round him could cope with the legions of Rome. Still, that firm and pious belief which was so deeply ingrained in the heart of the Jews, that God specially interested himself in them, that he personally directed everything that befell them, and intervened in every incident of their history, had its effect upon him.

His training taught him that he was an instrument in God's hands; and although he hardly even hoped that he was destined to be a deliverer of Jerusalem, he thought that God might intend him to do great things for his people. At any rate, while never claiming any special authority, or to have, more than those around him, any special mission, he was careful not to damp the enthusiasm of his followers by disclaiming the mission they attributed to him, knowing how much such a belief added to his authority and to the efficiency of the force under his command.

Chapter Twelve

DESULTORY FIGHTING

After having gone through the camps of the whole of the companies, John assembled the leaders round him and held a council as to future operations. It was agreed that it would be best to leave alone for the present the legion at Scythopolis, for rumors of the gathering would almost certainly have reached that city, and the Romans might be on their guard against attack. It was resolved, therefore, to cross the Jordan a few miles below Tarichea, to traverse the hills between Endor and Gelbus, and by a long march to gain the range of hills extending from Carmel to Samaria and forming the boundary between the latter province and Galilee. They would then be looking down upon the camp of Vespasian at Cæsarea.

The country between these hills and the city was too flat for them to engage with any hopes of success, for although by a surprise that might inflict great damage on the Romans, they would be wholly unable to withstand the charges of the Roman horse. They would therefore maintain a lookout from the mountains, and attack the Roman camp the first time it was pitched on ground whence a rapid retreat could be effected to the hills.

As the Jordan was unfordable between Scythopolis and the lake, all who could not swim were ordered to carry with them on their march down to the river logs of light wood sufficient to support them crossing.

Those who could swim were to assist in piloting over those unable to do so. This would be a work of no great difficulty, for the width of the

Jordan was not great, and it was only a short distance in the center that it would be unfordable. As was to be expected, the companies raised near the shore of the lake contained but few men unable to swim, while those from the mountain districts were almost wholly ignorant of the art.

The bands were therefore linked together for the purpose of crossing, one of those from the plains and a company of mountaineers marching down to the stream together. The preparations were all complete by the afternoon, and just as it was becoming twilight the leading bands arrived on the banks of the Jordan. The crossing was effected without difficulty, and in two hours all were over. Then the companies formed up under their leaders and started independently, men who knew the country well being assigned as guides to each.

They crossed the hill between Endor and Gelbus, marched through Jezrael, and then, just as morning was breaking, ascended the slopes of Mount Carmel, leaving Legio on their right. It was a march of about fifty miles, but the men were all active and vigorous, lightly armed, and sustained by enthusiasm and excitement, and not a man dropped behind during the journey. Once among the hills, they threw themselves down for a rest of some hours. From the crest of the hill it was but some twelve miles down to Cæsarea, and the blue line of the sea extended right and left as far as the eye could reach.

In the afternoon Jonas was sent down to the city to learn how matters stood there, and when Vespasian was going to move. He was to remain there that night and return with the news on the following morning. He came back, however, at midnight, saying that the Romans had marched on the previous day, that they had taken the southern road which skirted the mountains for some distance, and would probably cross the central range at Sichen, and either proceed to Scythopolis or join the legion thence on the plain of Aulon, west of the Jordon. This was a disappointment, but at daybreak the companies were afoot.

It was decided they should march separately, each taking its own line to the east, following infrequented roads, and keeping among the hills as far as possible so that no report of the passage of any large gathering of men should reach the Romans. Although no time had been lost, John, when he approached the Jordan, learned that Vespasian had already joined the legion from Scythopolis and had crossed the river into Peræa, and was marching with all speed against Gadara, its chief city.

Halting for the night near the Jordan, John crossed the river by a ford next morning, and then moved forward cautiously to commence operations as soon as the Romans were engaged upon the siege of the city. But ere many hours had passed he learned that the inhabitants had sent forward a deputation to Vespasian, and that the war party, taken by surprise by the rapid advance of the Romans, had hastily evacuated the city after slaying many of those who were willing to admit the Romans.

When Vespasian arrived he had been received with acclamations by the inhabitants, who had already destroyed a portion of their walls, to prove that they never thought of resistance. Having thus established the Roman authority in Peræa, Vespasian left a garrison there and set out with the main body of his army for Cæsarea, leaving a garrison in the town and dispatching Placidus with Five hundred horse and three thousand foot in pursuit of the fugitives who had fled from Gadara before he entered it.

As Vespasian marched back the band under John began their work. Wherever the road led through the mountains they rolled down rocks upon the column. The light-armed allies of the Romans were sent out on each flank, and climbing the hills, attacked their assailants. As soon, however, as they neared the crests, which were, as they believed, held by small parties only of the enemy, the Jews rushed upon them with fury, overthrew them, and drove them down the hills until the heavy-armed troops were obliged to advance to their assistance, upon which the Jews at once fell back to the higher slopes.

Growing bolder by success they even ventured to rush down upon the baggage, breaking through its guard and killing great numbers of animals. A party of Roman horse which came up at full gallop was charged just as they reached the spot by two more companies from the hill, and these, before the Romans could face about and oppose their line of long spears to their assailants, were among them, stabbing the horses, leaping up behind the soldiers and slaying them with their knives, and throwing the whole into confusion. Then the sound of a horn was heard on the hillside, and the whole of the Jews instantly relinquished their work and took to the mountains just as a large body of cavalry, headed by Titus, came thundering up.

At night the Romans were disturbed by constant alarms. Men crept up to the sentries and slew them in the darkness. Numbers of the enemy penetrated into the camp, killing the soldiers as they slept, hocking the horses, and setting fire to the camp in several places; and it was not until the whole army got under arms that the attack ceased. The next day they were similarly harassed upon the march, and it was not until they had crossed the mountains and descended on to the western plain that the Jews drew off, highly satisfied with the result of their first encounter with the Romans. Their loss had been slight, not more than twenty having fallen, while they had killed more than two hundred of the light-armed troops, had inflicted some loss upon the Romans themselves, had slain numbers of baggage animals, and had shown the enemy that however formidable the Roman soldiers might be on the plains, the legions of Vespasian were no more invincible than was that of Cestius among the hills. They regretted, however, that instead of engaging the main army they had not followed the force under Placidus, of whose dispatch from Gadara they had not learned until it was too late.

The fugitives of whom Placidus was in pursuit had taken possession of the village of Bethennabris. He pursued the stratagem which had already succeeded so well. He feigned a retreat, and the Jews sallied out and attacked him. He cut off the greater part from returning to the village, and at night attacked Bethennabris, captured it, and put all within it to the sword. Those who had escaped were joined by great numbers of the country people, and made for the Jordan, intending to cross by the ford opposite Jericho, but the river was swollen with rain and they were unable to cross. Placidus overtook and attacked them. Vast numbers were killed, and more were driven into the river and drowned.

Fifteen thousand fell, twenty-five hundred were taken prisoners, with a vast number of animals of all kinds. Placidus then reduced the whole of Peræa and the coast of the Dead Sea as far as Machærus.

Vespasian soon moved down from Cæsarea, keeping near the sea, and capturing Antipatris, Lydda, and Thamna, and blocking Emmaus; then continuing his course southward he wasted the country to the frontier of Idumea, and captured the towns Betaris and Caphartobas, putting to the sword about ten thousand men. Then he marched back by Emmaus and Sichem, descended the hills and marched to Jericho, where he was joined by Placidus with the troops from Peræa. The city had been deserted by its inhabitants, and the Roman army rested here for some time, until, just as Vespasian was about to march upon Jerusalem, the news arrived of the death of Nero, and, unwilling to weaken his army by besieging the city, strong in itself and defended by a host, Vespasian withdrew to Cæsarea, and for another two years Jerusalem had time for preparation or submission.

As Vespasian's march had, except when he was crossing the mountains from Emmaus to Sichem, lain entirely in the plains, John had been able to do but little. Half the force had been sent across the Jordan, and its operations had greatly added to the difficulties Placidus had met with in subduing Peræa. The other companies had closely followed the march of Vespasian, had made many attacks upon parties dispatched to pillage the country, and after the Romans marched north again besieged and captured some of the small places in which they had left garrisons. They had united when the two Roman armies met at Jericho, and were prepared to defend desperately the rugged mountain roads leading thence to Jerusalem, when to their surprise they saw the Roman host moving away to the north again.

As soon as they ascertained that Vespasian had for the present entirely abandoned the idea of attacking Jerusalem and that his troops had gone into permanent quarters, John held a council with the other commanders. Some were in favor of remaining in arms, and of constantly attacking the Roman garrisons; others were for scattering and returning to their homes, from which they had now been absent three months, until the Romans again set themselves in motion against Jerusalem. Opinions were about equally divided, and John remained silent until all had spoken; then he said:

"I think that we had better disperse. If we remained in arms we might gain some successes, we might surprise and slay some Roman garrisons, but the others would speedily prepare themselves against attack by strengthening their walls and taking every precaution. But did we succeed in destroying the garrisons in every one of the towns they have captured, of what benefit would it be? It would rather excite the Romans yet more against the people; yet more would they march through the land, burning, destroying, and slaying. They would turn the country into a desert, and either slay or carry away all the people captives.

"We should irritate without seriously injuring the Romans, and the very people, whose sufferings we should heighten by our work, would turn against us. Now that the whole country has been scoured, all the towns which have resisted destroyed, and all the men who defended them put to the sword, there may be breathing space for the land until the Romans advance against Jerusalem. It may be that those in Jerusalem may come to terms with the Romans, in which case there need not be any more bloodshed. Therefore I say that it seems to me that it would be wrong to continue the war so long as the Romans rest peacefully in their camps; but should Jerusalem have need for us in her defense, every one of us will again take the field."

Johns counsel was finally adopted. May of the men were longing to return to their homes, where they knew that they would be welcomed and honored for the deeds they performed; for although they had achieved no grand successes, they had done much by compelling the Romans to keep together, and had thus saved many towns from plunder and destruction. Their operations too had created a fresh sensation of hope, and had aroused the people from the dull despair in which they were sinking. Had messengers been now sent out on all sides a great multitude of men would have collected; but John knew well that numbers would be no avail, and that in a pitched battle the Romans could defeat many times their number of undisciplined and ill-armed Jews.

John himself stood even higher in the estimation of his followers than he did at the commencement of the campaign. His own band had been particularly successful and had several times encountered parties of the Romans almost equal to themselves in numbers. His plans had been always well laid, and on no occasion had the Romans cut off and killed any numerous parties. Altogether the justness of his views had been established by experience, the men had gained confidence in themselves and in him, and now only regretted that they had had no opportunity of attacking the Romans in anything like equal numbers.

Therefore when the news spread that John was of opinion that the wisest course was for them to return to their homes and there to hold themselves in readiness to reassemble whenever the Romans moved against Jerusalem, the decision was willingly accepted, and a few hours after the Roman column had marched out from Jericho the Jewish companies started for their respective homes, all promising to take up arms again when the signal was given.

Although the success that had attended them had not been so great as they had hoped, it had been sufficiently marked to inspire them with confidence in themselves and their leader; but few lives had been lost and they had learned that so long as they persisted in the tactics their leader had laid down there was but little chance of the Romans striking a heavy blow at them.

Surprise was mingled with joy in the greeting John received on his return home.

"No disaster has befallen your bands, I hope, John?" Simon asked anxiously. "We heard that the Romans had reached Jericho, and we have been praying the Lord night and day for his protection for you, believing that you would doubtless fall upon the enemy as they marched through the mountains toward Jerusalem."

"We should have done so, father, and already had taken up a position on the heights commanding the roads, but there was no fighting, simply because Vespasian has marched away with his army to Cæsarea, and will not, as we believe, make any movement against Jerusalem this year."

"The Lord be praised!" Simon said piously. "There is time yet for the city to repent in sackcloth and ashes for its sins, and to come to such terms with the Romans as may save the Temple."

"So far as I have heard, father, Jerusalem is little likely either to repent or to negotiate. The news of what is passing there is even worse than that which the Rabbi Solomon told us; but I will not pain you by talking of these matters now. You have heard what we have been doing. We have done no great deeds, but we have harassed the Romans sorely, so that they could not say that they held the country behind the flight of their arrows. We have taken many cities where they had left small garrisons, we have cut off very many small parties, have captured many flocks and herds which they had carried off, and have lost but few men while inflicting much damage. Moreover, we have gained experience and confidence, and when the time comes for fighting hand to hand with the Romans we shall enter upon the struggle without fear."

"But what could have induced the Romans to retire when almost within sight of Jerusalem?"

"Partly, no doubt, because Vespasian considered it better to let the Jews go on slaying each other than to waste his strength in killing them; but partly, I believe, because of news from Rome. We heard a rumor that a messenger had arrived in the Roman camp with the news that Nero is dead, and Vespasian may well wish to keep his army together to watch the course of events."

This was indeed Vespasian's main object in retiring, and for nearly two years he kept his army in hand, waiting for his opportunity, while Galba, Otho, and Vitellius in turn gained and lost the imperial crown. John remained at home, except that he went out with the companies in the spring of 69, when Vespasian for a time set his troops in motion. As before, the Romans marched down into the south of Judea and reduced the country on the western shore of the Dead Sea, while Cerealis entered Idumea and completely subdued it, so that there now remained only the towns of Herodium, Masada, Machærus, and Jerusalem itself which still remained unconquered.

John's troops had pursued precisely the same tactics as in the previous year, and had contented themselves with harassing the Romans whenever the latter entered difficult country, and in preventing them from sending out small foraging parties. John himself would not have called his men under arms, as he saw that no real advantage was gained; but the men were eager to go, and he saw that there was a considerable advantage in their continued practice in arms, in the quickness with which they worked together, and in the confidence which they had in themselves.

The company suffered but slight loss in the operations, but John himself had an adventure which nearly cost him his life. Vespasian with the bulk of his army was encamped at Hebron, while Titus was at Carmelia, near the Dead Sea. John's company were in the hills near Hebron, and he, wishing to examine the Roman position at Carmelia and the road between the two towns, started by himself. He carried, as usual, his buckler, two light javelins, and a sword. The road led down a series of precipitous valleys, and John, knowing that he could instantly gain the hills out of reach of danger, did not hesitate to descend into it.

He was now nineteen, strong, active, and sinewy. The position in which he had been placed had given him the habit of command, and the heavy responsibility which had devolved upon him had added two or three years to his apparent age. He was taller than most of his countrymen, broad across the shoulders, and a match for any single man under his command. As he walked along he heard the sound of a horse's footsteps coming up the valley. He sprang a short distance up the craggy hillside, and then paused as a single horseman came in sight.

As he came a little nearer John saw by the splendor of his armor, and that of the horse he was riding, that he was an officer of rank and distinction. John scorned to fly before a single foe, and stood quietly watching him till he came nearly abreast of him. The horseman reined up his charger, and without a word seized his javelin and hurled it at the armed figure standing on the hillside some thirty feet above him. John sprang lightly aside, and the missile struck the rock with a sharp clang close to him. In return he threw a javelin at the Roman, which struck him on the armor and fell blunt.

"Well thrown!" the Roman said calmly, and hurled a second javelin. The stroke was too swift to avoid; but John threw up his buckler so as to receive it at an angle, and the javelin glanced off and flew far up the hillside. This time John sprang down the rocks with the activity of a goat till within a few feet of the Roman. Then he threw his javelin at the horse, with so true an aim that it struck at a spot unprotected by armor, and the animal fell.

With an exclamation of anger the Roman threw himself off as the animal sank beneath his legs. He had already drawn his sword as John approached, and stood at once on the defensive. Without a moment's hesitation John sprang at him, and the combat commenced. John trusted to his activity, while the Roman had an immense advantage in his heavy armor. The Roman stood calm and confident, while John attacked, moving quickly round and round him, springing in to deliver a blow, and then bounding out of reach of the sweep of the heavy Roman sword.

For some time the combat continued. John had received two or three sever wounds, while although the Roman was bleeding his armor protected him from any serious hurt. Suddenly John sprang in at the Roman, throwing himself with all his force against him; he partially warded with his sword the blow which the Roman struck at him as he came in, but his weapon was beaten down, and the Roman blade cut through his think headdress. But the impetus of his spring was sufficient. The Roman, taken by surprise by this sudden attack, tottered, and then fell with a crash, John falling on top of him.

John was almost blinded by the blood which streamed down his forehead from the blow he had last received; but he dashed it aside, seized his long knife, and in another moment would have slain his enemy had not the latter exclaimed:

"Strike, Jew! I am Titus."

John was confused by the last blow he had received; but a thousand thoughts whirled in his brain. For an instant he grasped the knife more firmly to slay the son of the chief enemy of his country; then the possibility of carrying him away a captive occurred to him; but he saw that this was out of the question. Then another thought flashed across his brain.

"Swear," he said in Greek, for he was ignorant of Latin, "by your gods, to spare the Temple, or I will kill you."

There was a moment's hesitation. The knife was already descending, when Titus exclaimed in the same language:

"I swear to do in all in my power to save the Temple."

John's knife fell from his hand. He tried to rise to his feet; then everything seemed to swim round, and he fell insensible. Titus rose to his feet; he was shaken by the fall, and he too had lost much blood. Panting from his exertions he looked down upon his prostate foe, and the generosity which was the prevailing feature of his character, except when excited in battle, mastered him.

"By Hercules," he exclaimed, "that is a gallant youth, though he is a Jew, and he has well-nigh made an end of me? What will Vespasian say when he hears that I have been beaten in fair fight, and owe my life to the mercy of a Jew! How they think of their temple, these Jews! Why, I would not injure it were it in my power to do so. Have not our emperors sent offerings there? Besides, we war not with the gods of the people we conquer. Ah, here come Plancus and the others! This will be a lesson to me not to trust myself alone among these mountains again. It is the first time I have done so, and it shall be the last."

A messenger had, in fact, arrived at Carmelia with an order from Vespasian for him to go to Hebron, as he had a desire to speak with him, and ordered Plancus, a centurion, to follow with his troop, Titus had sprung on his horse and ridden off at once. The Romans were soon upon the spot, and were loud in exclamation of surprise and grief at seeing their commander covered with dust, and bleeding from several wounds, while his horse lay dead beside him. To their inquiries whether he was seriously wounded, Titus replied lightly:

"I am more dirty than hurt. Though, had it not been for my armor, there would have been a different tale to tell, for these Jews fight like demons. As you see, he first slew my horse with his javelin, and then we fought it out on foot."

"Was there only this one?" the centurion asked in surprise, pointing to John's body.

"Only that one," Titus said, "and he nearly got the best of it. Fighting with these Jews is like fighting with wild cats, so fierce are they in the attack, and so quick are their movements. I tell you that for a moment my life was at his mercy. See if he is dead, Plancus."

"No, he breathes," Plancus said, stooping over him.

"Let four of the men make a litter with their spears," Titus said, "and take him down to Carmelia, and let my own leech attend him. I would gladly save his life if I can. I began the fray, and truly he has shown himself so gallant a young man that I would not that he should die."

Accordingly, when John opened his eyes he found himself lying in a Roman tent, where and old man was sitting by his couch, and a Roman sentry pacing backward and forward before the entrance of the tent.

"Drink this," the old man said, placing a cordial to his lips. "You need have no fear, you are in the camp of Titus, and he himself has ordered that all attention shall be paid to you."

John was too weak from loss of blood, and confused from the effects of the blow on his head, even to feel the sensation of wonder. He drank the potion and closed his eyes again, and went off into a sleep that lasted for many hours. It was not until the next day that he thoroughly awoke. The leech continued to attend him, and at the end of the four days he was able to sit up.

In the afternoon he head a clash of arms as the sentry gave the military salute, and a moment later Titus entered, accompanied by one whom John instantly recognized as Josephus. John rose to his feet.

"I told you he was but a young man," Titus said to Josephus; "but now that I can see him more nearly, or at any rate more calmly, I can see that he is little more than a lad, and yet, as you have heard me say, he is a man of valor, and defeated me in a fair fight."

"I seem to know his face," Josephus said, and then addressed John in Hebrew.

"Who are you, young man?"

"I am that John whom you saved in the storm on the Sea of Galilee, and who fought with you at Jotapata."

"Is it possible!" Josephus exclaimed in surprise. "I thought that I alone was saved there."

"I lay hidden with the boy Jonas, who told us of the track down to the water," John said quietly, "and have since then been fighting the Romans. While you—"

"While I have been their prisoner," Josephus broke in. "I know that all my countrymen are enraged against me, but truly without a cause." Josephus then translated to Titus what John had told him, adding that the young man had served him with zeal and devotion, and that he had an affection for him.

"Then I am the more glad that he has not lost his life," Titus said courteously. "And now, my antagonist," he said in Greek to John, "I would tell you that I bear you no malice, though you have shed my blood and brought somewhat of disgrace upon me; for truly it is a disgrace for a Roman soldier in heavy armor to be overthrown by one who carries but a light buckler as his protection. But I love a brave man, even though he be a foe, and I honor those who are fighting for what they believe to be the cause of their country. If I let you go free, will you promise me not to bear arms against Rome?"

"I could not promise that, Titus," John said quietly, "even were you to order me now to be taken out and slain. It is the first duty of all Jews to fight for the Holy City, and so long as I live, and the Holy City is in danger, so long I must fight for her. These are the commands of my religion, and I cannot, even to save my life, disobey them."

"I will not press you to do so," Titus said; "though Josephus here will tell you that Rome is not an unkind lord to those who have most withstood it. When you are well enough to leave us you shall go unharmed, though, could you have seen your way to desist from hostility to us, I

would have been a good friend to you and have promoted you to posts
of honor, and that in countries where you would have been opposed to
your countrymen. But if you will not have it so you are free to go; and
remember that at any time you have a friend in Titus, and that when
this war is over, and peace restored, if you come to me I will repeat the
offer that I have now made. Moreover, you may rely upon it that in the
last extremity I will do all in my power to save the Temple, and indeed,
in no case would I have injured a building so venerable and holy."

Titus then left the tent, but Josephus remained for some time talking
to John.

"I suppose you, like all others, have looked upon me as a traitor,
John?" he began.

"Not so," John replied. "I knew that you fought bravely at Jotapata,
and risked your life many times in its defense. I knew, too, that you from
the first opposed the revolt against the Romans, and it is not for me to
judge as to your position among them."

"I am a prisoner," Josephus said. "I am kindly treated, indeed, and
Vespasian frequently asks my opinion of matters connected with the
country, but surely I am doing more good to my countrymen by softening
his heart toward them than if I had died at Jotapata; still more if I had
been, like John of Gischala, a scourge to it. I trust even yet that, through
my influence, Jerusalem may be saved. When the time comes Vespasian
will, I hope, grant terms; and my only fear is that the madness of the
people will lead them to refuse all accommodation, and so force him
into taking the city by storm, in which case it cannot but be that terrible
misery will fall upon it, and that vast numbers will lose their lives. And
now, tell me how you are at home, and what you have been doing since
I last saw you."

John thought it as well not to mention to Josephus the prominent
part which he had taken among those who had so harassed the Romans,
but he said that he had joined bands raised in Galilee, and had been
among those who had hung upon the Roman flank and rear wherever
they marched.

"The Jews have behaved with prudence and valor," Josephus said, "and I now see that it would have been far better had I trusted more in mountain warfare than in fenced cities, but it would have been the same in the end. I know the Jews. They would have fought bravely for a time, but the thought of each would have turned to his farm and his vineyard, and they would never have kept the field for any length of time. The Romans, therefore, would in the end have tired them out, and perhaps the fate which has befallen the cities that resisted would have fallen upon all the land. And now remember that, although but a prisoner, I have much influence with Vespasian, and that at any time, should you fall into their hands again, I will exert that influence in your favor."

John remained about ten days at Carmelia. Titus had several interviews with him, and at the last of these said:

"I have conceived a strong friendship for you, young man, and would willing do you service. Take this signet-ring. At all times and in all places it will pass you to my presence. If a Roman sword be raised to strike you, and you show this ring, it will be lowered. That you should fight against us to the last is, as you believe your duty, and as I myself would so fight for Rome I seek not further to dissuade you; but when resistance is at an end, and it is useless any longer to hold the sword, your death cannot benefit your country. Therefore, when that time comes, if not before, use this ring and come to me, and I will grant you not only your life, but that of such friends as you wish to save. I do not forget that you had my life in your hands, and that you spared it. It is a life that may yet be valuable to Rome, and though even now when I speak of it, my cheek flushes with humiliation, I am none the less grateful. It pleases me to see that, in the conversation you have had with my officers, you have borne yourself so modesty, and have made no mention of this, for although I myself do not hesitate to speak of the mishap which befell me, it is pleasant for me that it is not spoken of by others. Believe me, then, that at all times you will find a sincere friend in Titus."

John replied in suitable terms, thanking Titus for the promises he had made, and disclaiming any merit in his success, which was but the last effort of a beaten man, and was the result of a sudden surprise, and not of any skill or bravery. Upon the following morning Titus furnished him with an escort far beyond the confines of the camp, and then taking to the hills, John rejoined his companions, who had long since given him up as dead. They could scarce credit him when he told them that he had been lying wounded in the hands of the Romans, and were still more surprised at hearing that he had been engaged in a personal encounter with Titus. Of this John gave no details beyond the fact that after throwing their javelins the horse of Titus had fallen, and they had fought hand to hand, until at last he had fallen bleeding from a sever wound, and that Titus himself had been wounded.

"But how was it he did not slay you?" was the question. "It seems almost a miracle, especially after wounding Titus himself."

"Doubtless the Lord put it into his heart to spare me," John said. "Titus only said that he preserved my life as that of a brave foe. The Romans esteem bravery, and as I had withstood Titus for some time he was pleased to think that I had done well."

"Ah, if you had killed him, what rejoicings there would have been in the land!"

"No," John said earnestly, "there would have been mourning. You may be sure that Vespasian would have avenged his blood upon all the people. It would have been a misfortune, indeed, had Titus fallen. It is well that it ended as it did."

John was, however, far too weak to be able to accompany his band upon its rapid marches, and therefore for a time resigned its command to one of his captains. He determined to go, until his strength returned to him, to a small community of which he had heard as dwelling in an almost inaccessible valley on the shore of the Dead Sea. He was told that they took no part in the commotion of the times, and that they lived in such poverty that even the robbers of Simon had not cared to interfere with them. They practiced hospitality to strangers, and spent their lives in religious observances. As John had often heard from his father of this sect, which was at one time numerous in the land, but had been sorely persecuted by the priests and Pharisees, he determined to stop for a time among them, and learn somewhat of their doctrines.

Accompanied by Jonas, he made his way across the mountains to the valley where they dwelt. As wounded and a stranger he was received without question among them, and a little hut, similar to that in which they all lived, was placed at his disposal. These huts were ranged in a square, in the center of which stood a larger building, used as their synagogue. Here John remained nearly a month, and was greatly struck by their religious fervor, the simplicity and austerity of their lives, and the doctrines that they held. He learned that the more rigorous of the sect abstained altogether from the use of meat and wine, and that celibacy was strictly enjoined. Those who married did not separate themselves from the sect, but were considered as occupying an inferior position in it.

Their food was of the simplest kind, and only sufficient to sustain life; the community raised the grain and vegetables necessary for their use. But it was the religious doctrines that they held which most greatly surprised John. They attached no importance whatever to the ceremonial law of the Jewish Scriptures, maintaining, in the first place, that the Scriptures had a spiritual signification wholly apart from the literal meaning alone understood by the world, and that this spiritual meaning could only be attained by those who, after long probation, were initiated into the inner mysteries of the sect.

In the second place, they held that the written law had been altogether superseded by the coming of the great prophet, Christ, who had been put to death by the Jewish priests. John learned that there were already large numbers of Jews who had accepted the doctrines taught by this Christ, although they did not all embrace the strict rules and modes of life of the ascetics. John was greatly struck with their doctrines, although he did not hear enough to do more than to dimly understand their meaning. He determined, however, that if he went safely through the war he would inquire further into these mysteries. At the end of the four weeks, his strength being comparatively restored, he took his leave of the community, and rejoined his band.

Chapter Thirteen

THE TEST OF DEVOTION

Although John was able to join his companions, he was still far from strong, and was glad to have a valid excuse for handing over his command to his lieutenant and returning home. The campaign was nearly over, and he could not have followed those rapid marches through the hills which enabled the band to appear now on one side, now on the other of the Romans, and to keep them in a constant state of watchfulness. At the same time he was glad of the excuse to leave, for although he had declared to Titus that he would fight against in defense of Jerusalem, he felt that, after the kind treatment he had met with, he could not take part in the daily skirmishes with the Romans.

Mounting a donkey, which was among the many animals captured in the attacks upon the Romans' baggage train, John bade adieu to his comrades, and with Jonas, now grown into a sturdy young fellow, started for home. He journeyed by the road to the west of Jerusalem, in order to avoid bandits of Simon, son of Gioras, who still scourged the neighborhood of Masada and Herodium, lying between Jerusalem and the Dead Sea. He avoided all the towns in which there were Roman garrisons, for the bandages on his head would have shown at once that he had been engaged in fighting. He traveled slowly, and was six days before he arrived home.

"This time, my son, you have not come home unharmed," Simon said. "Truly you are a shadow of your former self."

"I shall soon be strong again, father, and these are honorable scars, for I had them in single combat with Titus himself in the valley between Hebron and Carmelia."

"Then how is it that you live to tell the tale, my son?" Simon asked, while exclamations of wonder broke from Mary and Martha. "Surely God did not deliver him into your hands?"

"I wish not to boast, father, and I have told the true story to none; but truly God did deliver him into my hands."

"And he is dead?" Simon exclaimed.

"No, father, he lives, for I spared him."

"Spared him!" Simon exclaimed. "What, you did not avenge the miseries of our people upon the son of the oppressor?"

"No, father; and I rejoice that I did not, for had I done so, surely the Romans would have avenged his death upon all the land. But I thought not of that at the time. I was sore wounded and bleeding, and my sense was well-nigh gone; but as I knelt upon him, and lifted my hand to slay him, and I said, 'swear by your gods that you will spare the Temple, or I slay you;' and he swore that, so far as lay in his power, he would spare the Temple."

An exclamation of joy burst from his hearers, and Simon said;

"Verily, my son, God has raised you up as a deliverer of his Temple, not, as some hoped, by defeating our oppressors, but by binding one of their mightiest ones to do it no harm."

"I pray, father, say naught of this to any one. It is between ourselves and Titus and the Lord, and I would not that any man should know of it. Moreover, Titus behaved with the greatest generosity to me. My victory over him was but a surprise. I was sorely wounded, while he was almost unharmed, when I sprang upon him and by the sudden impulse threw him to the ground, he being burdened with his heavy armor. I had but strength to hear him swear, and then I fell as one dead. Titus might have slain me as I lay, but he not only did me no harm, but when his soldiers came up, he gave me into their care, and directed me to be carried down to his camp, placed in a tent, and tended by his own leech, and when I recovered he let me go free."

"Truly it is a marvelous tale, John. That you should have fallen into the hands of the Romans and come forth unharmed after discomfiting their leader is as marvelous to me as Daniel coming unharmed from the lions' den. We will say naught of your story, my son. Tell us only what you told your own companions, so that we may know what to say when we are questioned."

"I told them the truth, father, although not all the truth. I said that I met Titus and fought with him, that I wounded him somewhat, but that by virtue of his armor I did him no great harm, while he wounded me so seriously that I fell down as one dead; that he, feeling that I had fought like a brave foeman, had me carried to his tent and tended and cared for until I was able to go forth, when he sent me away free and unharmed."

"Truly men say of Titus that he is clement and merciful, and therein differs much from Vespasian his father, and the clemency which he showed to the people of Gischala and other places which he has taken proves that is so; but this deed of his to you shows that he must have a great heart, for few men of rank and warlike fame who had been discomfited by one yet scarce a man, but would have left him by the road to die so that none might know what had happened."

"Titus made no secret of it, father," John said; "he told Josephus, in my hearing, that I had spared his life. He said naught of the oath which he had taken, but I know that he will keep it as far, as he said, as lies in his power."

"What is he like?" Mary asked.

"He is not of very tall stature, but stoutly built and strong; his face, clean shaven as is their custom, has a pleasant and kindly expression that tallies with his disposition, for he is greatly beloved by his soldiers. In action they say he is brave to rashness, quick to anger, but as quickly appeased. Had he been in command of the Roman legions they would have been not less formidable in fight, and perhaps, when the passions of Titus were roused, not less savage, but they would not have wrought such wholesale cruelty and destruction as they have done."

"It is rarely that pity enters into the heart of a Roman," Simon said; "and yet it is hardly for us to complain, for when we crossed over the Jordan and conquered Canaan we put all to the sword and spared none. It may be that in future times, if wars do not altogether cease in the world, they will be waged in another spirit; but so far, from the commencement of the world until now, it has ever been the same, war has brought desolation and destruction upon the vanquished."

The next morning John went early into the garden, not that he was strong enough for heavy work, but in order that Mary might, as usual, join him there.

"Do you know, John," she said, after their first greeting, "you have made me happier than I have been for some time."

"How is that, Mary?"

"It seemed to me, John, that you were getting away from me."

"Getting away, Mary!" he repeated; "how do you mean?"

"You were becoming a great leader, John. I was proud that it should be so, proud to think that you might become a deliverer of the nation, and then it would have been meet and right that you should take to yourself as a wife a daughter of one of the great ones of the land."

"Mary!" John exclaimed indignantly.

"It might have been necessary, John. The tillers of the soil can marry where they please; those who have power must wed for other reasons than that of love. They must make alliances that will strengthen their position, and it would have been your duty to have sacrificed your love for the sake of your country. I should have been the first to bid you do so. I should have been content to make my sacrifice, too, on the alter of our country, content with knowing that you, the deliverer of Israel, would have chosen me from among all other women had you only had your own pleasure and happiness to consult; but after what you told us yesterday I think perhaps that this need not be so, and that the way in which you were to save the Temple was not the way we thought. Your mission has been fulfilled, not by great victories, which would have made you the hero of Israel, but in that contest in the valley where no eyes but those of God beheld you, and should the Temple be saved none will know that you were its savior save we who love you. Therefore, John, once again I can look forward to the time when you and I can dwell together in the house of your fathers."

Mary so earnest that John did not attempt to laugh her out of her fancies, as was his usual way; he only said quietly:

"Perhaps you are right, Mary, as to my mission, but I do not think, dear, that even had I been made ruler of Israel I would have gone elsewhere for a wife; but as you say, circumstances might have been too strong for me, and at any rate I am well pleased that there is no chance of my happiness being set in one scale and the good of my country in another."

"And now, John, I believe that you will come back to me even if Jerusalem falls. This is the third time your life has been spared, and if we count that day when we were so nearly drowned together on the lake, we may say that four times your life has been saved when it seemed all but lost, and I believe now that it will be saved to the end."

"I hope for your sake, Mary, and for my father and mother's that it may be so. I have so much to make my life happy that I will assuredly do all in my power to save it. As you know, I have never held with those who would destroy themselves when all seemed lost. My idea is, a man should fight until the last, but should, if possible, provide some way of escape when fighting is no longer of avail. Fortunately, if I do not fall in battle I have a talisman which will bring me safe to you. Titus has given me a signet-ring which will at all times procure me access to him. He has promised that at all times he will be my friend, and should I fall into the hands of his soldiers again he will let me go free and will give me the lives of any who may be dear to me."

"This Titus must be a noble enemy," Mary said, with tears in her eyes; "he is strong, and kind, and generous. Had such a man been raised up as the leader of our people, instead of the leader of our foes, how different it might have been!"

"Yes," John agreed; "truly we are sheep without a shepherd, nay, we are sheep whose leaders are ravening wolves, who devour their own flock."

The time passed quietly and happily save for the grief which the tidings of the terrible doings in Jerusalem caused. The two years' respite which the city had obtained when Vespasian marched away from Jericho, instead of being turned to good account, had brought even greater evils than before. Simon son of Gioras, having wasted all the country toward Idumea, began to threaten Jerusalem. The Zealots marched out against him, but were driven back to the city. Simon, thinking that the Idumeans, believing him to be occupied with Jerusalem, would have grown careless, suddenly entered their country at the head of twenty thousand men.

The Idumeans flew to arms and met him with twenty-five thousand men, and a furious battle ensued, in which neither party gained the advantage. Simon retreated, and the Idumeans dispersed. Simon raised an even larger force than before, and advanced, with forty thousand irregular troops besides his heavy-armed soldiers. They took Hebron and wasted Idumea with fire and sword.

The Zealots, in Simon's absence, succeeded in capturing his wife, and carried her off to Jerusalem, hoping by this means to force him to come to terms. On receiving the news he hurried back with his forces, surrounded Jerusalem, and slew every one who ventured to leave the city, except some whom he sent back, having cut off their hands, to tell those within that unless his wife were returned he would storm the city and slay every man within it. Even the Zealots were alarmed at his threats and fury and restored his wife, whereupon he withdrew.

This had happened in the previous year before Cerealis and Vespasian had entered Idumea. As soon as the Romans had retired Simon again sallied forth from Masada, collected a great number of Idumeans and drove them before him into Jerusalem, then he encamped before the city and slew all who quitted the protection of its walls.

But at length the party of John became divided; the Idumeans, who were in considerable numbers in the city, rose and drove John and the Zealots into the palace built by Grapte, which had served them as their headquarters and the storehouse where they piled up the treasure which they had amassed by the plunder of the people. But the Idumeans attacked them here and drove them into the Temple, which adjoined the palace, and took possession of all the plunder that they had amassed. The Zealots, however, were in great force in the Temple and threatened to pour out and destroy the whole city by fire. The Idumeans called an assembly of the chief priests and they decided to admit Simon within the gates.

The high-priest, Matthias, went out in person to invite him to enter, and, amid the joyful greetings of the population, Simon marched through the gates with his followers and took possession of the upper city. This was the last and most fatal mistake of the people of Jerusalem. The sheep had invited the tiger to save them from a wolf, and now two tyrants instead of one lorded it over the city. As soon as Simon entered he proceeded to attack the Zealots in the Temple, but the commanding position of that building enabled them to defend themselves with success.

To obtain still further advantage they reared four strong towers, and on these placed their military engines and bowmen, and so swept the approaches to the Temple that Simon was forced to desist from the attack. All through the winter fighting went on without intermission, and the streets of Jerusalem ran with blood. A further division took place among the Zealots. Eleazar, who had been their head before the arrival of John of Gischala, jealous of the supremacy of that leader, got together a party and suddenly seceded from the main band and seized the inner court of the temple.

Now fighting went on within as well as without the holy buildings. The party of Eleazar were well supplied with provisions, for the stores in the Temple were of immense extent. They were too few in numbers to sally out to attack the party of John; but they were strong enough to defend the walls of the inner court, which looked down upon the rest of the Temple and enabled them to command the positions of John's troops. Day and night the struggle went on. The inner court of the Temple was desecrated by blood—dying men lay on the steps of the altar, and the shouts and songs of the savage soldiery rose where they hymns of praise of the Levites had been wont to ascend.

John's troops continued their attack upon the inner court, while they successfully resisted the assaults of Simon, who tried to take advantage of the internecine strife waging between the two parties of Zealots; but the superior height of the positions held by John's men enabled them to defend themselves as successfully as did those of Eleazar, against their attacks.

And yet during all this terrible strife the services of the Temple continued in the midst of blood and carnage. Free ingress and egress were, as at all times, permitted to the pious, who made their way unharmed through the fierce combatants, passed over the pavement slippery with blood, and laid their offering on the altars, often paying with their lives for their pious services, being smitten down even as they prayed at the altar by the missiles which the followers of John poured incessantly into the inner court.

Sometimes, drunk with the wine obtained from the abundant stores of the Temple, the followers of Eleazar would sally out against John; sometimes John would pour out against Simon, wasting and destroying the city as far as his troops could penetrate. Thus the Temple became surrounded by a waste of ruins, held in turn by one or other of the factions. Even the rites of burial, so dear to the Jews, were neglected, and the bodies of the slain lay unburied where they fell. And yet the forces of the three factions which thus desolated the city were comparatively small, and had the wretched population who were tyrannized by them possessed any unanimity or been led by any man of courage, they could easily have overthrown them all, for Simon's force amounted to about fifteen thousand, that of John to six thousand, while Eleazar would count but twenty-four hundred men; and yet in Jerusalem were gathered a population amounting, with the original inhabitants and the fugitives from the country around, to over a million people.

At length the long interval of suspense was drawing to an end. At the death of Vitellius, Vespasian had been called upon by the general voice of the people to ascend the throne, and had some time before left for Rome to assume the imperial purple. He was joyfully acknowledged by the whole Roman empire, who had groaned under a succession of brutal tyrants, and now hailed the accession of one who was at once a great general and an upright and able man, and who would rule the empire with a firm, just, and moderate hand. When winter was over Vespasian sent Titus, who had in the mean time gone to Egypt, back to Palestine, and ordered him to complete the conquest of Judea.

The Twelfth Legion, that which had been defeated when under the command of Cetius, was ordered to reinforce the three already in Judea, and the gaps made in the ranks during the war, and by the withdrawal of the men who had accompanied Vespasian to Rome were filled by an addition of two thousand picked troops from Alexandria and three thousand from the legions stationed on the Euphrates. The Syrian kings sent large contingents, and Tiberius Alexander, an intimate friend of Titus, a man of wisdom and integrity, was appointed to high command. His knowledge of the country, which he had once governed, added to his value in the Roman councils.

As soon as the news spread that the Roman army was collecting for its march against Jerusalem the signal fires were kindled on the hills above Gamala, and John, after a tender farewell to his parents and Mary, set out with Jonas. In twenty-four hours the band had again assembled. When they were gathered John addressed them. He pointed out to them that the campaign that they were not about to undertake differed widely from those which had preceded it.

"Hitherto," he said, "you have but skirmished around the Romans, and have run but comparatively little danger; but now those who go with me must make up their minds that they are going to Jerusalem to die. It may be that the Lord will yet deliver the Holy City from her enemies as he delivered it in days of old. But you know what has been doing in Jerusalem for the last four years, that not only the streets but the altar itself have been flooded with the blood of the people, how the Jews themselves have desecrated the Temple, and how wickedness of all kinds has prevailed in the city.

"Thus you can judge for yourselves what chance there is that God will interfere on behalf of the people who have forsaken and insulted him. If he does not interfere, in my opinion the fate of the city is sealed. I have seen the Romans at work at Jotapata and Gamala, and I know how the strongest walls go down before their engines and battering rams. Moreover, I hear that in the wars which have been raging within the gates, the magazines, which contain sufficient food to last even her great population for years, have been entirely destroyed, and thus those who go to defend her have to face not the Roman sword only, but famine.

"Therefore I say that those who go up to defend the Temple must make up their minds that they go to die for the Temple. It is for each of you to ask yourselves whether you are ready to do this. I ask no one to go with me; let each before it is too late ask himself whether he is ready to do this thing. I blame none who find the sacrifice too great; it is between them and their conscience. Therefore I pray you let all tonight disperse among the hills, each by himself, so that you may think over what I have said, and let all who come to the conclusion that they are not called upon to go to certain death in defense of the Temple depart to their homes without reproach from their comrades. Each man here has done his duty so long as hope remained. Now it is for each to decide for himself whether he feels called upon to give his life for the Temple."

Silently the crowd dispersed, and John joined the captains and passed the night with them.

"I fear we shall have but a small gathering in the morning," one of them said as they sat down by the fire. "Many will fight as long as there is hope, but few will go down to certain death."

"It is better so," John said; "misery and ruin have fallen upon the country. As you saw for yourselves Judea and Idumea are but deserts, and more have fallen by famine and misery than by the sword. We would not have our nation blotted out, and as in the days after the captivity in Babylon, God again collected his people and restored their land to them, so it may be his intention to do now when they have paid the full penalty of their disobedience and wickedness. Therefore I would not that any should go down to die, save those who feel that God has called them to do so.

"Already the victims who have fallen in these four years are well-nigh countless, and in Jerusalem, there are a million people, sufficient, if they have spirit and strength and the Lord is with them, to defend the walls. Thus, then, however small the number of those who may gather tomorrow, I shall be content. Had the Romans advanced against Jerusalem at the commencement of the war, there was not a Jew capable of bearing arms but would have gone up to the defense of the Holy City; but now their spirit is broken by the woes that have come upon them, and still more by the civil wars in Jerusalem herself. A spirit of hopeless and despair has come upon us. It is not that men fear to die or that they care to live, it is that they say, What matters it whether we live or die? All is lost; why should we trouble as to what may come upon us?"

"Then you no longer believe in your mission, John?" One of the party said gloomily.

"I have never proclaimed a mission," John said; "others have proclaimed it for me. I simply invited a score of men to follow me, to do what we could to hinder the Romans, and because God gave us success others believed that I was sent as a deliverer. And yet I believe that I had a mission, and that mission has been fulfilled. I told you not before, but I tell you now for your comfort what happened between me and Titus, but I wish not that it should be told to others. I told you that I fought with him, and that being wounded and insensible I was carried into his tent; but that was not all. When we fought, although sorely wounded I sprang upon him and we fell to the ground, I uppermost. I drew my knife and would have slain him, when the Lord put a thought into my mind, and I called upon him to swear that he would spare the Temple.

"He swore that if it lay in his power he would do so. Then he was but in inferior command, but he is general of the army and should be able to keep his oath. Thus, if I had a mission to save the Temple, I trust that I have fulfilled it, and that whatever fate may fall upon the city the Temple will yet remain erect and unharmed."

John's words gave new life and energy to the before dispirited men gathered round him. It seemed to them not only that the Temple would be saved, but that their belief in their leader's mission as a deliverer was fully justified, and a feeling of enthusiasm succeeded that of depression.

"Why did you not tell us before, why did you not let all your followers know what a great thing you had done, John?" one of them asked presently.

"For two reasons," John replied. "I did not wish to seem to exalt myself or to boast of the success which God had given me over the Roman, for it was assuredly his strength and not mine, for I myself could do naught against the strength and skill of Titus, and as I told you I was wounded nigh to death while he received small hurt. In the next place, I thought that if I made it public it would be noised abroad through the land, and that Titus, when he heard that all men knew that he had been worsted in fight with a Jew, might repent of his oath, or might even ask to be sent to some other command so that he might not be called upon to keep it."

John's companions agreed that the second reason was a valid one, though they did not agree that the first should have weighed with him.

"It is not by hiding a light under a bushel," one of them said, "that men gain the confidence of their followers. The more men believe in their leaders the more blindly will they follow him, the greater the efforts they will make for him. It was the belief in your mission which gathered eight thousand men on these mountains to follow you, and the proof that you have given us that that belief was well founded, and that you had a mission to save the Temple, the knowledge that you had single-handed forced the Roman general to swear an oath to save the Temple, would have so heightened that enthusiasm that they would have followed you had you bidden them attack the whole Roman army. I agree that for your second reason it was wise to say nothing of what took place; but your first was, I think, a mistaken one."

"At any rate," another said, "the hand of God is plainly marked in the matter, for it has placed Titus in full command, and has thus given him the power of carrying out the oath which he swore. Now, my friends, we can go up with light hearts with John to Jerusalem, for thought we may die, yet do we feel assured that the Lord purposes to save the Temple, and that one day he will restore the glories of Judah."

In the morning, as John had expected, the number of those who gathered at the sound of the trumpet was comparatively small. The night's reflection, the feeling that the sacrifice of their lives would be of no avail, and the dull despair that had seized the whole nation had had their effect, and of the eight thousand men who had gathered there the night before, but six hundred now obeyed the summons.

These gathered stern and silent, but with an expression of desperate resolution on their faces. At the earnest request of his captains, John allowed them to go among the men and to tell them that although the manner in which it was done was a secret, John had given to them undoubted proofs that he had a mission from God, and that they believed that whatever might happen to Jerusalem, it was the Lord's will that the Temple should be saved. The joyous expression of their leaders' faces even more than their words assured their followers of enthusiasm seized them; and when, an hour later, John took his place on a rock to address them, the shouts of greeting which broke forth showed him how great was the change in their spirit.

"My friends," he said, "I greet you who have decided to die with me, if need be, in defense of Jerusalem. I blame not those who have gone. They would not have gone had the Lord required them to stay; but to you he has spoken, and has told you that he has need of your services. Henceforth we will act as one band—a band of men inspired with one thought and one aim. And now, though our numbers may not be great, yet a force so composed of men who hold their lives as naught may do wonders. You remember how Gideon sent the greater party of his army away, and with a mere handful defeated the hosts of the enemy!

"We look not for victory; but we will show the Romans what men can do to avenge their bleeding country—what deeds Jews can perform when fighting for the Temple. We shall go into Jerusalem; there we will hold all of from all parties. If we are attacked we will defend ourselves. But our aim will be to act as a body apart from others, ready to undertake the most desperate services, and to set an example of courage and devotion. Now let us count our numbers and arrange ourselves anew into companies."

It was found that the bands composed of men from Tiberias and the other cities of the lake had entirely disappeared, and that those who had stayed were principally hardly dwellers among the hills. They are again divided into twenty companies of thirty men each; and after examining their arms and seeing that all were well provided, John gave the order and the band set off. Keeping on the eastern side of Jordan they stopped at a large village near the ford opposite Jericho; and here a quantity of grain was purchased and was made up into sacks, each weighting fifty pounds.

"The granaries that remain will be principally in the hands of the troops of John or Simon," John said; "and it is as well that we should have our own store to depend upon. So long as we can buy food we will do so, and we can fall back upon our own magazine if necessary. It will be best for two or three of us to go into the city first and find a quarter where we can lodge close together, and as far removed as possible from the factions. Simon holds the upper town and John the temple; therefore we will establish ourselves in the lower town. We will not go in in a body, for they might refuse us admittance; but as the Romans approach there will be a stream of fugitives entering the city; we will mingle with them and pass in unobserved.

"Many of the fugitives will be carrying the goods they most value, and many doubtless will take in provisions with them, therefore our sacks of grain will not excite attention."

It was five years since John had journeyed up with his parents to Jerusalem, and he therefore knew but little of the city. Some of his followers, however, had been there more recently; and he picked out four of these, one of whom was a captain of a company, to enter the city and find a suitable post for them. The whole band crossed the Jordan together, and made a détour to avoid éericho, where the Tenth Legion had been quartered during the winter. Then they took their way up the steep road through the hills, until, passing through Bethany, they came out on the crest of the hill looking down upon the Valley of Jehoshaphat, with the Temple rising immediately opposite to them, and the palace of Agrippa and the crowded houses of the city in the background.

The men laid down their sacks and stood for a long time looking at Jerusalem. Many were move to tears as they looked on the stately beauty of the Holy City, and thought how low it had fallen, with civil tumult within and a terrible enemy approaching from without. Even now there is no fairer scene in the world than the view of Jerusalem from the spot where they were standing, called then as now the Mount of Olives; and it must have been superb, indeed, in the days when the Temple stood intact and the palaces of Agrippa and Herod rose on the brow of Mount Zion.

After a long pause they resumed their way, crossed the upper end of the Valley of Jehoshaphat, and established themselves for the night in a grove of trees near the Grotto of Jeremiah, four chosen men at once entering the city by the Old Gate on the north side of the city. The country here, and indeed all the hills around Jerusalem, were covered with the houses of the wealthy, surrounded by gardens and orchards. They belonged not only to the Jews of the city, but to those who dwelt in foreign countries, and who were accustomed each year to come to Jerusalem for the Passover and to spend some time there before they returned to their distant homes. Even now, undismayed by the dangers of the times and the knowledge that the Romans would shortly besiege the city, pilgrims were arriving from all the cities of Asia Minor, Greece, and Egypt, for the time of the Passover was close at hand.

At the foot of the walls and on the slopes around large numbers of pilgrims were encamped, the rich in gorgeous tents, the poor in shelters constructed of boughs or carpets. This overflow of people was an occurrence which was witnessed every year on the same occasion, but its proportions were this time of greater magnitude than usual, partly owing to the difficulty of procuring lodgings in the town owing to the crowds of fugitives there, partly because many thought it safer to camp outside, and to enter the city only to pay their devotions and take part in the ceremonial than to put themselves wholly into the power of the ruffians of Simon and John.

In the following morning the men returned and reported that they had found a spot in the inner lower town, between the Corner Gate and the

Gate of Ephriam in the second wall, where was a large house inhabited now but by two or three persons; here a great number of them could take up their quarters, while the others could find lodging near. The reason why so many houses were empty there was that it was somewhat exposed to the irruptions of Simon's men from the upper town, as they frequently came down and robbed those who entered the city at the Damascus Gate, from which led the great north road.

Crowds of fugitives were making their way by this road to the city, flying before the advance of the Romans, who were, they said, but a few hours' march in their rear. Many were men coming to take their part in the defense of the city, but the great proportion were old men, women, and children flying for refuge. John shook his head as he watched the stream of fugitives, for he well knew the horrors that would befall the besieged town.

"Better a thousand times," he said to Jonas, "that these poor people should have remained in their villages. They have nothing which would tempt the cupidity of the Roman soldiers, and no evil might have befallen them; whereas now they will perish by famine or disease or be slain by the Romans, besides consuming the food which would have sustained the fighting men. Were I master of Jerusalem I would, when I heard the Romans were approaching, have cleared out the city all who could not aid in the defense. It would have seemed a harsh action, but it would have been a merciful one, and would greatly strengthen the power of resistance."

Chapter Fourteen

JERUSALEM

Mingling with the crowd, John and his followers made their way through the Damascus Gate into Jerusalem, and followed the Damascus Street to the Gate of Ephraim. An air of somber misery pervaded the whole population. In their hearts the greater portion of the population had for many months been longing for the approach of the Romans; even death would be preferable to the misery which they suffered. There were but few people in the streets, for all remained in their houses with closed doors, save when necessity drove them out to make purchases. Turning sharp round by the wall the members of the band made their way along by it until they were met by one or another of those who had gone on in advance, and were conducted to the house which had been hired for them.

The inhabitants of the houses near looked out of their windows in alarm when they saw so many armed men arriving, but they gained courage on observing their quiet and orderly demeanor, and doors were presently unbolted and men came out to inquire who were the new-comers. When they were told that they were from Galilee and Peræa and had come down only to fight for the Holy City, that they would harm no one, and had nothing in common with any of the factions, confidence was restored, and offers were at once made to take in ten, fifteen, or twenty men, according to the size of the houses; for the people soon saw that the new arrivals would prove a protection from the attacks and insults of small numbers of Simon's men, who had hitherto pervaded the lower town, breaking into houses, robbing and murdering wheresoever they chose.

The grain was all stored in the house that had been hired; and here John took up his quarters with the men of his own company and those of Asher, one of his bravest and most determined captains. The rest were all accommodated in houses in the same street. And as this, like most of the streets of Jerusalem, was very narrow, John felt that it could be defended against an attack by a greatly superior force.

It was but half and hour after the band had been settled in their quarters that a shriek was heard at the end of the street. John ran out in time to see a woman struck down, while a body of some twenty half-drunken soldiers with drawn swords were trying to force in the door of the house. John sounded his bugle, and there was a rush of armed men into the street. John put himself at the head of the two companies with him and advanced against the soldiers and sternly ordered then to desist. The soldiers, astonished by the sudden appearance of so large a body of armed men, drew back in astonishment.

"Who are you?" one who seemed to be their leader asked.

"It matters not who I am," John said quietly. "It is enough, as you see, that I have a force here sufficiently strong to make myself obeyed. This street henceforth is mine; and beware of attempting plunder or violence here, for whoever does so surely dies!"

Muttering threats below their breath the soldiers sullenly withdrew. An hour later one of the inhabitants ran in to inform John that a large body of men were coming down from the upper city. John immediately called his men to arms, and at their head took up his position at the end of the street.

Ere long a crowd of soldiers were seen approaching. At their head strode one whom John at once guessed to be Simon himself. When he arrived within ten paces Simon stopped, surprised at the compact order and resolute appearance of the band which filled the street.

"Who are you?" he asked John imperiously.

"My name is John, and I am generally called John of Gamala, although that is not my birthplace."

Simon uttered an exclamation of astonishment, for the tales of John's attacks upon the Roman camp at Gamala, and of his subsequent actions against the Romans, were well known in Jerusalem.

"You are but a lad," Simon said contemptuously, "and John of Gamala must be a warrior!"

"I am John of Gamala," John repeated quietly, "and these men are part of my band. We have come down to defend Jerusalem, since there is no more to be done in the open country. We wish to interfere with none, to take part with no faction, but simply to defend the city. We war with Romans and not with Jews. We assault no one; but woe be to him that assaults us! Here are six hundred of us, each man ready to die; and though you have twenty men to one, yet will we withstand you if you meddle with us. By tonight the Romans will be outside the walls. Is this the time that Jews should fall upon each other like wild beasts?"

Simon hesitated. The idea of opposition excited him, as usual, to fury; but, upon the other hand, he saw that this determined body were not to be overcome save with great loss, and he wanted his men for his struggles with the Zealots.

"You are not in correspondence with John of Gischala?" he asked doubtfully.

"I am in correspondence with none," John said. "As I have told you, we come only to fight for Jerusalem, and will take no part on one side or other in your dissensions. We have taken up this street between the gate and the Corner Gate, and this street we will hold."

Simon still hesitated. He saw that round this nucleus of determined men the whole of the citizens of the lower town might gather, and that he might be forced to confine himself to the upper town. This, however, would be of no great importance now. The inner lower town was the poor quarter of Jerusalem. Here dwelt the artisans and mechanics in the narrow and tortuous lanes, while the wealthier classes resided either in the upper town, where stood the palaces of the great, or in the new town between the second and third walls. The new town had indeed until lately been a suburb outside the walls. Agrippa had begun the third wall, which was to inclose this, and had he been allowed to build it according to his design, he would have made Jerusalem absolutely impregnable save by famine; but the authorities at Rome, knowing how turbulent were the population of Jerusalem, and foreseeing that at some time they might have to lay siege to the city, had forbidden its construction, and the new wall had been hastily erected by the Jews themselves after they had risen and defeated Cestius four years before.

This wall inclosed a vast number of villas with gardens and open spaces, now thickly tenanted by the temporary habitations of the fugitives and pilgrims. The lower town then contained but little to tempt the cupidity of Simon's troops. Its houses had indeed been ransacked over and over again, and Simon reflected that even should his men be prevented from descending into it it would matter but little, while, as it was separated from the upper town by the Tyropœon Valley and the first wall, no rising there could be a formidable danger to him. Still, it galled him to be resisted, and had it not been that the Romans were close at hand he would at once have given his men orders to attack the strangers. He stood for some minutes stroking his beard, and then said:

"I will give you no answer now. I will think over what you say till tomorrow, then we will talk again."

"I doubt not what your decision will be," John said. "You are a brave man, Simon, and although you have done much harm to the Jews, yet I know that you will defend Jerusalem to the end against the Romans. You need feel no jealousy of me. I aspire to no leadership or power. I am here only to fight, and six hundred such men as mine are not to be despised in the day of trial. Should the Romans march away baffled before the walls, I, too, shall leave, and you who remain can resume your mad struggles if you will; but I think that in the presence of the enemy all strife within the city should cease and that we should be as one man in the face of the Romans."

Simon looked with surprise and some admiration at the young man who so boldly addressed him. Savage and cruel as he was, Simon was a man of the greatest bravery. He had none of the duplicity and treachery which characterized John of Gischala, but was straightforward and in his way honest. As only his picture has come down to us as described by the pen of Josephus, who at the time of his writing his history had become thoroughly a Roman, and who elevated Titus and his troops at the expense of his own countrymen, great allowance must be made for the dark colors in which he is painted.

The fact that he was regarded with affection and devotion by his troops, who were willing to go to certain death at his orders, shows that at least there must have been many good qualities in him, and history records no instance of more desperate and sustained bravery than he exhibited in defense of Jerusalem. The frankness of John's speech, instead of angering him, pleased him much.

"Enough," he said; "I need no further time to reflect. A man who had thought of treachery would not speak so boldly and fearlessly as you do. Let us be friends. I have often wondered what sort of man was the John of Gamala of whom I have heard so much, and who has so long kept the field against the Romans; and although I wonder greatly at seeing you so young a man, yet I rejoice that so valiant a fighter should be here to aid us in the struggle. Here is my hand in token of amity."

John took the hand held out to him, and a shout of satisfaction rose from the armed men on either side, the followers of John being rejoiced that they would not be called upon to engage in civil strife, those of Simon well satisfied that they were not to be called upon to attack a body of men who looked such formidable antagonists. Just at this moment a man rode in at the gate saying that the Romans were but two miles distant, and would speedily make their appearance over the Hill of Scopus. Simon ordered a party of his men to proceed at once to Damascus Gate, and to close it as soon as the Romans were visible. Then he turned again to John.

"Come up with me," he said, "to the Palace of Herod. From its summit we can see the enemy approaching."

Giving orders to his men to lay aside their arms, and calling Jonas to accompany him, John without hesitation turned to accompany Simon.

The latter had hardly expected him to accept his invitation, and the readiness with which he did so at once pleased and gratified him. It was a proof of fearlessness, and a testimony to John's belief in his faith and honor. John of Gischala, treacherous himself, would not have placed himself in his power, whatever guarantee he gave for his safety; while he himself would not have confided himself to John of Gischala, though the latter had sworn to his safety with his band on the altar.

John himself was struck with the rugged grandeur of Simon's appearance. He was far above the stature of ordinary men, and of immense strength, and there was nevertheless an ease and lightness in his carriage which showed that he was no less active than strong. His face was leonine in expression; his long hair fell back from his forehead; his eyebrows were heavy; his eyes were gray and clear, with a fierce and savage expression when his brows met in a frown and his lips were firmly set, but at other times frank, open , and straightforward in their look. The mouth was set and determined without being hard, and a pleasant smile at times lit up his features. He was a man capable of strong affections and generous impulses.

He was cruel at times; but, it was an age of cruelty, and Titus himself, who is held up as a magnanimous general, was guilty of far more hideous cruelties than any committed by Simon. Had the latter been master of Jerusalem from the first, and had not the granaries been destroyed in the civil war, the legions of Titus would never have achieved the conquest of the city.

Ascending the steep slope of the valley the passed through the gate in the first wall, and turning to the right entered the Palace of Herod, which was at once a royal dwelling and a fortress of tremendous strength.

Much as John's thoughts were otherwise occupied, he could not help being struck by the magnificence and splendor of this noble building but he said nothing as Simon strode along through the forum, passed out beyond the palace itself, entered the strong and lofty tower of Phasaelus, and ascended to its summit. An involuntary exclamation burst from John as he gained the platform. From the point on which he stood he commanded a view of the whole city and of the country round. Far below at his feet lay the crowded streets of the inner town, between which and the outer wall the ground was thickly occupied by houses of the better class standing half-embowered in trees. Close beside him rose the stately towers of Hippicus and Mariamne. Behind him was the palace of Herod, standing on the ground once occupied by the Castle of David. On the east the Palace of Agrippa partly obscured the view of the Temple; but a portion of the building could be seen standing on its platform on the summit of Mount Moriah; to its left, and connected with it by two lines of cloisters, was the Castle of Antonia, while still further along was the fort known as Acra. Behind the Palace of Herod and its superb gardens were scattered the palaces and mansions of the wealthy Jews and strangers, which, with their gardens, occupied the whole of the upper part of Mount Zion. On the lower slope of Mount Moriah, lying between the Valley of Jehoshaphat and that of the Tyropœon, was a densely populated suburb known as the New Town.

Westward, beyond the Tower of Hippicus, lay the valley of Hinnom with the Dragon Pool glistening in the sun, while at a distance of four or five miles to the southward could be seen the village of Bethlehem. The whole country outside the walls was a garden, with countless villas, mansions, and groves of trees. For some minutes John looked round in admiration of the scene, while Simon stood with his eyes fixed upon the road crossing Mount Scopus. Suddenly he uttered an exclamation, and John joined him and looked in the direction in which he was gazing. The white line of road was darkened by a moving mass, sparkling as the sun shone on arms and armor.

"They come at last," Simon said, and as he spoke cries of wailing and lamentation were heard from the walls far below them. The four years that had elapsed since danger first threatened Jerusalem had deepened the impression in the minds of the Jews that the enemy would not be permitted to approach the Holy City. It was true that their faith had been sorely shaken by many strange prodigies. A strange light had shone about the altar and the Temple, and it was said that voices had been heard from the Holy of Holies, saying, "Let us depart hence."

The beautiful Gate of the Temple, which required the strength of twenty men to close it, had opened of its own accord. War chariots and armies had been seen contending in the clouds, and for months a great comet, in shape like a flaming sword, had hung over the city. Still men had hoped, and the cry from the watchers that the Roman army was in sight struck dismay among inhabitants. There was still many without the walls; some of these rushed wildly into the gates and entered the city, while the wiser fled away to the hills and made their way to their homes.

Titus, as he reached the brow of Mount Scopus, reined in his horse and looked for some time in silence at the great and magnificent city which extended before him, and there can be little doubt that he would fain have spared it had it been possible. Even a Roman could not gaze on the massive beauty of the Temple unmoved. It was the most famous religious edifice in the world. From all parts pilgrims flocked to it, and kings made offerings to it. It was believed by the Jews to be the special seat of their deity; and the Romans, partly from policy, partly from superstition, paid respect and reverence to the gods of all the nations they subdued, and annual offerings had been sent by Rome to the Temple.

Titus may well have wished to spare the city the ruin and misery of a siege, to preserve the Temple intact, and to hand over to King Agrippa uninjured his palace and capital. In all the wide dominions of Rome there was not a city which approached Jerusalem in beauty and grandeur; and Titus must have felt that whatever honor would accrue to him from its conquest, would be dearly purchased by the linking of his name to all time as the destroyer of so magnificent a city. Similar emotions were felt by the group of officers who rode with Titus, and who reined up their horses as he did so. With them the military point of view was doubtless the most prominent, and as they saw from their lofty vantage-ground how the deep valleys of Hinnom and Jehoshaphat girt the city in on either side, and how stately and strong were the walls and towers, they may well have felt how mighty was the task which they had before them.

The scene was calm and peaceful. No sound of warlike trumpets came from the walls; no signs of an enemy appeared without; and Titus rode on past the deserted villas and beautiful grounds that bordered the road, until he neared the Damascus Gate. He was accompanied by six hundred horse, for the legions had encamped in the Valley of Thorns, near the village of Gaboth Saul, some four miles from Jerusalem.

The walls appeared deserted, but Titus, having experience of the desperate courage of the Jews, paused at some little distance from the gate, and turning to the right entered a lane which ran parallel to the wall, and made his way toward the Tower of Psephinus, or the Rubble Tower, at the northeastern angle of the outer wall. Suddenly a gate near the Tower of the Women was thrown open, and a crowd of armed men dashed out. Rushing forward at the top of their speed, some threw themselves across the road which Titus was following; but most of them rushed in behind him, cutting him off from the main body of his cavalry, and leaving him isolated with but a few followers.

The main body of Roman cavalry, furiously assailed, and ignorant that Titus was cut off from them, turned and fled. Titus hesitated a moment. In front of him was an unknown country, he knew not wither the lane he was following led, hedges rose on either side, and even did he burst the crowd in front of him he might be overwhelmed by missiles as he rode on. Therefore, calling upon his men to follow him he turned round and dashed into the crowd which barred his retreat.

He wore neither helmet nor breastplate, for as he had only advanced to reconnoiter, and with no thought of fighting, these had been left behind. Yet, though javelins flew around him in showers and arrows whizzed close to him, not one touched him as he struck right and left among those who barred his passage, while his war-horse, excited by the shouts and tumult, trampled them under his feet.

In vain the Jews, astonished at his bravery, and still more so at his immunity from harm amid the shower of missiles, strove to seize him. He and his little band cut his way onward, those in front drawing back with almost superstitious fear from his attack.

Two only of his followers were slain; one fell pierced with numerous javelins, another was pulled from his horse and killed; but with the rest he emerged unharmed from among his assailants and reached his camp in safety.

The soldiers of Simon, for it was his men who guarded this part of the wall, returned with mingled feelings. They were triumphant that they had caused the son of Cæsar himself to fly before them. They were humiliated that so great a prize should have escaped them when he seemed in their hands, and they had a superstitious feeling that he had been divinely protected from their assaults.

From their lookout Simon and John had seen the Roman cavalry turn off from the Damascus road into the lane, and had then lost sight of them. Then they heard the sudden din of battle and the shouts of the combatants, and saw the Roman cavalry riding off in full speed, but the clamor had continued, and in a short time another little party of horsemen were seen in issue from the lane and following their companions. Simon laughed grimly.

"We have taught the Romans early that the wasps have stings, and that if they think they are going to take the nest without trouble they will be mistaken. And now, John, what do you advise? You were, they say, at Jotapata and Gamala, and you have since shown how well you understand the Roman tactics. I am a soldier with an arm to strike, but so far I have not had experience in the Roman tactics at sieges. Tell me what would you do first were you commander of this city?"

"There is no doubt what is the first thing to be done," John said. "It is the duty of all within this city to lay aside their feuds and unite in her defense. It is for you, as the strongest, to make the first advance, and to send at once to John and Eleazar to propose that so long as the Romans are before the city there shall be a truce between you, and to arrange which part of the walls shall be held by the soldiers of each. You must also arrange to unite for common action, both in the defense and in attacking them without the walls; for it is only by disturbing them at their work, and by hindering them as they bring forward their engines of war, that you can hope to hold the city. Strong as your walls may be, they will crumble to ruins when the battering rams once begin their work against them."

Simon was silent for a minute; then he said:

"Your advice is good. I will send at once to John and Eleazar and ask them to meet me on the bridge across the Tyropæon, which separates our forces."

The sun was already setting, but the distance was short. Simon advanced to the bridge, and, hailing the Zealots on the other side, said that he desired an interview with John in reference to the defense of the city, and that he pledged his solemn oath that no harm should come to him. He sent a similar message to Eleazar. John shortly appeared, for from the summit of Antonia he too had watched the advancing Romans, and felt the necessity for common action for defense of the town.

Eleazar refused to come. He would have trusted Simon, but to reach the meeting-place he would have had to pass through the outer courts of the Temple held by John, and he knew that no confidence could be reposed in any oath that the latter might take. He sent word, however, that he was willing to abstain from all hostilities, and to make common cause with the others for the defense of the city. John of Gischala advanced alone on to the bridge, a wide and stately edifice carried on lofty arches across the Tyropæon Valley, from a point near the Palace of Agrippa to the platform of the Temple.

"Come with me," Simon said to his companion. John of Gischala paused in his advance as he saw that Simon was not alone.

"Let one of your men come with you if you like," Simon said with a grim laugh at his hesitation, "or two, or six if you like." But John of Gischala knew that the eyes of the soldiers on both sides of the bridge were upon him, and having faith in the oath of Simon he again advanced.

John looked with curiosity at the man of whom he had heard so much, and who, having been a scourge to Upper Galilee with his horde of robbers, had now brought such misery upon Jerusalem. Without approaching his rival in size and strength, John of Gischala was a powerfully built man. He did not shrink from danger, and had upon occasion shown great bravery; but he relied upon craft more than force to gain his ends.

He possessed great power of oratory, could rouse men's passions or calm them at will. He could cajole or threaten, persuade or deceive, with equal facility, was always ready to break an oath if it was inconvenient to keep it. Although fond of power, he was still more greedy of gain; but in one respect he and Simon agreed, both hated the Romans with an intense and bitter hatred, both were ready to die in defense of Jerusalem.

"I think it is time, John," Simon said, "to cease from our strife for the present, and to make common cause against the enemy. If we continue our dissensions, and the Romans in consequence take the city, our names will be accursed in all generations as the men who gave Jerusalem into the hands of the Romans."

"I am ready to agree to a truce," John of Gischala said. "It is you who have been attacking me, not I who have been attacking you; but we need not talk of that now. It is to be an understood thing that if the Romans retire we shall both occupy the positions we hold now, whatever changes may have taken place, and we can then either come to an understanding or fight the matter out?"

"Yes, that is what I would propose," Simon replied. "Whatever changes may take place, when the Romans retire we can occupy exactly the positions we hold now. Will you swear to that by the Temple?"

"I will," John said.

The two men each took a solemn oath to carry out the terms they agreed upon, and throughout the siege to put aside all enemity toward each other, and to act together in all things for the defense of the city. They then arranged as to the portion of the wall which each should occupy, these corresponding very nearly to the lines which they at present held. Simon held the whole of the third wall, which, commencing from Hippicus, the tower at the north corner of the high town, ran northward to Psephinus, or the Rubble Tower, then eastward to the Valley of Jehoshaphat, again south to the Temple platform.

The second wall, inclosing the inner low town, or Inner Acra, as it was sometimes called, was divided between the two. Simon also held the first wall from Hippicus right round at the foot of Zion across the lower end of the Tyropæon Valley, and round the outer low town as far as the platform of the Temple. John held the Temple platform, the middle low town, and some parts of the city immediately adjacent, both on the south slope of Mount Moriah or Ophel, as this portion of the hill was called, and part of the inner low town.

The line, therefore, which Simon had to defend was vastly greater than that held by John's troops, but in fact the whole line bordering the valleys of Himnom and Jehoshaphat was practically unassailable, the wall being built along the edge of precipices, where it could not be attacked either with battering-rams or by escalade and it was really the north face of the city only that was exposed to serious assault. The outer wall on this side that against which the assault would first be made, was entirely occupied by Simon's troops; but it was not anticipated that any successful resistance could be made here, for the walls hastily raised by the Jews after turning out the Romans were incapable of offering a long resistance to such a force as was now to assail it. It was, then, at the second wall that the first great stand would be made, and John's and Simon's troops divided this between them, so that the division was fair enough when it was considered that Simon's force was more than double that of John, when this matter had been arranged, John of Gischala said to Simon:

"Who is this young man who accompanies you?"

"He is one who has done much more for the cause than either you or I, John of Gischala, and indeed hitherto it may be doubted whether we have not been the two worst enemies of Jerusalem. This is John of Gamala, of whom we heard so often during the last three years."

"This John of Gamala!" John repeated in a tone of incredulity; "you are mocking me, Simon."

"I mock no one," Simon said sternly. "I tell you this is John of Gamala; and when we think that you and I men of war, have as yet struck no single blow against the Romans since I aided in the defeat of the legions of Cestius—for you fled from Gischala like a coward at night, while I have been fighting for my own hand down here—we may well feel ashamed, both of us, in the presence of this youth, who has for three years harassed the Romans, burning their camps, driving out small garrisons, hindering pillagers from straying over the country, cutting off their convoys, and forcing them to keep ever on the watch. I tell you, John, I feel ashamed beside him. He has brought here six hundred men of his band, all picked and determined fellows, for the defense of the city. I tell you they will be no mean assistance, and you would say so also had you seen how they drew up to-day in solid order ready to withstand the whole of my force. He is not of my party or of yours; he comes simply to fight against the Romans, and, as I understand him, when the Romans retire he will leave also."

"That is certainly my intention," John said quietly; "but before I go I hope that I shall be able to act as mediator between you both, and to persuade you to come to some arrangement which may free Jerusalem from a renewal of the evils which, between you, you have inflicted upon her. If you beat back the Romans you will have gained all the honor that men could desire, and your names will go down to all posterity as the saviors of Jerusalem and the Temple. If you desire treasure, there is not a Jew but that will be ready to contribute to the utmost of his power. If you desire power, Palestine is wide enough for you to divide it between you, only beware lest by striving longer against each other your names go down as those who have been the tyrants of the land, names to be accursed as long as the Hebrew tongue remains."

The two men were silent. Bold as they were, they felt abashed before the outspoken rebuke of this stripling. They had heard him spoken of as one under the special protection of Jehovah. They knew that he had had marvelous escapes, and that he had fought single-handed with Titus; and the air of authority with which he spoke, his entire disregard of their power, his fearlessness in the presence of men before whom all Jerusalem trembled, confirmed the stories they had heard, and created an impression almost to awe.

"If we three are alive when the Romans depart from before the city," Simon said in his deep voice, "it shall be as you say, and I bind myself beforehand to agree to whatever you shall decide is just and right. Therefore, John of Gischala, henceforth I shall regard this not as a truce, but as the beginning of peace between us, and our rivalry shall be who shall best defend the Holy City against her foes."

"So be it!" John of Gischala replied; "but I would that Eleazar were here. He is an enemy in my midst, and just as, whenever I was fighting with you, he fell upon me from behind, so will it be that while I am struggling with the Romans he may be attacking me from the Inner Temple. He has none of the outer walls to defend, and will therefore be free to choose the moment when he can fall upon me unawares."

"Make peace with him at any price," John said, "only put an end to this strife and let there be no more blood-shed in the Temple. How can we hope for God's assistance in defending the city when his altars are being daily desecrated with blood?"

"I will see what I can do," John said. "Somehow or other this strife must be brought to an end, and it shall be done without bloodshed if possible."

"There is another thing, John," Simon said. "Our comrade here has been telling me that from what he saw at Jotapata and Galama he is convinced that by passive resistance only we cannot defeat the Romans; but that we must sally out and attack them in their camps and at their work, and therefore let us agree that will we meet here from time to time and arrange that, issuing together through the gates in our portions of the wall, we may unite in falling upon the Romans."

"The council is good," John of Gischala said. "It will keep up the courage of the men to fight in the open. Whenever an opportunity presents itself my men shall act with yours. You have given Titus a lesson to-day. The next time we will divide the honor."

Chapter Fifteen

THE SIEGE IS BEGUN

The Fifth Legion, which had been stationed at Emmaus, half-way between Jerusalem and Jaffa, marching the greater part of the night, joined the Twelfth and Fifteenth at their halting-place at Gaboth Saul, and the next morning the three advanced together. The Twelfth and Fifteenth marched half-way down the Hill of Scopus and encamped together on a knoll, while the Fifth Legion encamped three furlongs to their rear, so that in case of an attack by the Jews its weary soldiers should not have to bear the brunt of the conflict. As these legions were marking out their camp the Tenth Legion, which had marched up from Jericho, appeared on the Mount of Olives, and Titus sent word for them to encamp there.

Thus Jerusalem was overlooked throughout its length and breadth by the Roman camps on the hills to the north and east sides. John had at the earnest request of Simon taken up his residence with him in the palace of Herod, and from the top of the Tower of Phasaelus watched the Roman legions at work.

"It seems to me," he said to Simon, "that now is the time for us to make an assault. The Romans raise veritable fortifications round their camp, and when once these are completed we can scarcely hope to storm them, whereas if we fall suddenly upon them now we can fight on even terms. The legion on the Mount of Olives is widely separated from the rest, and we might overcome it before the others could come to its assistance."

"I agree with you," Simon said; "let us strike a blow at once."

Simon at once sent off to John to propose that the latter should issue out from the Golden Gate in the middle of the Temple platform, while he himself would lead out his troops by the gate to the north of that platform. In accordance with the suggestion of John he requested John of Gischala to place a watchman on a conspicuous position on the wall, with orders to wave his mantle as a signal to both parties to charge, as from his position he would be better able than they to see what the Romans were doing, and both parties could see him, while they might be invisible to each other.

John of Gischala sent back at once to say that he approved of the plan, and would join in it. Simon called his troops together, and leaving the outer wall strongly manned lest the Twelfth and Fifteenth legions might take advantage of the absence of so large a portion of the garrison to make a sudden attack upon it, marched toward the northeastern gate, being joined on the way by John with his band. They waited until a messenger came from John of Gischala, saying that he was ready, then the gates were thrown open and the troops poured out. John had given strict orders to his men to keep together in their companies, each under his commander, and not to try to maintain regular order as one band, for this would be next to impossible fighting on such hilly and broken ground; besides, they would be sure to get mixed up with the masses of Simon's troops.

At the same moment that Simon's force poured through the northeastern gate, that of John of Gischala issued from the Temple platform, and in rivalry with each other both dashed down the steep declivity into the bottom of the Valley of Jehoshaphat, and then climbed the sharp slope of the Mount of Olives. Then with loud shouts they fell, in wild disorder, each as he reached the spot, upon the Tenth Legion.

The Romans, anticipating no attack and many of them unarmed as they worked at the intrenchments, were unable to resist the fierce onslaught. Accustomed to regular warfare, this rush of armed men from all sides upon them surprised and disconcerted them. Every moment added to the number of their assailants as fresh combatants continued to pour out from the city, and fighting stubbornly and sullenly the Romans were driven out of their half-formed intrenchments up the slope and over the crest of the Mount of Olives.

The Jews fought regardless of life; single men dashed into the midst of the Romans and fell there fighting fiercely; John's compact companies hurled themselves upon the line and broke it. Simon fought desperately at the head of his men, cutting down all who stood in his way. The Romans were wavering and would soon have broken into open flight, when rescue arrived. The general in command had, immediately the Jews had been seen issuing out, sent off a horseman to Titus with the news, and he, putting himself at the head of this body-guard, started instantly to their assistance.

Falling suddenly upon the flank of the Jews he bore them down by the impetuosity and weight of the charge. In vain Simon and John of Gischala tried to rally their men, and John's bands gathering round him at the sound of his bugle opposed a firm and steady resistance. The Roman legion rallied, and, ashamed of having been driven back before the eyes of Titus, attacked the Jews with fury and the latter were driven down the hill into the valley.

Here John's band refused to retire further, Simon and John of Gischala rallied their troops, and an obstinate contest ensued, the Romans being unable to push the Jews further back now that the latter were in turn fighting with the ground in their favor. For some time the battle raged; then Titus, seeing that he could not drive the Jews back into the city, ordered a portion of the Tenth Legion to reascend the Mount of Olives and complete the work of fortifying their camp, so that at the end of the day the legion could fall back to a place of safety.

The watchman on the wall saw the movement, and thought that the Romans were retreating. He waved his mantle wildly, and at the signal the Jews again burst down upon their foes, and fresh forces poured down from the gates to their assistance. In vain the Roman line tried to hold the bottom of the valley; the Jews burst through them and drove them in disorder up the hill, Titus alone, with a few followers, making a stand on the lower slopes. The Jews, rushing on, surrounded his party and fell upon him from all sides, while their main body swarmed up the hill, and the Romans, panic-stricken, dispersed in all directions.

Victory seemed in the hands of the Jews, when some of the Romans discovered that Titus was not with them, but was cut off and surrounded at the bottom of the hill. They shouted to others, and the news rapidly spread through the fugitives. Overwhelmed with shame at having deserted their general, and knowing the severe punishment which according to Roman military law would befall them for their cowardice, the Romans paused in their flight.

Their discipline came to their aid, and they quickly fell in in companies, and with a shout of fury advanced upon the scattered Jews, who, although vastly superior in numbers, had no order or formation which would enable them to resist the downward impetus of the solid masses of heavy-armed Romans. Again they were driven down the hill, and the Romans, pressing upon them, found to their delight that Titus and his band had successfully resisted the attacks of their foes.

The Jews were driven some distance up the side of the slope and there the combat was renewed, until, seeing that they could make no further impression upon the enemy, the Jews retired sullenly through their gates into the city. They were, however, well satisfied with their day's work. Numbers had fallen, but they had inflicted heavy loss upon the Romans. They had forced one of the legions to retreat in fair fight, had all but captured Titus, and had proved to the Romans the formidable nature of the task they had undertaken.

The next day, the 13th of April, was the day of the Passover, and all Jerusalem prepared as usual to celebrate the day of the great sacrifice. The gates of the Temple were as usual thrown open, and the multitude thronged in to worship. John of Gischala had sworn to Eleazar, as he had to Simon, to lay aside all hostility, but as usual he did not allow his oath to prevent him from carrying out his designs. A number of his men concealed their arms under their garments, and entered the Temple with the worshippers.

At a signal the swords were drawn and the cry of battle was raised. Eleazar and his followers at once fled in dismay to the vaults under the Temple. The multitude in the courts above, panic-stricken at the threatened conflict, strove to escape. Many were trampled under food and killed; some were wantonly slain by John's followers, to whom murder had become a pastime.

When order was restored John of Gischala went to the entrance of the vaults and shouted to Eleazar that he desired to keep his oath and would do no harm, but that for the general safety of the city he could be no longer permitted to hold the inner Temple, but must with his men take his share in the defense of the walls. If Eleazar would agree to do this he promised that no harm whatever should be done to him or his followers. Eleazar being at the mercy of his foe, accepted the terms and with his followers ascended into the Temple.

For once John of Gischala kept his word; Eleazar was permitted to retain the command of his own two thousand men, but his force henceforth formed a part of the Zealot army of John. Thus from this time forward there were by to factions in the city.

Josephus, always the bitter enemy of John of Gischala, speaks in terms of the utmost reprobation of his conduct on this occasion, and the occasion and manner in which the deed was effected cannot for a moment be defended. At the same time it must be admitted that the occasion was an urgent one, that the existence of this enemy in his midst crippled John of Gischala's power to defend his portion of the city, and that the suppression of Eleazar's faction and the conversion of his troops from enemies into allies was an act of high policy, and was indeed a necessity, if Jerusalem was to be successfully defended.

The desecration of the Temple, however, upon so sacred an occasion as the feast of the Passover, filled all pious Jews with horror, and caused John to be regarded with even greater detestation than before. For the opinion of the unarmed multitude, however, he cared little. He had crushed the faction of Eleazar, had added two thousand men to his strength, and was now ready, without fear of trouble within, to face the

Roman enemy without.

The desperate sortie of the Jews had convinced Titus that if Jerusalem was to be taken it must be by means of regular siege operations, conducted with the greatest care and caution, and having made a circuit of the city he perceived that it was impregnable save on the north and northwestern sides, that is, the part defended by the third wall.

He reluctantly, therefore, gave orders that all the villas, mansions, gardens, and groves standing between that wall and the foot of Mount Scopus should be destroyed, and placing strong bodies of troops opposite the gates to prevent any sortie of the defenders, he set the whole of the three legions encamped on that side to carry out the work of destruction.

A feeling of grief and dismay filled the city at the sight of the devastation that was being wrought and there were very many among the multitude who would gladly have avoided further evils by submitting to the Romans; but such and idea did not enter the heads of the military leaders, Simon determined upon sortie. A number of the citizens were ordered to take their places upon the walls, and to cry out to the Romans that they desired peace, and to implore them to enter the town and take possession.

In the meantime a number of Simon's men issued out from the Women's Gate in confusion as if expelled by the peace party. They appeared to be in a state of extreme terror, sometimes advancing toward the Romans as if to submit to them, at other times retreating toward the wall as if afraid of putting themselves into the hands of the Romans, but as they neared the walls they were assailed by a shower of missiles above. Titus suspected that a trick was being played, and ordered the troops to stand fast; but the battalion facing the gate, seeing it stand open, were unable to resist the impulse to rush in and take possession. They therefore advanced through the crowd of Jews outside until close to the gate; then Simon's men drew out their concealed weapons and fell upon them in the rear, while a fresh body of armed men rushed out from the gate and attacked them in front, while from the two flanking towers a storm of javelins, arrows, and stones was poured upon them.

The Romans fought desperately, but numbers of them were slain, and the rest took to flight, pursued by the Jews, and did not halt until they reached the tombs of Helen, half a mile from the walls, while the Jews with shouts of triumph reentered the city.

John had taken no part in this sortie. He had lost more than fifty men in the fight on the Mount of Olives and determined to hold the rest in reserve until they were needed in a moment of extreme peril. The manner in which the bands had held together, and had steadfastly resisted the Roman attacks, had greatly excited the admiration of Simon.

"I see now," he said on the evening of the sortie, when talking the matter over with John, "the secret of the successes you have gained over the Romans. Your men fight as steadily and with as much discipline as they do, while they are far quicker in their movements. They unite the activity of my men with the steadiness of the Romans. I wish now that I had spent the last year in training and disciplining my men to act with equal steadiness and order, but it is too late to try to do so now. Each will do his best and will die fighting; but were I to attempt now to introduce regularity among them they would lose the fierce rush with which they assault the Romans, without acquiring sufficient discipline to enable them to keep their order as yours do in the confusion of the battle."

"Mine are all picked men," John said. "I had eight thousand under my orders during the last two years of fighting, but I bade all leave me, when I advanced to Jerusalem, save those who were ready and prepared to die; therefore I can reply upon every man as upon myself. Unless I see some exceptional opportunity I do not think I shall lead them out beyond the walls again. The time will come as the siege goes on when you will need a body of men to hold a breach or arrest the advance of a Roman column, men who will die rather than give way a foot. When that time comes my band shall fill the gap."

"I think you are right," Simon agreed. "Your men are too good to be wasted in desultory fighting. They shall be kept as a last resource, and I know that when the time comes they can be relied upon."

The clearing of the ground occupied four days, and Titus then determined to advance his camp nearer to the city, and fixed upon a

spot which was the highest on the plateau, a quarter of a mile to the
northwest of the Rubble Tower. Before moving into it the position was
strongly fortified, and so much impressed was Titus by the sallies which
the Jews had made that he formed up his whole army along the north
and northwest side of the city. The heavy-armed troops, three deep, were
the first line; behind them came a rank of archers, and behind these the
cavalry three deep.

Brave as were the Jews they did not venture to sally out to endeavor to
break through this living wall, which stood all day immovable, while the
baggage animals, aided by a great crowd of artisans and camp-followers,
moved the war engines, reserves, and baggage of the army from Mount
Scopus down to the new camp. Here the Twelfth and Fifteenth Legions,
under Titus himself, took up their position. The Fifth Legion, under
the command of Cerealis, formed their camp on a knoll a quarter of a
mile from the Jaffa Gate, and divided from it by the Valley of Hinnom,
which is here of no great depth. It lay about a third of a mile south of
the camp of Titus. The Tenth Legion remained on the Mount of Olives.
Their camp had now been very strongly fortified, and was in a position
to repel any attack that might be made against it.

Now that his dispositions were complete Titus determined to save the
city if possible from the horrors of siege. He therefore sent Nicanor and
Josephus with a flag of truce toward the walls to offer them terms. No
sooner had they come within bow-shot than an arrow was discharged
from the wall and struck Nicanor upon the shoulder. The ambassadors at
once retired, and Titus, indignant alike at the insult of his messengers and
the violation of the flag of truce, immediately began to make preparations
for the siege. Could the population of the city have been consulted they
would have declared by an immense majority of voices to surrender; but
Simon and John of Gischala, whose men held the walls, were absolute
masters of the city, and the inhabitants were to pay now, as they had paid
in the past, for their cowardice in allowing themselves to be tyrannized
over by a body of men whom they outnumbered by ten to one.

Titus, after a careful examination of the walls, determined to attack at a spot between the Jaffa Gate and Psephinus. In former times all assaults of the enemy had been directed against the north, and it was here, consequently, that the wall was strongest. At its foot, too, a wide and deep fosse had been cut in the solid rock, rendering it impossible for the assailants to advance to the attack until this was filled up.

But on the northwest the walls had not been made equally strong, nor had the fosse been continued from Psephinus to the Jaffa Gate. It had no doubt been considered that the projecting angle of the wall at Psephinus and the fortifications of the Palace of Herod covered this portion of the wall, which was, moreover, to some extent protected by the Valley of Hinnom. But between the top of the slope of that valley and the foot of the walls was a level space of ground sufficiently wide for the establishment of machines for breaching the wall.

Here, therefore, Titus determined to make his attack. On the 22d of April the troops began the work. Each legion was to erect a bank, mount a battering-ram, and construct a tower. A vast quantity of timber was required, and the desolation already effected between the north wall and Scopus was now widely extended, the whole of the trees for a great distance round Jerusalem being cut down and brought to the spot. The towers were constructed about ninety feet in height and with a wide face. They were put together beyond the range of the missiles of the defenders, and were to be advanced upon wheels up the bank until they neared the wall.

As the three banks approached the wall hurdles covered the hides were erected to protect the workers, and on each side javelin men and archers were posted, together with the war engines for casting missiles. Simon was not idle. He possessed the war engines taken when Antonia was surrendered by the Romans and those captured from the legion of Cestius, but his men had no experience in the working of these machines. They could only manipulate them slowly, and their aim was bad. They were able, therefore, to interfere but little with the work of the Romans.

The archers and slingers, however, did great damage and killed many, while at times the gate would be thrown open and Simon would dash out at the head of his men, and do much damage before the Romans could drive him back within the walls. The Tenth Legion did more injury to the defenders than did the others, being provided with more powerful war machines. Their balistæ threw stones weighing a hundred weight a distance of a quarter of a mile. The Jewish watchmen on the walls kept vigilant watch upon these machines, and each time a stone was coming shouted a warning, and the defenders threw themselves on their faces until the stone passed over. Even at night the whiteness of the newly cut rock rendered the masses visible as they flew through the air, and Titus then ordered the stones to be painted black before they were discharged, and thus added to their effect, as their approach could be no longer seen.

Night and day the Romans toiled at the work, night and day the Jews with missiles and sorties hindered their approach, until the banks had approached so close to the walls that the battering rams would be within striking distance. Then the towers were brought up and the rams began to strike their mighty blows upon the wall, while from the top of the lofty towers and from the stories below, the archers and war machines poured a storm of missiles down upon the defenders of the walls.

As it was evident now that the danger lay solely in this quarter, and that the whole strength of the besieged was needed here, Simon sent John of Gischala to urge that the line of demarcation agreed upon by them between their respective troops should no longer be observed. John would not trust himself in the power of Simon, but gave leave to his soldiers to go down and aid in the defense, and they, who had been chafing at their forced inactivity while Simon's men were bearing the brunt of the fighting, went down to take their share in the struggle.

Regardless of the storm of missiles the Jews maintained their place upon the walls, shooting blazing arrows and hurling combustibles down upon the Roman works, and executing such frequent and desperate sorties that Titus was obliged to keep the greater part of his force constantly under arms, and to gather round the towers large bodies of archers and horsemen to repel the attacks. At length a corner tower fell before one of the battering-rams, but the wall behind stood firm and no breach was effected. Nevertheless the Jews appeared dispirited at this proof of the power of the battering-rams, and fell back into the city.

The Roman legionaries, under the belief that the fighting was over for evening, were drawn back into their camps. Suddenly, from a small gate hitherto unnoticed by the Romans, situated at the foot of the tower of Hippicus, the Jews poured out with flaming brands in their hands, and dashed at the Roman banks, swarming up the banks and surrounding the towers, to which they endeavored to set fire. They were, however, plated with iron outside, and the beams inside were so massive a description that the Jews were unable to set light to them.

While some of the Jews were striving to do this, the rest fell with such fury upon the Roman troops who hurried up to the protection of the works that they were driven back. A body of Alexandrian troops only, posted near the towers, maintained themselves against the attack until Titus with his cavalry charged down upon the Jews, who, although a match for the Roman infantry, were never throughout the war able to resist the charges of the bodies of heavy horsemen. Titus is said to have killed twelve Jews with his own hand, and, fighting desperately to the end, the assailants were driven back into the city. One prisoner only was taken, and him Titus, with the barbarity which afterward distinguished his proceedings during the siege, ordered to be crucified close to the walls.

Among those killed on the Jewish side was John, the commander of the Idumeans, who formed part of Simon's force. He was shot by an Arab while he was parleying with a Roman soldier. He was a man of great courage and excellent judgment, and his loss was a serious one for the besieged. At night all was still and silent; both parties were exhausted with their long and desperate struggle, and even the machines ceased to hurl their missiles. Suddenly a terrific crash was heard, and the very ground seemed to shake. Both parties sprang to arms—the Jews fearing that the wall had fallen; the Romans not knowing what had happened, but apprehensive of another of the sorties, which they had begun to hold in high respect.

Something like a panic seized them until Titus, riding about among them, reassured them by his presence and words. They knew, indeed, that a repetition of the defeats they had suffered at the Jewish hands would not be forgiven. The battalion which has been defeated at the sortie at the Women's Gate had been sternly rebuked by Titus, who had ordered the military law to be carried into effect, and a certain number of soldiers to be executed, and had only pardoned them upon the intercession of the whole army on their behalf. Therefore the legionaries now fell into their ranks at the order of Titus and drew up on order of battle, while parties were sent forward to ascertain what had happened.

It was found that a series of misfortune had befallen them. The Jews in their attack had been unable to set fire to the towers, but they had worked so vigorously, in their attempt to destroy the bank that they had weakened that portion of it upon which one of the towers stood; this had given way beneath the tremendous weight resting upon it, and the great tower had fallen with a crash to the ground. In the morning the combat recommenced, but although the Jews exposed their lives on the walls unflinchingly, they were unable to withstand the terrible shower of missiles poured upon them from the remaining towers, or to interrupt the steady swing of the huge rams which day and night beat against the walls.

One of these especially did material damage, and the Jews themselves christened it "Nico," or the Conqueror. At length, wearied out by their efforts, disheartened by the failure of their attempts to interfere with the work of destruction, and knowing that the inner lines were vastly stronger than those without, the Jews abandoned the defense of the tottering wall and retired behind their next line of defense. The Romans soon discovered that they were unopposed, and scaled the wall. As soon as they found that the whole space between it and the second wall was abandoned they set to work and threw down a large portion of the third wall, and took up their post inside. Titus established himself at the spot known as the camp of the Assyrians, at the front of the Tower of Psephinus.

As soon as his arrangements were completed he gave orders for the assault to be recommenced. The date of the capture of the outer wall was on the 6th of May, fifteen days after the commencement of the siege. The capture of Bezetha, or the New Town, enabled the Romans to make an attack directly on the Palace of Herod on the one side and Mount Moriah upon the other, without first assaulting the second wall, which defended the inner lower town; but two or three days' fighting convinced Titus that these positions could not be successfully attacked until the lower town was in his power.

The three great towers Pasaelus, Hippicus, and Mariamne, desperately defended by Simon's soldiers, formed an impregnable obstacle on the one side, while Antonia and the steep ascent up to the Temple platform was defended with equal stubbornness and success by the soldiers of John of Gischala. Titus therefore prepared for the assault of the second wall. The point selected for the attack was the middle tower on the northern face, close to which were the wool mart, the clothes mart, and the braziers' shops.

There were no natural obstacles to the approach, and the battering-ram was soon placed in position, while a strong body of archers prevented the defenders showing themselves above the parapet. The wall was of far less strength than that which the Romans had before encountered, and soon began to totter before the blows of the battering-ram. The Jews, indeed, were indifferent as to its fall, for they knew that the possession of the inner town was of slight importance to them, and that its fall would not greatly facilitate the attack upon what was the natural line of defense, namely, the heights of Zion and Moriah.

For a short time the Roman advance was delayed by the proceedings of Castor, the Jewish officer commanding the tower which they had assaulted. He, with ten men, alone had remained there when the rest of the defenders had retired, and he got up a sham battle among his men, the Romans suspending operations under the belief that a party of defenders were anxious to surrender. Castor himself stood on the parapet and offered Titus to surrender. Titus promised him his life, and when an archer standing near sent an arrow which pierced Castor's nose he sternly rebuked him.

He then asked Josephus, who was standing beside him, to go forward and assure Castor and his companions that their lives should be spared. Josephus, however, knew the way of his countrymen too well, and declined to endanger his life. But upon Castor offering to throw down a bag of gold, a man ran forward to receive it, when Castor hurled a great stone down at him, and Titus, seeing that he was being fooled, ordered the battering-ram to re-commence its work.

Just before the tower fell Castor set fire to it, and leaped with his companions, as the Roman supposed, into the flames, but really into a vault, whence they made their escape into the city. As soon as the tower fell Titus entered the breach with his body-guard and a thousand heavy-armed troops. The inhabitants, almost entirely of the poorer class, surrendered willingly, and Titus gave orders that none save those found with arms upon them should be killed. The Romans dispersed through the narrow and winding streets, when suddenly Simon and his men poured down from the upper city, and John at the head of his band issued from his quarters.

While some fell upon the Romans in the streets, others entered the houses and rained missiles upon them from above; while another party, issuing from the gate by Phasaelus, attacked the Romans between the second and third walls and drove them into their camp. For a time Titus and those in the lower town suffered terribly; but at last Titus posted archers to command the lanes leading toward the breach, and managed, but with considerable loss, to withdraw his troops through it.

The Jews at once manned the wall, and formed in close order behind the breach. Titus led his heavy-armed troops against it, but John and Simon defended it with the greatest valor, and for three days and nights beat back the continued attacks of the Roman soldiers; but at the end of that time they were utterly exhausted, while the Romans incessantly brought up fresh troops. Even Simon, who had fought desperately at the head of his men, and had performed prodigies of valor, could no longer continue the struggle, and slowly and in good order the defenders of the breach fell back to the upper city, and the lower remained in the possession of the Romans.

In order to avoid a recurrence of the disaster which had befallen them, Titus ordered a considerable portion of the second wall to be leveled, so that the troops could, if necessary, pour in or out without difficulty. But Simon had no thought of repeating his sortie. A large number of his best men had already fallen, and he determined to reserve his force for the defense of the almost impregnable position of the upper city. Two hundred of John's band had fallen round the breach, he himself had received several wounds, and the fighting strength of his band was now but one-half of what it was at the commencement of the siege.

He had, before the Romans first entered the inner town, had the remainder of his store of grain removed to the building in the upper town which Simon had assigned to his band. It had as yet been but little trenched upon as Simon had ordered that rations similar to those issued to his own men from the few granaries which had escaped destruction should be given to John's band.

"What do you think now of the prospect?" Simon asked as John and he stood together on the Tower of Phasaelus on the day after the Romans had taken possession of the lower town.

"I think, as I did at first," John said, "that nothing but a miracle can save the Temple."

"But the difficulties that the Romans have overcome," Simon said, "are as nothing to those still before them."

"That is quite true," John agreed, "and had we but a good supply of food I believe that we might hold for months; but the grain is already nearly exhausted, and cannot support even the fighting men much longer, while the inhabitants are dying from hunger. Well and strong, we might resist every attack that the Romans can make, but when we can no longer lift our swords they must overcome us. Still, as long as I can fight, I am ready to do so, in hopes that God may yet have mercy upon us, and deliver his Temple."

Chapter Sixteen

THE SUBTERRANEAN PASSAGE

For a few days after the capture of the lower city the Jews had a respite. Titus knew that famine was sapping the strength of the defenders, and that every day weakened their power of resistance. He saw that the assault upon their strong position would be attended with immense difficulty and loss, and he was desirous of saving the city from destruction. He ordered, therefore, a grand review of the troops to take place, and for four days of great army at his command—the splendid cavalry, the solid masses of the Roman infantry, and the light-armed troops and cavalry of the allies—defiled before him. The Jews, from the height of the city, watched with a feeling of dull despair the tremendous power assembled against them, and felt the hopelessness of further resistance.

An intense desire for peace reigned throughout the multitude, but John of Gischala and Simon had no thought of yielding. They believed that whatever mercy Titus might be ready to grant to the inhabitants of the town, for them and their followers there was no hope whatever of pardon, and they were firmly resolved to resist until the last. Titus, finding that no offers of submission came from the city, sent Josephus to parley with the defenders.

He could not have made a worse choice of an ambassador. Divided as the Jews were among themselves, they were united in a common hatred for the man whom they regarded as a traitor to his country, and the harangue of Josephus to the effect that resistance was unavailing and that they should submit themselves to the mercy of Titus was drowned by the execrations from the walls. In fact, in no case could his words have reached any large number of inhabitants, for he had cautiously placed himself out of bow-shot of the walls, and his words could not scarcely have reached those for whom they had been intended even if silence had been observed. His mission, therefore, was altogether unavailing.

John felt his own resolution terribly shaken by the sights which he beheld in the city. The inhabitants moved about like specters, or fell and died in the streets. He felt now that resistance had been a mistake, and that it would have been far better to have thrown open the gates when Titus appeared before them, in which case the great proportion at least of those within would have been spared, and the Temple and the city itself would have escaped destruction. He even regretted that he had marched down to take part in the defense.

Had he known how entirely exhausted were the granaries he would not have done so. He had thought that at least there would have been sufficient provisions for a siege of months, and that the patience of the Romans might have been worn out. He felt now that the sacrifice had been a useless one; but although he himself would now have raised his voice in favor of surrender, he was powerless. Even his own men would not have listened to his voice. Originally the most fervent and ardent spirits of his band, they were now inspired by a feeling of desperate enthusiasm equal to that which animated Simon and John of Gischala, and his authority would have been at once overthrown had he ventured to raise his voice in favor of surrender.

Already he had once been made to feel that there were points as to which his influence failed to have any effect whatever. He had, the morning after they retired to the upper city, spoken to his men on the subject of their store of grain. He had urged on them the horrors which were taking place before their eyes, that women and children were expiring in thousands, and that the inhabitants were suffering the extreme agonies of starvation, and had concluded by proposing that their store should be distributed among the starving women. His words had been received in silence, and then one of the captains of the companies had risen.

"What you say, John, of the sufferings which the people are undergoing is felt by us all, but I, for one, cannot agree to the proposal that we should give up our store of food. Owing to the number of us that have fallen there are still well-nigh fifty pounds a man left, which will keep us in health and strength for another two months. Were we to give it out it would not suffice for a single meal for a quarter of the people assembled here, and would delay their death but a few hours; thus it would profit them nothing, while it will enable us to maintain our strength, and maybe, at a critical moment, to hurl back the Romans from the very gates of the Temple.

"It would be wickedness, not charity, to part with our store. It would defeat the object for which we came here, and for which we are ready to die, without any real benefit to those on whom we bestowed the food."

A general chorus of approval showed that he speaker represented the opinion of his comrades. After a pause he went on:

"There is another reason why we should keep what we ourselves have brought in here. You know how the soldiers of Simon persecute the people, how they torture them to discover hidden stores of food, how they break in and rob them as they devour the secret provisions they have concealed. I know not whether hunger could drive us to act likewise, but we know the lengths to which famished men can be driven. Therefore I would that we should be spared the necessity for such cruelties to keep life together. We are all ready to die, but let it be as strong men, facing the enemy, and slaying as we fall."

Again the murmur of approval was heard, and John felt that it would be worse than useless to argue the point. He admitted to himself that there was reason in the argument, and that while a distribution of their food would give the most temporary relief only to the multitude, it would impair the efficiency of the band. The result showed him that, implicit as was the obedience given to him in all military matters, his influence had its limits, and that beyond a certain point his authority ceased.

Henceforth he remained in the house, except when he went to his post on the walls immediately adjoining, and he therefore escaped being harrowed by the sight of sufferings that he could not relieve. Each day, however, he set apart the half of his own portion of grain and gave it to the first starving woman he met when he went out.

The regulation issue of rations had now ceased, the granaries were exhausted, and henceforth Simon's troops lived entirely upon the food they extorted from the inhabitants.

John of Gischala's followers fared better. Enormous as had been the destruction of the grain, the stores in the Temple were so prodigious that they were enabled to live in comparative abundance, and so maintained their strength and power.

But the sufferings of the people increased daily, and great numbers made their escape from the city, either sallying out from unguarded posterns at night, or letting themselves down from the lower part of the walls by ropes.

Titus allowed them to pass through, but John of Gischala and Simon, with purposeless cruelty, placed guards on all the walls and gates to prevent the starving people leaving the city, although their true policy would have been to facilitate in every way the escape of all save the fighting men, and thus to husband what provisions still remained for the use of the defenders of the city.

In the daytime, when the gates were open, people went out and collected vegetables and herbs from the gardens between the walls and the Roman posts, but on their return were pitilessly robbed by the rough soldiers, who confiscated to their own use all that was brought in. The efforts to escape formed a fresh pretext to Simon and John of Gischala to plunder the wealthy inhabitants, who, under the charge of intending to fly to the Romans, were despoiled of all they had, tortured and executed. Titus soon changed his policy, and instead of allowing the deserters to make their way through, seized them and those who went out from the city to seek food, scourged, tortured, and crucified them before the walls. Sometimes as many as five hundred were crucified in a single day. This checked the desertion, and the multitude, deeming it better to die of hunger than to be tortured to death by the Romans, resigned themselves to the misery of starvation.

For seventeen days the Romans labored at their embankments, and only one attack was made upon the walls. This was carried out by the son of the King of Commagene, who had just joined the army with a chosen band, armed and attired in the Macedonan fashion. As soon as he arrived he loudly expressed his surprise at the duration of the siege. Titus, hearing this, told him that he was at perfect liberty to assault the city if he liked. This he and his men at once did, and fought with great valor, but with no success whatever, a great number of them being killed, and scarcely one escaping uninjured.

For a fortnight John had bestowed the half of his ration upon a poor women whose child was sick, and who stood at the door of her house every morning to wait his passing. One day she begged him to enter.

"I shall need no more food," she said; "thanks to God, who sent you to our city, my child is recovered and can now walk, and I intend to fly tonight from this terrible place."

"But there is no escape," John said; "the soldiers allow none to pass, and if you could pass through them the Romans would slay you."

"I can escape," the woman said; "and that is why I have called you in. My husband, who was killed by Simon's robbers three months ago, was for many years employed in working in the underground passages of the city, and in repairing the conduits which carry the water from the springs. As I often carried down his food to him when he was at work, I know every winding and turn of the underground ways.

"As you know, the ground beneath the city is honeycombed by passages whence stone was in the old time obtained for buildings.

"There are many houses which have entrance by pits into these places.

"This in one of them, and my husband took it for that convenience. From here I can find my way down to the great conduit which was built by King Hezekiah to bring the water from the upper springs of the river Gihon down into the city. Some of these waters supply the pool known as the Dragon Pool, but the main body runs down the conduit in the line of the Tyropœon Valley, and those from the Temple could in old times go down and draw water thence should the pools and cisterns fail. But that entrance has long been blocked up, for when the Temple was destroyed and the people carried away captives, the ruins covered the entrance and none knew of it.

"My husband when at work once found a passage which ran for some distance by the side of some massive masonry of old time. One of the great stones was loose, and he prized it out to see what might lie behind it; when he did so he heard the sound of running water, and passing through the hole found himself in a great conduit. This he afterward followed up, and found that it terminated at the upper end of the Valley of Hinnom in a round chamber, at the bottom of which springs bubble up.

"There was an entrance to this chamber from without through a passage. The outer exit of this was well-nigh filled up with earth, and many bushes grew there, so that none passing by would have an idea of its existence.

"When the troubles here became great he took me and showed me the conduit, and let me to the exit, saying that the time might come when I might need to fly from Jerusalem. The exit lies far beyond the camps that the Romans have planted on either side of the Valley of Hinnom; and by going out at night I and my child can make our way unseen to the hills. Since you have saved our lives I tell you of this secret, which is known, I think, to none but myself; for, after showing me the place, my husband closed up the entrance to the passage, which was before well-nigh filled up the stones.

"It may be that the time may come when you, too, will need to save yourself by flight. Now, if you will come with me I will show you the way. See, I have mixed here a pot of charcoal and water, with which you can mark the turnings and the passages, so that you will afterwards be able to find your way, for without such aid you would never be able to follow the path through its many windings after only once going through it."

John thanked the woman warmly for her offer, and they at once prepared to descend into the pit. This was situated in a cellar beneath the house, and was boarded over, so that plunderers entering to search for provisions would not discover it. Upon entering the cellar the woman lit two lamps. "They are full of oil," she said, "and I have often been sorely tempted to drink it; but I have kept it untouched, knowing that my life might some day depend on it."

Rough steps were cut in the side of the pit, and after descending some thirty feet John found himself in a long passage. The woman led the way. As they went on John was surprised at the number and extent of these passages, which crossed each other in all directions, sometimes opening into great chambers from which large quantities of stone had been taken, while he passed many shafts, like that by which they had descended, to the surface above. The woman led the way with an unfaltering step, which showed how thorough was her acquaintance with the ground, pausing when they turned down a fresh passage to make a smear at the corner of the wall with the black liquid. Presently the passage began to descend rapidly.

"We are now under the Palace of King Agrippa," she said, "and are descending by the side of the Tyropœon Valley."

Presently, turning down a small side passage, they found their way arrested by a pile of stones and rubbish. They clambered up this, removed some of the upper stones, and crawled along underneath the roof. The rubbish heap soon slanted down again, and they continued their way as before. Another turn and they were in a wider passage than those they had lately traversed.

"This is the wall of the conduit," the woman said, touching the massive masonry on her right hand. "The opening is a little further on."

Presently they arrived at a great stone lying across a passage, corresponding in size to a gap in the wall on the right. They made their way through this and found themselves in the Conduit of King Hezekiah; a stream of water ankle-deep was running through it.

"We need not go further," the woman said; "once here you cannot miss your way. It will take nigh an hour's walking through the water before you arrive at the chamber of the springs, from which there is but the one exit."

"I will come down again with you tonight," John said, "and will carry your child to the entrance. You will both need all your strength when you sally out, so as to get well beyond the Romans, who are scattered all over the country, cutting wood for their embankments. Moreover, I shall be able to see, as I come down with you, whether all the marks are plainly visible, and that there is no fear of mistake, for once lost in these passages one would never find one's way again, and there would be the choice between dying of hunger and of being found by the Romans, who will assuredly search all these passages for fugitives as they did at Jotapata. Truly I thank you with all my heart; I feel you have given me the means of saving my life; that is, if I do not fall in the fighting."

As they made their way back to the house, John examined the marks at every turning, and added to those that were not sufficiently conspicuous to catch the eye at once. When they had gained the cellar and replaced the boards the woman said:

"Why should you not also leave the city tonight? All say that there is no hope of resistance, and that John of Gischala and Simon are only bringing destruction upon all in the city by thus holding out against the Romans.

"Why should you throw away your life so uselessly?"

"I have come here to defend the Temple," John said, "and so long as the Temple stands I will resist the enemy. It may be it is useless; but no one can say what is the purpose of God, or whether he does not yet intend to save his Holy Seat; but when the Temple has fallen I shall have no more to fight for, and will then, if I can, save my life for the sake of those who love me."

That evening on his return from the wall John proceeded to the house of the woman. She was in readiness for the journey. The child, who was seven or eight years old, was dressed, and the mother had a little bundle with her valuables by her. As soon as they descended into the passage below, John offered to carry the child, but her mother refused.

"She can walk well," she said, "for a time, and you could not carry her upon your shoulder, for the passages are in many places just high enough for you to pass under without stooping. At any rate, she can walk for a time."

It was not long, however, before the child, weakened by its illness, began to drag behind, and John swung her up on his back. The marks, he found, were easily made out, and in half an hour they arrived at the entrance to the conduit. Here they were forced to walk slowly; in some places the water, owing to the channel having sunk, deepened to the knee, and other times stones had fallen from the roof and impeded their passage, and it was nearly two hours before they reached the arched chamber at the termination of the conduit. There was a stone pavement round the edge of the pool, and upon this they sat down to rest for an hour, for both John and the woman were exhausted by the labor they had undergone.

"It is time for me to be moving," the woman said, rising; "it must be nigh midnight, and I must be some miles on my way before morning. The child has walked but a short distance yet, and will do her best now when she knows that those wicked Romans will kill her and her mother if they catch them. Won't you, Mariamne?"

The child nodded; the Romans were the bogy with which Jewish children had for the last five years been frightened, and she announced her intention of walking till her feet fell off.

"I will carry you as much as I can," her mother said; "but it can only be for a short distance at a time, and I, too, am weak, and your weight is too much for me. And now God bless you, my friend," she said, turning to John; "and may he keep you safe through the dangers of the siege, and lead you to your home and parents again!"

They made their way to the end of the passage together, climbed over the rubbish which nearly blocked the entrance, crawled through the hole, and found themselves in the outer air. Thick low bushes covered the ground around them, and no sound was to be heard. John rose to his feet and looked around. Behind him, at the distance of more than a quarter of a mile, the light of the Roman watch-fires showed where the legions were encamped. Beyond and above could be seen here and there a light in the city. No sound was to be heard save the occasional call of a Roman sentinel. On the other side all was dark, for the working parties always returned to camp at night in readiness to repel any sortie the Jews might make against the camps or working parties.

"It is a very dark night," John said doubtfully. "Do you think you can find your way?"

"There are the stars," the woman replied confidently. "Besides, I was born at Bethlehem, and know the country well. I shall keep on west for a while, and then turn off into the deep valleys leading down toward Masada. God be with you!" and taking the child's hand, she emerged from the bushes and glided noiselessly away into the darkness. John set out on his return journey, which he found very much shorter than he had done coming, for the weight of a child for two hours when walking over difficult ground is trying even to a strong and active man. He carefully replaced the boards across the mouth of the pit, placed the lamps in a position so he could find them in the dark, and, upon going out of the house, closed the door carefully.

The next morning, that of the 29th of May, the Roman attack began. The Fifth and Twelfth Legions had raised embankments near the Struthion or Soapwort Pool, facing the Castle of Antonia, while the Tenth and Fifteenth raised theirs facing the great towers of Hippicus, Phasaelus, and Mariamne. They had not carried out their work unmolested, for the Jews had now learned the art of constructing and managing war machines, and had made three hundred scorpions for throwing arrows and caused terrible annoyance and great loss to the Romans. But now all was prepared. On the evening of the 28th the last stroke had been given to the embankment, and the troops stood in readiness for the attack.

Suddenly a smoke was seen stealing up round the embankments facing Antonia, and the Roman officers called back their men, not knowing what was going to occur. Then a series of mighty crashes was heard; the great embankments, with their engines and battering-rams, tottered and fell; dense smoke shot up in columns, followed rapidly by tongues of fire, and soon the vast piles of materials, collected and put together with so much pains, were blazing fiercely; while the Jews laughed and shouted in triumph upon the walls.

The moment John of Gischala perceived where the Romans were going to construct their embankments he had begun to run a mine from behind the wall toward them. When the gallery was extended under them a great excavation was hollowed out, the roof being supported by huge beams, between which were piled up pitch and other combustibles. When the Romans were seen advancing to the attack fire was applied, and as soon as the supports of the roof were burned away, the ground with the embankments upon it, fell in.

Simon, on his side, was equally ready to receive the enemy, but he trusted rather to valor than stratagem; as soon as the Roman engines facing the towers began to shake the walls Tepthaus, Megassar, and Chagiras rushed out with torches in their hands, followed by a crowd of Simon's soldiers. They drove the Romans before them, and set fire to the great machine. The Romans crowded up to the assistance of the working parties, but as they advanced they were received with showers of missiles from the walls, and attacked fiercely by the Jews, who poured out from the city in a continuous stream.

The flames spread rapidly, and seeing no hope of saving their engines and embankments, the Romans retreated to their camp. The triumphant Jews pressed hard on their rear, rushed upon the intrenchments, and assailed the guards. Numbers of these were killed, but the rest fought resolutely, while the engines on the works poured showers of missiles among the Jews. Careless of death, the assailants pressed forward, stormed the interenchment, and the Romans were on the point of flight, when Titus, who had been absent upon the other side, arrived with a strong body of troops, and fell upon the Jews.

A desperate contest ensued, but the Jews were finally driven back into the city. Their enterprise had, however, been crowned with complete success. The embankments, which had occupied the Romans seventeen days in building were destroyed, and with them the battering-rams and the great part of their engines. The work of reconstruction would be far more difficult and toilsome than at first, for the country had been denuded of timber for many miles off. Moreover, the soldiers were becoming greatly disheartened by the failure of all their attacks upon the city.

Titus summoned a council, and laid before them three plans; one for an attempt to take the city by storm; the second to repair the works and rebuild the engines; the third to blockade the city and starve it into surrender. The last was decided upon, and as a first step the whole army was set to work to build a trench and wall around the city. The work was carried on with the greatest zeal, and in three days the wall, nearly five miles in circumference, was completed. Thus there was no longer any chance of escape to the inhabitants, no more possibility of going out at night to search for food.

Now the misery of the siege was redoubled. Thousands died daily. A mournful silence hung over the city. Some died in their houses, some in the streets, some crawled to the cemeteries and expired there, some sat upon their house-tops with their eyes fixed upon the Temple until they sank back dead. No one had strength to dig graves, and the dead bodies were thrown from the walls into the ravines below. The high-priest Matthias, who had admitted Simon and his followers into the city, was suspected of being in communication with the Romans, and he and his three sons were led out on to the wall, and executed in sight of the besiegers, while fifteen of the members of the Sanhedrim were executed at the same time.

These murders caused indignation even on the part of some of Simon's men, and one Judas, with ten others, agreed to deliver one of the towers to the enemy, but the Romans, rendered cautious by the treachery which had before been practiced, hesitated to approach; and before they were convinced that the offer was made in good faith Simon discovered what was going on, and the eleven conspirators were executed upon the walls, and their bodies thrown over.

Despair drove many again to attempt desertion. Some of these, on reaching the Roman lines, were spared, but many more were killed, for the sake of the money supposed to be concealed upon them. Up to the 1st of July it was calculated that well-nigh six hundred thousand had perished, in addition to the vast numbers buried in the cemetery and the great heaps of dead before the walls. Great numbers of the houses had become tombs, the inhabitants shutting themselves up and dying quietly together.

But while trusting chiefly to famine, the Romans had labored steadily on at their military engines, although obliged to fetch the timber for ten miles, and at the beginning of July the battering-rams began to play against Antonia. The Jews sallied out, but this time with less fury than usual, and they were repulsed without much difficulty by the Romans. All day long the battering-rams thundered against the wall, while men, protected by hurdles and penthouses, labored to dislodge the stones at the foot of the walls, in spite of the storm of missiles hurled down from above.

By nightfall they had got out four large stones. It happened that these stones stood just over the part under which John of Gischala had driven his mine when he destroyed the Roman embankments, and thus, doubly weakened, the wall fell with a crash during the night. John, however, had built another wall in the rear; and the Romans rushed to the assault of the breach in the morning, they found a new line of defense confronting them. Titus addressed the troops, and called for volunteers. Sabinus, a Syrian, volunteered for the attack and eleven men followed him.

In spite of the storm of missiles he reached the top of the wall. The Jews, believing that many were behind him, turned to fly, but his foot slipped, and he fell, and before he could regain his feet the Jews turned round upon him and slew him. Three of his companions fell beside him on top of the wall, and the rest were carried back wounded to camp.

Two days later, in the middle of the night, twenty Roman soldiers, with a standard-bearer and trumpeter, crept silently up to the breach, surprised and slew the watch. The trumpeter blew the charge, and the Jews, believing that the whole Roman army was upon them, fled in a sudden panic. Titus at once advanced with his men, stormed the new wall, entered the Castle of Antonia, and then advanced along the cloisters which connected it with the Temple; but John of Gischala had by this time arrived at the spot and opposed a desperate resistance to the assault, until Simon, crossing from the upper city by the bridge, came to his assistance, and John, finding that the Temple was attacked, also led his band across.

For ten hours the struggle raged. Vast numbers fell on both sides, till the dead formed a bank between the combatants. Titus, finding that even the courage and discipline of his troops did not avail against the desperate resistance of the Jews, at last called them off from the assault, well satisfied with having captured Antonia. During the fight the Romans had several times nearly penetrated into the Temple. Indeed, a centurion, named Julian, a man of great strength, courage, and skill at arms, had charged the Jews with such fury that he had made his way alone as far as the inner court, when his mailed shoes slipped on the marble pavement, and he fell, and the Jews, rushing back, slew him, after a desperate resistance to the end.

Titus commanded that the fortress of Antonia should be leveled to the ground, and then sent Josephus with a message to John of Gischala, offering him free egress for himself and his men if he would come out to fight outside, in order that the Temple might be saved further defilement. John replied by curses upon Josephus, whom he denounced as a traitor, and concluded that he feared not that the city should be taken, for it was the city of God. Then Titus sent for a number of persons of distinction, who had from time to time made their escape from the city, and these attempted in vain to persuade the people, if not to surrender, at least to spare the Temple from defilement and ruin. Even the Roman soldiers were adverse to an attack upon a place so long regarded as preeminently holy, and Titus himself harangued the Jews.

"You have put up a barrier," he said, "to prevent strangers from polluting your Temple. This the Romans have always respected. We have allowed you to put to death all who violated its precincts, yet you defile it yourselves with blood and carnage. I call on your gods—I call on my whole army—I call upon the Jews who are with me—I call on yourselves—to witness that I do not force you to this crime. Come forth and fight in any other place, and no Roman shall violate your sacred edifice." But John of Gischala and the Zealots would hear of no surrender. They doubted whether Titus would keep his promise, and feared to surrender the stronghold which was now their last hope. Above all, they believed that God would yet interfere to save his Temple. Titus, finding that the garrison were obstinate, raised his voice and called out:

"John, whom I met near Hebron, if you are there, bear witness that I have striven to keep my oath. I will strive to the end; but blame me not if, not through my fault, but by the obstinacy of these men, destruction comes upon the Temple."

John, who was standing within hearing, called out:

"I am here, Titus, and I bear witness, yet, I pray you strive to the end to keep the oath which you swore to me."

"What is this oath, John?" Simon, who was standing close by, asked, "What compact have you with the Roman general?"

"We met in battle alone," John said quietly, "and it chanced that he fell. I might have slain him, but it came to me that I were better to try to save the Temple than to slay one of its enemies, and therefore swore him to save the Temple if it lay in his power. He has offered to spare it. It lay with you and John of Gischala to save the Temple from destruction by accepting his terms. You have not done so. If the Temple is destroyed it is by the obstinacy of its defenders, not by the cruelty of the Romans."

"It would be madness to accept his offer," Simon said angrily. "Titus knows well that in the plains we should be no match for his troops. Did you ever hear before of a garrison giving up a position so strong that it could not be taken from them, and going out to fight beyond the walls? Besides, who can tell that the Romans will keep their promises? Once we were at their mercy they might level the Temple."

"In that case the sin would be upon their heads. Besides, there is no occasion to retire beyond the walls. Why should not all the fighting men retire into the upper city, and leave the Temple to God? If it is his will that the Romans should destroy it, they will do so. If it is his will that they should respect it, they will do so. He can save or destroy at his will. If we retreat to the upper town and break down the bridge after us, they could never take it."

"And how long could we hold out?" Simon said with a hard laugh. "Is there a day's food left in the city? If there is my men are less sharp than I give them credit for. No, we will fight here to the end for the Temple, and the sooner the Romans attack the better, for if they delay many days there is not a single man will have strength enough to lift a sword."

Chapter Seventeen

THE CAPTURE OF THE TEMPLE

Although abhorring the general conduct of Simon and John of Gischala, and believing that conditions could be made with the Romans which would save the Temple, John still retained the hope cherished by every Jew that God would yet himself save Jerusalem, as in the old times. He was conscious that the people had forfeited all right to expect his aid; that by their wickedness and forgetfulness of him, and more especially by the frightful scenes which had desecrated the city and Temple during the last four years, they must have angered God beyond all hope of forgiveness. Still the punishment which had been inflicted was already so terrible that he, like others, hoped that God's anger might yet relent, as it had done in old times, and that a remnant might yet be spared.

But above all, their hope lay in the belief that the Temple was the actual abode of the Lord, and that though he might suffer the whole people to perish for their sins, he would yet protect at the last his own sanctuary. Surely, John thought as he stood on the roof of the Temple, this glorious building can never be meant to be destroyed.

The Temple occupied a square six hundred feet every way. The lofty rock on which it stood had been cased with solid masonry, so that it rose perpendicularly from the plain. On the top of this massive foundation was built a strong and lofty wall round the whole area. Within the wall was a spacious double cloister, fifty-two and one-half feet broad, supported by one hundred and sixty two columns. On the south side the cloister was one hundred and five feet wide, being a triple cloister, and was here called the King's Cloister. Within the area surrounded by the cloisters was an open court paved with marble; this was the Court of the Gentiles, and was separated from the second court, that of the Jews, by a stone railing five feet high.

An ascent of fourteen steps led to a terrace seventeen and one-half feet wide, beyond which rose the wall of the inner court; this was seventy feet high on the outside, forty-four feet on the inside. Round the inner court was another range of cloisters. There were ten gates in the inner court. The doors of nine of these gateways were fifty-two and one-half feet high, and half that breadth; the gateways rose to the height of seventy feet. The tenth, usually called the Beautiful Gate of the Temple, was larger than the rest, the gateway being eighty-seven and one-half feet in height, the doors seventy feet.

In the center of the inner court was the Temple itself. The great porch was one hundred and seventy-five feet in width, the gateway tower one hundred and thirty-two feet high and forty-three feet wide, and through it was seen the Beautiful Gate. The Temple itself was built of white marble, and the roof was covered with sharp golden spikes.

Now that it was evident that on the side of the Temple alone would the enemy make an attack, the division between Simon and John of Gischala's men was no longer kept up. All gathered for the defense of the Temple. The Jews kept up a vigilant watch, for the Romans could assemble in great force in Antonia unseen by them, and could advance under cover by the cloisters which flanked the platform connecting Antonia with the Temple on either side. The interval between Antonia and the Temple was but three hundred feet. The cloisters were considered to form part of the Temple, and the Jews were therefore reluctant to destroy them, although they greatly facilitated the attack of the Romans.

Finding that his offers were all rejected, Titus spent seven days in the destruction of a large portion of Antonia, and then prepared for a night attack. As the whole army could not make the assault, thirty men were picked from each hundred. Tribunes were appointed over each thousand, Cerealis being chosen to command the whole. Titus himself mounted a watch-tower in Antonia in order that he might see and reward each act of bravery. The assault began between two and three o'clock in the morning. The Jews were on the watch, and as soon as the massive columns moved forward the cries of the guards gave the alarm, and the Jews sleeping in and around the Temple seized their arms and rushed down to the defense.

For a time the Romans had the advantage; the weight of their close formation enabled them to press forward against the most obstinate resistance, and even in the darkness there was no fear of mistaking fried for foe; while the Jews, fighting in small parties, often mistook each other for enemies, and as many fell by the swords of their friends as by those of the enemy. The loss was all the greater since the troops of John of Gischala and Simon had no common password, and, coming suddenly upon each other, often fought desperately before they discovered their mistake; but as daylight began to break these mistakes became less frequent. The presence and example of their leaders animated the Jews to the greatest exertions; while the knowledge that Titus was watching them inspired the Romans with even more than their usual courage and obstinacy.

For nine hours the conflict raged, and then the Romans, unable to make the slightest submission upon the resistance of the Jews, fell back again into Antonia. Finding that in hand-to-hand conflict his soldiers could not overcome the Jews, Titus ordered the erection of small embankments, two on the platform between the cloisters, the other two outside the cloister walls. But the work proceeded slowly owing to the difficulty of procuring wood. The Jews as usually hindered the work as much as possible with showers of missiles, and attempted to create a diversion by a sortie and attack upon the camp of the Tenth Legion on the Mount of Olives. This, however, was repulsed by the Romans without great difficulty.

As the cloisters leading to Antonia afforded great assistance to the Romans in their attacks the Jews set fire to the end of the cloisters touching the Temple wall, and a length of from twenty to thirty feet of each cloister was destroyed. The Romans destroyed a further portion, so as to afford more room for the men at work upon the embankments. The action of the Jews was to a certain extent a necessity, but it depressed the spirits of the inhabitants, for there was a prophecy, "When square the walls, the Temple falls!" Hitherto Antonia and the connecting cloisters had been considered as forming part of the Temple and had given it an irregular form, but the destruction of these cloisters left the Temple standing a massive square.

The embankments presently rose above the height of the wall, and it was evident that this would soon be taken. The Jews retired from the roof of the cloister facing the embankment as if despairing of further resistance, but they had previously stored great quantities of combustibles in the space between the cedar roof of the cloisters and the upper platform. The Romans on the embankment, seeing that the Jews had retired, without waiting for orders ran down, and planting ladders scaled the wall.

The Jews set up cries as if of despair, and the Romans poured up on to the walls until a great mass of men were collected on the roof of the cloister; then on a sudden flames shot up in all directions beneath their feet, and they found themselves enveloped in a sea of fire. Many were burned or smothered by the smoke, some stabbed themselves with their swords, some leaped down into the outer court and were there killed by the Jews, many jumped down outside the walls and were picked up dead or with broken limbs, others ran along upon the top of the walls until they were shot down by the Jewish missiles. But one man seems to have escaped. A soldier named Artorius, standing on the wall, shouted to the Romans below, "Whoever catches me shall be my heir." A soldier ran forward to accept the terms, Artorius jumped down upon him, killing him by his fall, but himself escaping unhurt.

The fire extended along the whole of the western cloister, and the northern cloister was next day burned by the Romans, and thus on the west and north sides the inner Temple was now exposed to the invader.

All this time famine had been continuing its work. The fighting men were so weakened that they had scarcely strength to drag their limbs along or to hold their weapons, while horrible tales were told of the sufferings of such of the inhabitants who still survived—one woman maddened by despair, cooking and eating her own infant. Occasionally a baggage animal or a Roman cavalry horse strayed near the walls, when a crowd of famishing wretches would pour out, kill and devour it. Titus, however, cut off even this occasional supply by ordering a solder whose horse had thus fallen into the hands of the Jews to be put to death for his carelessness.

John's band had been greatly diminished in number in the two days they had been fighting opposite Antonia. The stores they had brought to the city were now exhausted, although for a long time only the smallest amount had been issued daily to eke out the handfuls of grain still served out to each of the fighting men. A few only had in their sufferings refused to obey the orders of John and their officers, and had joined the bands of Simon and John of Gischala in the revolting cruelties which they practiced to extort food from the inhabitants. These had not yet been allowed to rejoin the band, which was no reduced to a little over fifty—stern, gaunt, and famineworn figures, but still unshaken in their determination to fight to the end.

The Romans now pushed on a bank from the western wall across the smoldering ruins of the cloister and inner court, and a battering-ram began to play against the inner Temple; but after six days' efforts, and bringing up their heaviest battering-ram, the Romans gave it up in despair, for the huge stones which formed the masonry of the wall defied even the ponderous machines which the Romans brought to play against it. An embankment from the northern side was also carried across the outer court to the foot of the most easterly of the four northern gates of the inner Temple.

Still anxious to save the Temple itself and its cloisters if possible, Titus would not resort to the use of fire, but ordered his men to force the gate with crowbars and levers. After great efforts a few of the stones of the threshold were removed; but the gates supported by the massive walls and the props behind defied all their efforts.

Titus now ordered his soldiers to carry the walls by storm. Ladders were brought up, and the soldiers, eager for revenge upon the foe who had so long baffled and humiliated them, sprang to the assault with shouts of exultation. The Jews offered no resistance until the Romans reached the top of the wall; but as they leaped down on to the roof of the cloister they threw themselves upon them. Numbers were slain as they stepped off the ladders on to the wall, and many of the ladders were hurled backward, crushing the soldiers crowded upon them on the pavement beneath.

Then Titus ordered the standards of the legions to be carried up, thinking that the soldiers would rally round these, the emblems of military honor. The Jews, however, permitted the standards and numbers of the legionaries to ascend on to the roof of the cloisters, and then again fell upon them with such fury that the Romans were overpowered, the standards were taken, and their defenders killed. Not one of the Romans who had mounted the wall retired from it.

Titus could no longer resist the appeals of his infuriated soldiers, who, maddened by the losses they had suffered and the disgrace of the loss of the standards, could not understand why this loss was entailed upon them when such an easy way of destroying the gate and entering the Temple was in their power. Most reluctantly Titus gave the permission they clamored for, and allowed his troops to set fire to the gate. The dry wood-work caught like tinder, and the flames mounted instantly. The silver plates which covered the wood-work melted and ran down in streams, and the fire at once communicated with the cloisters inside the wall.

Appalled at the sight of the inner court in flames, the Jews stood despairing, while the shouts of triumph of the Romans rose high in the air. During the rest of the day and all through the night the conflagration continued and extended all round the cloisters. Thus the Temple itself was surrounded by a ring of fire.

The next day, the 4th of August, Titus called a council of his generals to deliberate on the fate of the Temple. There were present besides Titus, Tiberias Alexandria, the second in command; the commanders of the Fifth, Tenth, and Fifteenth Legions; Fronto, the commander of the Alexandrian troops; and Marcus Antonius Julianus, the procurator of Judea.

Some were for leveling the Temple to the ground; others advised that, if abandoned by the Jews, it might be preserved, but it defended as a citadel it ought to be destroyed. Titus listened to the opinions of the others and then declared his own, which was, that whatever the use the Jews made of it, it ought to be preserved. Alexander, Cerealis, and Fronto went over to the opinion of Titus, and therefore by a majority of one it was agreed that the Temple should be spared, however fiercely the Jews might resist. Orders were given to prevent the fire spreading to the Temple, and to clear the ground for an assault against it.

The 5th of August broke. It was on that day that the Temple of Solomon had been burned by Nebuchadnezzar; but the courage of the Jews was not depressed by the omen. The brief pause had enabled them to recover from the despair which they had felt in seeing the inner cloister in flames, and at eight o'clock in the morning, sallying from the Eastern Gate, they rushed down upon the Romans. The latter formed in close order, and, covered by their shields, received the onslaught calmly. But so desperately did the Jews fight, and in such numbers did they pour out from the Temple, that the Romans had begun to give way, when Titus arrived with great reinforcements; but even then it was not until one o'clock that the Jews were driven back again into the walls of the inner Temple.

Titus, having seen his troops victorious, retired to his tent, and the soldiers continued their work of clearing the platform and extinguishing the smoldering fire of the cloisters. Suddenly the Jewish bands burst out again, and another deadly struggle commenced. Then one of the Roman soldiers, seizing a burning brand from the cloisters, hurled it into the window of one of the side chambers that inclosed the Temple on the north.

In the furious struggle that was going on none noticed the action, and it was not until the flames were seen rushing out of the window that the Jews perceived what had happened. With a cry of anguish they discontinued the conflict, and rushed back to try and extinguish the flames. But the wood-work, dried by the intense heat of the August sun, was ripe for burning, and in spite of the most desperate efforts the fire spread rapidly.

The news that the Temple was on fire reached Titus, and starting up, accompanied by his body-guard of spearmen, commanded by Liberatus, he hastened to the spot. His officers followed him, and as the news spread the whole of the Roman legionaries rushed with one accord to the spot. Titus pushed forward into the first court of the inner Temple, the Court of the Women, and then into the inner court, and by the shouts and gestures implored his own soldiers and the Jews alike to assist in subduing the flames.

But the clamor and din drowned his voice. The legionaries, pouring in after him, added to the confusion. So great was the crowd that many of the soldiers were crushed to death, while many fell among the ruins of the still smoldering cloisters and were either smothered or burned. Those who reached the sanctuary paid no attention to the remonstrances, commands, or even threats of Titus, but shouted to those in front of them to complete the work of destruction.

Titus pressed forward with his guards to the vestibule, and then entered, first the Holy, and then the Holy of Holies. After one glance at the beauty and magnificence of the marvelous shrine he rushed back and again implored his soldiers to exert themselves to save it, and ordered Liberatus to strike down any who disobeyed. But the soldiers were now altogether beyond control, and were mad with triumph, fury, and hate. One of the body-guard, as Titus left the sanctuary, seized a brand and applied it to the wood-work. The flames leaped up, and soon the whole Temple was wrapped in fire.

The soldiers spread through the building, snatching at the golden ornaments and vessels, and slaying all they met, unarmed men, priests in their robes, women and children. Many of the Jews threw themselves into the flames. Some of the priests found their way on to the broad wall of the inner Temple, where they remained until compelled by famine to come down, when they were all executed. Six thousand of the populace took refuge on the roof of the Royal Cloister along the south side of the outer Temple. The Romans set fire to this, and every soul upon it perished.

As soon as they felt that their efforts to extinguish the fire were vain and that the Temple was indeed lost, John of Gischala, Simon, and John called their men together, and issuing out, fell with the fury of desperation upon the dense ranks of the Roman soldiers in the inner court, and, in spite of their resistance, cut their way through to the outer court and gained the bridge leading from the southwest corner across the Valley of the Tyropœon to the upper city, and were therefore for a time in safety.

John, bewildered, exhausted, and heart-broken from the terrible events of the past few days, staggered back to his house and threw himself on his couch and lay there for a long time crushed by the severity of the blow. Until now he had hoped that Titus would in the end spare the Temple, but he recognized now that it was the obstinacy of the Jews that had brought about its destruction. "It was God's will that it should perish," he said to himself; "and Titus could no more save it than I could do." After some hours he roused himself and descended to the room now occupied by the remnant of the band. Jonas and ten others alone were gathered there. Some had thrown themselves down on the ground, some sat in attitudes of utter dejection; several were bleeding from wounds received in the desperate fight of the morning, others were badly burned in the desperate efforts they had made to extinguish the flames. Exhausted by want of food, worn out by their exertions, filled with despair at the failure of their last hopes, the members of the little band scarce looked up when their leader entered.

"My friends," he said, "listen to me, if but for the last time. We at least have nothing to reproach ourselves with. We have fought for the Temple to the last; and if we failed to save it, it is because it was the will of God that it should perish. At any rate, our duty is done. God has not given us our lives, and preserved them through so many fights, that we should throw them away. It is our duty now to save our lives if we can. Now that the Temple is fallen, we are called upon to do no more fighting. Let the bands of John of Gischala and Simon fight to the last. They are as wild beasts inclosed in the snare of the hunter, and they merit a thousand deaths, for it is they who have brought Jerusalem to this pass, they who robbed and murdered the population, they who have destroyed the granaries which would have enable the city to exist for years, they who refused the terms by which the Temple might have been saved, they who have caused its destruction in spite of the efforts of Titus to preserve it—they are the authors of all this ruin and woe; they have lived as wild beasts, so let them die! But there is no reason why we should die with them, for their guilt is not upon our heads. We have done our duty in fighting for the Temple, and have robbed and injured none; therefore, I say, let us save our lives."

"Would you surrender to the Romans?" one of the band asked indignantly. "Do you, whom we have followed, counsel us to become traitors?"

"It is not treachery to surrender when one can no longer resist," John said quietly. "But I am not thinking of surrendering; I am thinking of passing out of the city into the country around. But first let us eat. I see you look surprised; but although the store we brought hither is long since exhausted, there is still a last reserve. I bought it with all the money that I had with me from one of Simon's men upon the day when we came hither from the lower town. He had gained it, doubtless, in wanton robbery, for at that time the fighting men had plenty of food; but as it was his I bought it, thinking that the time might come when one meal might mean life to many of us. I have never touched it, but it remains where I hid it in my chamber. I will fetch it now."

John ascended to his chamber and brought down a bag containing about fifteen pounds of flour.

"Let us make a bread of this," he said. "It will give us each a good meal now, and there will be enough left to provide food for each during the first day's journey."

The exhausted men seemed inspired with new life at the sight of the food. No thought of asking how they were to pass through the Roman lines occurred to them. The idea of satisfying their hunger overpowered all other feelings.

The door was closed to keep out intruders. Dough was made and a fire kindled with pieces of wood dry as tinder so that no smoke should attract the eyes of those who were constantly on the lookout for such a sign that some family was engaged in cooking. The flat dough-cakes were placed over the glowing embers, the whole having been divided into twenty-four portions. Some of the men could hardly wait until their portions were baked, but John urged upon them that, were they to eat it in a half-cooked state, the consequences might be very serious after their prolonged fast. Still none of them could resist breaking off little pieces to stay their craving.

"Let us eat slowly," John said when the food was ready. "The more slowly we eat the further it will go. When it is eaten we will take a sleep for four hours to regain our strength. There is no fear of our being called upon to aid in the defense. The Romans must be as exhausted as we are; and they will need thought and preparation before they attack our last stronghold, which is far stronger than any they have yet taken. If we had food we could hold Mount Zion against them for months."

As soon as the meal was over all lay down to sleep. None had asked any questions as to how their escape was to be effected. The unexpected meal which John's forethought had prepared for them had revived all their confidence in him, and they were ready to follow him wherever he might take them. It was night when John called them to awake, but the glare of the vast pile of the burning Temple lit up every object; the brightness was almost equaled that of day.

"It is time," John said as the men rose to their feet and grasped their arms. "I trust that we shall have no occasion to use weapons; but we will carry them, so that if we should fall into the hands of the Romans we may fall fighting, and not die by the torments that they inflict upon those who fall into their hands. If I could obtain a hearing so as to be brought before Titus he might give us our lives, but I will not trust to that. In the first place, they would cut us down like hunted animals did they come upon us; and in the second, I would not now owe my life to the clemency of the Romans."

A fierce assent was given by his followers.

"Now," John went on, "let each take his piece of bread and put it in his bosom. Leave your bucklers and javelins behind you, but take your swords. Jonas, bring a brand from the fire. Now let us be off."

None of those with him except Jonas had the least idea where he was going; but he had instructed the lad of the secret of the pit, and one day had taken him down the passages to the aqueduct.

"You and I found safety before, Jonas, together, and I trust may do so again; but should anything happen to me, you will now have the means of escape."

"If you die I will die with you, master," Jonas said. And indeed in the fights he had always kept close to John, following every movement and ready to dash forward when his leader was attacked by more than one enemy, springing upon them like a wild cat and burying his knife in their throats. It was to his watchful protection and ready aid that John owed it that he had passed through so many combats comparatively unharmed.

"Not so, Jonas," he said, in answer to the lad's declaration that he would die with him. "It would be no satisfaction to me that you should share my fate, but a great one to know that you would get away safely. If I fall I charge you to pass out by this underground way, and to carry to my father and mother and Mary the news that I have fallen fighting to the last in the defense of the Temple. Tell them that I thought of them to the end, and that I sent you to them to be with them, and to be to my father and mother a son until they shall find for Mary a husband who may fill my place and be the stay of their old age. My father will treat you as an adopted son for my sake, and will bestow upon you a portion of the lands. You have been as a brother to me, Jonas; and I pray you promise me to carry out my wishes."

Jonas had reluctantly given the pledge, but from that hour until John had declared that he would fight no more, Jonas had been moody and silent. Now, however, as he walked behind his friend, his face was full of satisfaction. There was no chance now that he would have to take home the news of his leader's death. Whatever befell them, they would share together. They soon reached the door of the house in which the pit was situated. It was entered and the door closed behind them. The lamps were then lit. John led the way to the cellar and bad the men remove the boards.

"I will go first with one of the lamps," he said. "Do you, Jonas, take the other end and come last in the line. Keep close together, so that the light may be sufficient for all to see."

Strengthened by the meal and by their confidence in John's promise to lead them through the Romans, the band felt like new men, and followed John with their usual light active gait as he led the way. Not a word was spoken till they reached the hole leading into the aqueduct.

"This is the Conduit of King Hezekiah," John said. "When we emerge at the other end we shall be beyond the Roman lines."

Exclamations of satisfaction burst from the men. Each had been wondering, as he walked, where their leader was taking them. All knew that the ground beneath Jerusalem was honeycombed by caves and passages; but that their leader could not intend to hide there was evident, for they had but one meal with them. But that any of these passages should debouch beyond the Roman lines had not occurred to them.

Each had thought that the passages they were following would probably lead out at the foot of the wall into the Valley of Hinnom or of Jehoshaphat, and that John intended to creep with them up to the foot of the Roman wall, and to trust to activity and speed to climb it and make their way through the guard placed there to cut off fugitives. But none had even hoped that they would be able to pass the wall of circumvallation without a struggle.

An hour's walking brought them to the chamber over the springs.

"Now," John said, "we will rest for half an hour before we sally out. Let each man eat half of the food he has brought with him. The rest he must keep till tomorrow, for we shall have to travel many miles before we can reach a spot that the Romans have not laid desolate, and where we can procure food. I trust," he went on, "that we shall be altogether unnoticed. The sentries may be on the alert on their wall, for they will think it likely that many may be trying to escape from the city, but all save those on duty will be either asleep after their toils or feasting in honor of their success. The fact, too, of the great glare of light over Jerusalem will render the darkness more intense when they look in the other direction. But if we should be noticed, it is best that we should separate and scatter in the darkness, each flying for his life and making his way home as best he may; if we are not seen, we will keep together. There is no fear of meeting with any Roman bands when we are once fairly away. The parties getting wood will have been warned by the smoke of what has taken place, and will have hurried back to gain their share of the spoil."

At the end of the half-hour John rose to his feet and led the way along the passage to the entrance. When he came to the spot where it was nearly blocked up he blew out his light and crawled forward over the rubbish until he reached the open air. The others followed until all were beside him, then he rose to his feet. The Temple was not visible, but the whole sky seemed on fire above Jerusalem, and the outline of the three great towers of the Palace of Herod and of the buildings of the upper city stood black against the glare.

There was no sign of life or movement near as with a quick, noiseless step the little party stole away. None of them knew more than the general direction which they had to follow, but the glare of the great fire served as a guide as to their direction, and even at this distance made objects on the ground plainly visible, so that they were enabled to pick their way among the stumps of the fallen plantations and orchards, through gardens, and by ruined villas and houses, until they reached the edge of the plateau, and plunged down into the valleys descending to the Dead Sea. After walking for two hours John called a halt.

"We can walk slowly now," he said, "and avoid the risk of breaking our legs among the rocks. We are safe here, and had best lie down until morning, and then resume our way. There is no fear whatever of the Romans sending out parties for days. They have the upper city to take yet, and the work of plunder and division of the spoil to carry out. We can sleep without anxiety.

It was strange to them all to lie down to sleep among the stillness of the mountains after the din and turmoil of the siege, when at any moment they might be called upon to leap up to repel an attack; but few of them went to sleep for some time. The dull feeling of despair, the utter carelessness of life, the desire for death and the end of trouble which had so long oppressed them, these had passed away now that they were free and in the open air, and the thoughts of the homes they had never thought to see again, and the loved ones who would greet them on their return as men who had almost come back from the dead, fell upon them. They could go back with heads erect and clear consciences. They had fought so long as the Temple stood. They had over and over again faced the Romans hand to hand without giving way a foot. They had taken no share in the evil deeds in the city, and had wronged and plundered no one. They did not return as conquerors, but that was the will of God and no fault of theirs.

At daybreak they were on their feet again, and now struck off more to the left, following mountain paths among the hills, until at last they came down to the plain within half a mile of the upper end of the Dead Sea. John here called his companions round him.

"Here, my friends," he said, "I think it were best that we separated, laying aside our swords, and singly or in pairs finding the way back to our homes. We know not in what towns there may be Roman garrisons or where we may meet parties of their soldiers traversing the country. Alone we shall attract no attention. One man may conceal himself behind a tree or in the smallest bush, but the sight of a party together would assuredly draw them upon us, therefore it were best to separate. Some of you will find it shorter to cross the ford of the Jordan there miles away, while others had best follow this side of the river."

All agreed that this would be the safer plan, and after a short talk each took leave of his leader and comrades and strode away, until Jonas alone remained with John.

"Will you cross the river, John, or follow this side?" Jonas asked.

"I think we had best keep on this side, Jonas; on the other the country is hilly and the villages few. Here at least we can gather fruit and corn as we go from the deserted gardens and fields, and two days' walking will take us to Tarichea. We can cross there or take a boat up the lake."

After waiting until the last of their comrades had disappeared from sight John and his companion continued their way, keeping about half-way between Jericho and the Jordan. They presently bore to the left until on the great road running north from Jericho. This they followed until nightfall, rejoicing in the grapes and figs which they picked by the roadside, where but a few months since little villages had nestled thickly. Just before darkness fell they came upon a village, which, although deserted, had not been burned, probably owing to some body of Roman soldiers having taken up their post there for a time. They entered one of the houses, lay down, and were soon fast asleep.

Chapter Eighteen

SLAVES

John was roused from sleep by being roughly shaken. He sprang to his feet, and found a number of men, some of whom were holding torches, in the room. Two of these had the appearance of merchants. The others were armed, and by their dress seemed to be Arabs.

"What are you doing here?" one of the men asked him.

"We are peaceful travelers," John said, "injuring no one, and came in here to sleep the night."

"You look like peaceful travelers!" the man replied. "You have two wounds yet unhealed on your head. Your companion has one of his arms bandaged. You are either robbers or some of the cut-throats who escaped from Jerusalem. You may think it lucky you have fallen into my hands instead of that of the Romans, who would have finished you off without a question. Bind them," he said, turning to his men.

Resistance was useless. The hands of John and Jonas were tied behind their backs, and they were taken outside the house. Several fires were burning in the road and lying down there three or four hundred men and women, while several men with spears and swords stood as a guard over them. John saw at once that he had fallen into the hands of a slave dealer, one of the many who had come from various parts to purchase the Jews whom the Romans sold as slaves, and already the multitude sold was so vast that it had reduced the price of slaves throughout Italy, Egypt, and the East to one-third of their former value. There were, however, comparatively few able-bodied men among them. In almost every case the Romans had put these to the sword, and the slave-dealers, finding John and Jonas, had congratulated themselves on the acquisition, knowing well that no complaint that the captives might make would be listened to, and that their story would not be believed even if they could get to tell it to any one of authority. John and Jonas were ordered to lie down with the rest, and were told that if they made any attempt to escape they would be scourged to death.

"The villains!" Jonas muttered as they lay down. "Is it not enough to drive one mad to think that after having escaped the Romans we should fall into the hands of these rogues!"

"We must not grumble at fate. Hitherto, Jonas, we have been marvelously preserved. First of all, we two were alone saved from Jotapata, then we with ten others alone out of six hundred escaped alive from Jerusalem. We have reason for thankfulness rather than repining. We have been delivered out of the hands of death; and remember that I have the ring of Titus with me, and that when the time comes this will avail us."

From the day the siege had begun John had carried the signet-ring of Titus, wearing it on his toe, concealed by the bands of his sandals. He knew that were he to fall into the bands of the Romans he would get no opportunity of speaking, but, even if not killed at once, would be robbed of any valuable he might possess, and that his assertion that the ring was a signet which Titus himself had given him would, even if listened to, be received with incredulity. He had therefore resolved to keep it concealed, and to produce it only when a favorable opportunity seemed to offer.

"At any rate, Jonas, let us practice patience and be thankful that we are still alive."

In the morning the cavalcade got into motion. John found that the majority of his fellow-captives were people who had been taken captive when Titus for the second time obtained possession of the inner city. They had been sent up to Tiberias and there sold, and their purchaser was now taking them down to Egypt.

The men were mostly past middle age, and would have been of little value as slaves had it not been that they were all craftsmen, workers in stone or metal, and would therefore fetch a fair price if sold to masters of these crafts. The rest were women and children. The men were attached to each other by cords, John and Jonas being placed at some distance apart, and one of the armed guards placed himself near each, as there was far more risk of active and determined young men trying to make their escape than of the others doing so, especially after the manner in which they had been kidnapped. All their clothes were taken from them save their loin-cloths, and John trembled lest he should be ordered also to take off his sandals, for his present captors would have no idea of the value of the ring, but would seize it for its setting.

Fortunately, however, this was not the case. The guards all wore sandals, and had therefore no motive in taking those of the captives, especially as they were old and worn. The party soon turned off from the main road and struck across the hills to the west, and John bitterly regretted that he had not halted for the night a few miles further back than he did, in which case he would have avoided the slave-dealers' caravan.

The heat was intense, and John pitied the women and children, compelled to keep up with the rest. He soon proposed to a woman who was burdened with a child about two years old to place it on his shoulders, and as the guard saw in this a proof that their new captives had no idea of endeavoring to escape they offered no objection to the arrangement, which, indeed, seemed so good to them that as the other mothers became fatigued they placed the children on the shoulders of the male prisoners loosing the bands of the latter in order that they might prevent the little ones from losing their balance.

The caravan halted for the night at Sichem, and the next day crossed Mount Gerizim to Bethsalisa, and then went off to Jaffa. Here the slave-dealers hired a ship and embarked the slaves. They were crowded closely together, but otherwise were not unkindly treated, being supplied with an abundance of food and water, for it was desirable that they should arrive in the best possible condition at Alexandria, whither they were bound.

Fortunately the weather was fine, and in six days they reached their destination. Alexandria was at that time the largest city, next to Rome herself, upon the shores of the Mediterranean. It had contained a very large Jewish population prior to the great massacre five years before, and even now there were a considerable number remaining. The merchant had counted upon this, and, indeed, had it not been for the number of Jews scattered among the various cities of the East the price of slaves would have fallen even lower than it did. But the Jewish residents, so far as they could afford it, came forward to buy their country men and women in order to free them from slavery.

When, therefore, the new arrivals were exposed in the market many assuring messages reached them from their compatriots, telling them to keep up their courage, for friends would look after them. The feeling against the Jews was still too strong for those who remained in Alexandria to appear openly in the matter, and they therefore employed intermediaries, principally Greeks and Cretans, to buy up the captives.

The women with children were the first purchased, as the value of these was not great; then some of the older men, who were unfit for much work, were taken; then there was a pause, for already many cargoes of captives had reached Alexandria, and the resources of their benevolent countrymen were becoming exhausted. No one had yet bid for John or Jonas, as the slave-dealers had placed a high price upon them as being strong and active and fitted for hard work. Their great fear was that they should be separated, and John had over and over again assured his companion that should he, as he hoped, succeed in getting himself sent to Titus, and so be freed, he would, before proceeding home, come to Egypt and purchase his friend's freedom.

The event they feared, however, did not happen. One day a Roman, evidently of high rank, came into the market, and, after looking carefully round, fixed his eyes upon John and his companion and at once approached their master. A few minutes were spent in bargaining, then the dealer unfastened the fetters which bound them, and the Roman briefly bade them follow him. He proceeded through the crowded streets until they were in the country outside the town. Here villas with beautiful gardens lined the roads. The Roman turned in at the entrance to one of the largest of these mansions. Under a colonnade which surrounded the house a lady was reclining upon a couch; her two slave-girls were fanning her.

"Lesbia," the Roman said, "you complained yesterday that you had not enough slaves to keep the garden in proper order, so I have brought you two more from the slave-market. They are Jews, that obstinate race that have been giving Titus so much trouble. Young as they are they seem to have been fighting, for both of them are marked with several scars."

"I dare say they will do," the lady said. "The Jews are said to understand the culture of the vine and fig better than most people, so they are probably accustomed to garden work."

The Roman clapped his hands, and a slave at once appeared.

"Send Philo here." A minute later a Greek appeared. "Philo, here are two slaves I have brought from the market; they are for work in the garden. See that they do it, and let me know how things go on. We shall know how to treat them if they are troublesome." Philo at once led the two new slaves to the shed at a short distance from the house where the slaves employed out of doors lodged.

"Do you speak Greek?" he asked.

"As well as my native language," John replied.

"My lord Tibellus is a just and good master," Philo said, "and you are fortunate in having fallen into his hands. He expects his slaves to work their best, and if they do so he treats them well; but disobedience and laziness he punishes severely. He is an officer of high rank in the government of the city. As you may not know the country, I warn you against thinking of escape. The lake of Mareotis well-nigh surrounds the back of the city, and beyond the lake the Roman authority extends for a vast distance, and none would dare to conceal runaway slaves.

"We shall not attempt to escape," John said quietly, "and are well content that we have fallen in such good hands. I am accustomed to work in a garden, but my companion has not had much experience at such work, therefore I pray you be patient with him at first."

John had agreed with Jonas that if they had the good fortune to be sold to a Roman they would not for a time say anything about the ring. It was better, they thought, to wait until Titus returned to Rome, which he would be sure to do after the complete conquest of Jerusalem.

Even were they sent to him there, while he was still full of wrath and bitterness against the Jews for the heavy loss that they had inflicted upon his army, and for the obstinacy which compelled him to destroy the city which he would fain have preserved as a trophy of his victory, they might be less favorably received than they would be after there had been some time for the passions awakened by the strife to abate, especially after the enjoyment of the triumph which was sure to be accorded to him on his return after his victory.

The next day the ring, the badge of slavery, was fastened round the necks of the two new purchases. John had already hidden in the ground the precious ring, as he rightly expected that he would have to work barefooted. They were at once set to work in the garden. John was surprised at the number and variety of the plants and trees which filled it, and at the beauty and care with which it was laid out and tended. Had it not been for the thought of the grief that they would be suffering at home he would for a time have worked contentedly. The labor was no harder than that on his father's farm, and as he worked well and willingly Philo, who was at the head of the slaves employed in the garden, which was a very extensive one, did not treat him with harshness.

Jonas, although less skillful, also gave satisfaction, and two months passed without any unpleasant incident. The Roman slaves, save in exceptional instances, were all well treated by their masters, although these had power of life and death over them. They were well fed, and generally had some small money payment made them. Sometimes those who were clever at a handicraft were let out to other masters, receiving a portion of the wages they earned, so that they were frequently able in old age to purchase their freedom.

There were four other slaves who worked in the garden. Two of these were Nubians, one a Parthian, and the other a Spaniard. The last died of home-sickness and fever after they had been there six weeks, and his place was filled up by another Jew from a cargo freshly arrived.

From him John learned what had taken place after he had left Jerusalem. The bands of Simon and John of Gischala were so much weakened by death and desertion, and were so enfeebled by famine, that they could not hope to withstand the regular approaches of the Roman arms for any length of time. The two leaders therefore invited Titus to a parley, and the latter, being desirous of avoiding other great buildings in the upper city, and of returning to Rome at once, agreed to meet them. They took their places at opposite ends of the bridge across the Tyropœon Valley.

Titus spoke first, and expostulated with them on the obstinacy which had already lead to the destruction of the Temple and the great part of the city. He said that all the world, even to the distant Britons, had been homage to the Romans, and that further resistance would only bring destruction upon them. Finally, he offered their lives to all if they would lay down their arms and surrender themselves as prisoners of war.

Simon and John replied that they and their followers had bound themselves by a solemn oath never to surrender themselves into the hands of the Romans, but they expressed their willingness to retire with their wives and families into the wilderness and leave the Romans in possession of the city. Titus considered this language for men in so desperate a position a mockery, and answered sternly that henceforth he would receive no deserters and show no mercy, and that they might fight their hardest. He at once ordered the destruction of all the buildings standing round the Temple.

The flames spread as far as the palace of Helena on Ophel, to the south of the Temple platform. Here the members of the royal family of Adiabene dwelt, and also in the palaces of Grapte and Monobazus, and the descendants of Helena now went over to the Romans, and Titus, although he declared that he would in future spare none, did not take their lives, seeing that they were of royal blood. Simon and John of Gischala, when they heard that Adiabene princes had gone over to the Romans, rushed to the Palace of Helena, sacked it, and murdered all who had taken refuge in the building, seven thousand in number; they had sacked the rest of the outer lower town, and retired with their booty into the high town.

Titus, furious at this conduct, ordered all the outer lower town to be burned, and soon from the Temple platform to the Fountain of Siloam a scene of desolation extended. The Roman soldiers then commenced to throw up banks, the one against Herod's Palace, the other near the bridge across the valley close to the Palace of Agrippa. The Idumeans under Simon were opposed to further resistance, and five of their leaders opened communication with Titus, who was disposed to treat with them, but the conspiracy was discovered by Simon and the five leaders executed. Still, in spite of the watchfulness of Simon and John large numbers of the inhabitants made their escape to the Romans, who, tired of slaying, spared their lives, but sold the able-bodied as slaves and allowed the rest to pass through their lines.

On the 1st of September, after eighteen days' incessant labor, the bank on the west against Herod's Place was completed and the battering-rams commenced their work. The defenders were too enfeebled by famine to offer any serious resistance, and the next day a long line of the wall fell to the ground.

Simon and John at first thought of cutting their way through the Roman ranks, but when they saw how small was the body of followers gathered round them they gave up the attempt. They hesitated for a moment whether they should throw themselves into the three great towers and fight to the last, or endeavor to fight their way through the wall of circumvallation.

They chose the latter course, hurried down to the lower end of the upper city, and sallying out from the gate they rushed at the Roman wall; but they had no engines of war to batter it, they were few in number and weakened by famine, and when they tried to scale the wall the Roman guards, assembling in haste, beat them back, and they returned to the city and, scattering, hid themselves in the underground caves.

The Romans advanced to the great towers and found them deserted.

Titus stood amazed at their strength and solidity, and exclaimed that God indeed was on their side, for that by man alone these impregnable towers could never have been taken.

All resistance having now ceased, the Romans spread themselves through the city, slaughtering all whom they met without distinction of age or sex. They were, however, aghast at the spectacle which the houses into which they burst presented. Some of these had been used as charnel-houses, and had been filled with dead bodies. In others they found the remains of whole families who with their servants had shut themselves up to die of hunger. Everywhere the dead far outnumbered the living.

The next day Titus issued an order that only such as possessed arms should be slain, and that all others should be taken prisoners; but the Roman soldiers were too infuriated at the losses and defeats they had suffered even to obey the orders of Titus, and all save the able bodied who would be of value as slaves were confined in the charred remains of the Women's Court, and so weakened were these by the ravages of famine that eleven thousand of them are said to have perished.

Of the survivors some were selected to grace the triumphal procession at Rome; of the remainder, all under the age of seventeen were sold as slaves; a part of those above that age were distributed among the amphitheaters of Syria to fight as gladiators against the wild beasts; and the rest were condemned to labor in the public works in Egypt for the rest of their lives. When all above the surface had been slain or made prisoners, the Romans set to work methodically to search the conduits, sewers, and passages under the city. Multitudes of fugitives were found here, and all were slain as soon as discovered. Then the army was set to work to raze the city to the ground. Every building and wall was thrown down, the only exception being a great barrack adjoining Herod's Palace, which was left for the use of one of the legions which was to be quartered there for a time, and the three great towers, Hippicus, Phasaelus, and Mariamne, which were left standing in order that they might show to future generations how vast had been the strength of the fortifications which Roman valor had captured.

John of Gischala and Simon had both so effectually concealed themselves that for a time they escaped the Roman searchers. At the end of some days, however, John was compelled by famine to come out and surrender. Simon was much longer before he made his appearance. He had taken with him into his hiding-place a few of his followers and some stone masons with their tools, and an effort was made to drive a mine beyond the Roman outposts. The rock, however, was hard and the men enfeebled by famine, and the consequence was that Simon, like his fellow-leader, was compelled to make his way to the surface.

The spot where he appeared was on the platform of the Temple far from the shaft by which he had entered the underground galleries. He appeared at night clad in white, and the Roman guards at first took him for a specter, and he thus escaped instant death and had time to declare who he was. Titus had already left, but Terentius Rufus, who commanded the Tenth Legion, which had been left behind, sent Simon in chains to Titus at Cæsarea, and he as well as John of Gischala were taken by the latter to Rome to grace his triumph.

"It is strange," John said when he heard the story, "that the two men who have brought all these woes upon Jerusalem should have both escaped with their lives. The innocent have fallen and the guilty escaped, yet escaped, for it would have been better for them to have died fighting in the court of the Temple than to live as slaves in the hands of the Romans."

A month later John learned the fate that had befallen the two Jewish leaders. Bother were dragged in the triumphal procession of Titus through the streets of Rome; then, according to the cruel Roman custom, Simon was first scourged and then executed as the bravest of the enemies of Rome, while John of Gischala was sentenced to imprisonment for life.

The day after the news of the return to Rome and triumph of Titus arrived John asked Philo to tell Tibellus that he prayed that he would hear him, as he wished to speak to him on a subject connected with Titus.

Wondering what his Jewish slave could have to say about the son of the emperor, Tibellus upon hearing from Philo of the request at once ordered John to be brought to him.

"Let me bring my companion also with me," John said to Philo. "He is my adopted brother, and can bear witness to the truth of my statements."

When they reached the colonnade Philo told them to stop there, and a minute later Tibellus came out.

"I have, my lord," John said, and he advanced and held out the ring.

The Roman took it and examined it.

"It is a signet-ring of Titus!" he said in surprise. "How came you by this? This is a grave matter, slave; and if you cannot account satisfactorily as to how you came possessed of this signet, you had better have thrown yourself into the sea, or swallowed poison, than have spoken of your possession of this signet."

"It was given to me by Titus himself," John said.

The Roman made a gesture of anger.

"It is ill jesting with the name of Cæsar," he said sternly. "This is Cæsar's ring. Doubtless it was stolen from him. You may have taken it from the robber by force or fraud, or as a gift, I know not which, but do not mock me with such a tale as that Cæsar gave one of his signets to you, a Jew."

"It is as I said," John replied calmly. "Titus himself bestowed that ring upon me, and said that if I desired to come to him at any time and showed it to a Roman it would open all doors and bring me to his presence."

"You do not speak as if you were mad," Tibellus said, "and yet your tale is not credible. Are you weary of life, Jew? Do you long to die by torture? Philo has spoken to me of you and your young companion. You have labored well and cheerfully, he tells me, and are skilled at your work. Do you find your lot so hard that you would die to escape it, and so tell me this impossible story? For death, and a horrible death, will assuredly be your portion. If you persist in this tale, and, showing me this ring, say, I demand that you send me and my companion to Titus, I should be bound to do so, and then torture and death will be your portion for mocking the name of Cæsar."

"My lord," John said calmly, "I repeat that I mock not the name of Cæsar, and that what I have told you is true. I am not weary of life or discontented with my station. I have been kindly treated by Philo, and work no harder than I should work at my father's farm in Galilee; but I naturally long to return home. I have abstained from showing you this ring before, because Titus had not as yet conquered Jerusalem; but now that I hear he has been received in triumph in Rome he would have time to give me and audience, and therefore I pray that I may be sent to him."

"But how is it possible that Titus could have given you this ring?" Tibellus asked, impressed by the calmness of John's manner, and yet still unable to believe a statement which appeared to him altogether incredible.

"I will tell you, my lord, but I will tell you alone; for although Titus made no secret of it all the time, he might not care for the story to be generally told."

Tibellus waved his hand to Philo, who at once withdrew.

"You have found it hard to believe what I have told you, my lord," John went on. "You will find it harder still to believe what I now tell you; but if it is your command, I am bound to do so."

"It is my command," Tibellus said shortly. "I would fain know the whole of this monstrous tale."

"I must first tell you, my lord, that though as yet but twenty-one years old, I have for four years fought with my countrymen against the Romans. You see," he said, pointing to the scars on his head, arms, and body, "I have been wounded often, and, as you may see for yourself, some of these scars are yet unhealed, others are so old that you can scarce see their traces. This is a proof of so much at least of my story. My companion here and I were, by the protection of our God, enabled to escape from Jotapata when all else save Josephus perished there. This was regarded by my countrymen as well-nigh a miracle, and as a proof that I had divine favor. In consequence a number of young men, when they took up arms, elected me as their leader, and for three years we did what we could to oppose the progress of the Roman arms. It was as if a fly should try to stop a camel. Still we did what we could, and any of the Roman officers who served under Titus would tell you that of those who opposed them in the field there was no more active partizan than the leader, who was generally known as John of Gamala."

"You John of Gamala!" Tibellus exclaimed. "In frequent letters from my friends with the army I have read that name, and heard how incessant was the watchfulness required to resist his attacks, and how often small garrisons and parties were cut off by him. It was he, too, who burned Vespasian's camp before Gamala; and you tell me, young man, that you are that Jewish hero, for hero he was, though it was against Rome he fought?"

"I tell you so, my lord; and my adopted brother here, who was with me through these campaigns, will confirm what I say. I say it not boastingly, for my leadership was due to no special bravery on my part, but simply because the young men of the band thought that God had specially chosen me to lead them."

"And now Titus," Tibellus said briefly, more and more convinced that his slave was audaciously inventing this story.

"Once near Hebron," John said, "I was passing through a valley alone, when Titus, who was riding from Carmelia in obedience to a summons from Vespasian, who was in Hebron, came upon me. He attacked me and we fought—"

"You and Titus hand to hand?" Tibellus asked, with a short laugh.

"Titus and I hand to hand," John repeated quietly; "he had wounded me twice, when I sprang within his guard and closed with him. His foot slipped and he fell, for a moment I could have slain him if I would, but I did not; then I fainted from loss of blood. Titus was shortly joined by some of his men, and he had me carried down to his camp, where I was kindly nursed for a week, he himself visiting me several times. At the end of that time he dismissed me, giving me his signet-ring, and telling me that if ever again I fell into the hands of the Romans and wished to see him, I had but to show the ring to a Roman and that he would send me to him."

"And to him you shall go," Tibellus said sternly; "and better would it have been that you had never been born than that I should send you to him with such a tale as this."

So saying he turned away, while John and his companion returned to their work. The Roman officer was absolutely incredulous as to the story he had heard, and indignant in the extreme at what he considered the audacity of the falsehood. Still he could not but be struck by the calmness with which John told the story, nor could he see what motive he could have in inventing it. Its falsity would of course be made apparent the instant he arrived in Rome, whereas had he said, as was doubtless the truth, that he had obtained the ring from one who had stolen it from Titus, he might be obtained his freedom and a reward for its restoration.

After thinking the matter over for a time he ordered his horse and rode into the city. One of the legions from Palestine had returned there, while two had accompanied Titus to Rome, and a fourth had remained in Judea. Tibellus rode at once to the headquarters of the commander of the legion. He had just returned with some of his officers from a parade of the troops. They had taken off their armor, and a slave was pouring wine into goblets for them.

"Ah, Tibellus!" he said, "is it you? Drink, my friend, and tell us what ails you, for in truth you look angered and hot."

"I have been angered by one of my slaves," Tibellus said.

"Then there is no trouble in that," the Roman said with a smile; "throw him to the fishes and buy another; they are cheap enough, for we have flooded the world with slaves, and as we know to our cost they are scarce salable. We have brought two or three thousand with us and can get no bid for them."

"Yes, but this matter can't be settled so," Tibellus said; "but first I want to ask you a question or two. You heard, of course, of John of Gamala in your wars in Judea?"

There was a chorus of assent.

"That did we, indeed, to our cost," the general said; "save the two leaders of Jerusalem he was the most dangerous, and was by far the most troublesome of our foes. Many a score of sleepless nights, has that fellow caused us; from the time he well-nigh burned our own camp before Gamala, he was a thorn in our side. One never knew where he was or when to expect him. One day we heard of him attacking a garrison at the other end of the country, and the next night he would fall upon our camp. We never marched through a ravine without expecting to see him and his men appearing on the hills and sending the rocks thundering down among us; and the worst of it was, do what we would we could never get to close quarters with him. His men could march three miles to our one; and as for the Arabs, if we sent them in pursuit they would soon come flying back to us, leaving a goodly portion of their numbers dead behind them. He was the most formable enemy we had outside Jerusalem, and had all the Jews fought as he did, instead of shutting themselves up in their walled towns, we might have been years before we subdued that pestilent country."

"Did you ever see this John of Gamala? Do you know what he was like personally? Was he another giant like this Simon who was executed at the triumph the other day?"

"None of us ever saw him, that is, to know which was he, though doubtless we may have seen him in the fights; but all the country people we questioned, and such wounded men as fell into our hands, all asserted that he was little more than a lad. He was strong and skillful in arms, but in years a youth. They all believed that he was a sort of prophet, one who had a mission from their God. But why are you asking?"

"I will tell you presently," Tibellus said; "but first answer me another question. Was it not your legion that was at Carmelia with Titus when Vespasian lay at Hebron?"

There was a general assent.

"Did you hear of a wounded Jew being brought in and tended there by order of Titus?"

"We did," the general said; "and here is Plancus, who was in command of that part of the horse of the legion which formed the body-guard of Titus, and who brought him into the camp; he will tell you about it."

"Titus had received a message from Vespasian that he wished to see him," the officer signified by the general said, "and rode off at once, telling us to follow him. We armed and mounted as soon as we could, but Titus was well mounted and had a considerable start. We came up to him in a valley –he was standing by the side of his dead horse. He was slightly wounded, and his dirtied armor showed that he had had a sharp fight. Close by lay a Jew who seemed to be dead. Titus ordered him to be carried back to the camp and cared for by his own leech. That is all I know about it."

"I can tell you more," the general said, "for Titus himself told me that he had had a desperate fight with the Jew, that he had wounded him severely, and was on the point of finishing him when the Jew sprang at him suddenly, and the sudden shock threw him to the ground, and that, strange as it might seem, although knowing who he was, the Jew spared his life. It was a strange story, and any one besides Titus would have kept it to himself, and run his sword through the body of the Jew to make sure of his silence; but Titus had notions of his own, and he is as generous as he is brave. By what he said I gathered that the Jew abstained from striking, believing, as was truly the case, that Titus was more merciful than Vespasian, and that he would spare Jerusalem and their Temple if he could. And now, why all these questions?"

"One more on my part first; what became of the Jew and what was he like?"

"That is two questions," the general replied; "however, I will answer them. Titus let him go free when he was recovered from his wounds. He was a young man of some twenty years old."

"And do you know his name?"

"I know his name was John, for so he told Titus, but as every other Jew one comes across is John that does not tell much."

"I can tell you his other name," Tibellus said. "It was John of Gamala."

An exclamation of astonishment broke from the officers.

"So that was John of Gamala himself!" the general said. "None of us ever dreamed of it, and yet it might well have been, for, now I think of it, the young fellow I saw lying wounded in the tent next to that of Titus answered exactly to the description we have heard of him, and the fact that he overcame Titus in itself shows that he had unusual strength and bravery. But how do you know about this?"

"Simply because John of Gamala is at present working as a slave in my garden."

"You do not say so!" the general exclaimed. "We have often wondered what became of him. We learned from the deserters that he had entered into Jerusalem and was fighting there against us. They all agreed that the men he had brought with him took no part in the atrocities of the soldiers of Simon and John of Gischala, but that they kept together and lived quietly and harmed no man. It was they, we heard, who did the chief part in the three days' fighting at the breach of the lower town; but we never heard what became of him, and supposed he must have fallen in the fighting round the Temple. And so he is your slave, Tibellus! How did you know it was he, and what are you going to do? The war is over now, and there has been bloodshed enough, and after all he was a gallant enemy, who fought us fairly and well."

"He told me himself who he was," Tibellus said; "but I believed he was lying to me. I had heard of John of Gamala, and deemed that he was a brave and skillful warrior, and it seemed impossible that young man could be he. As to what I am going to do with him, I have nothing to do but what he has himself demanded, namely to be sent to Titus. He produced a signet-ring of Cæsar, said that it was given to him by the general himself, and that he told him that if he presented it to a Roman at any time he would lead him to his presence. I believed that he had stolen the ring, or had got it from somebody that had stolen it; and he then told me of the story very much as you have told it, save that he said that when he well-nigh conquered by Titus, and sprang upon him, Cæsar's foot slipped, and he fell, hinting that his success was the result of accident rather than his own effort. He spoke by no means boastingly of it, but as if it was the most natural thing in the world."

"There he showed discretion and wisdom," the general said; "but truly this is a marvelous story. If he had not appealed to Cæsar, I should have said, give him his freedom. You can buy a slave for a few sesterces. This young fellow is too good to be a slave, and now that Judea is finally crushed he could never become dangerous; but as he has demanded to be sent to Cæsar, you must, of course, send him there; besides, with the idea that Titus has, he may be really glad to see the youth again. But we shall like to see him also. We all honor a brave adversary, and I should like to see him who so long set us at defiance."

"I will bring him down tomorrow at this hour," Tibellus said, and then, taking his leave of the officers, he mounted and rode back.

On reaching home he at once sent for John. "I doubted your story when you told it to me," he said, "and deemed it impossible; but I have been down to the officers of the legion which arrived last week from Judea. It chances to be the very one which was at Carmelia when Vespasian lay at Hebron, and I find that your story is fully confirmed; although, indeed, they did not know that the wounded man Titus sent in was John of Gamala; but as they admit that he answered exactly to the description which they have heard of that leader, they doubt not that it was he. However, be assured that your request is granted, and that you shall be sent to Rome by the next ship that goes thither."

Chapter Nineteen

AT ROME

Tibellus at once ordered John to be released from all further work, the badge of slavery to be removed, and that he should be supplied handsome garments, removed into the house, and assigned an apartment with the freedmen. The bearer of the signet of Titus, now that it was ascertained that the signet had been really given to him by Cæsar, was an important person, and was to be received with consideration if not honor. When these changes had been made, John was again brought before Tibellus.

"Is there anything else I can do for your comfort as one who has been honored by Titus himself, our future emperor? You have but to express your wishes and I shall be glad to carry them out."

"I would ask, then," John said, "that my friend and companion may be set free and allowed to accompany me to Rome. He is my adopted brother. He has fought and slept by my side for the last four years, and your bounty to me gives me no pleasure so long as he is laboring as a slave."

Tibellus at once sent for Philo, and ordered the collar to be filed from the neck of Jonas, and for him to be treated in the same manner as John.

The next day Tibellus invited John to accompany him to the barracks, and as he would take no excuses he was obliged to do so.

Tibellus presented him to the general and his officers, who received him cordially, and were much struck with his quiet demeanor and the nobility of his bearing. John had for four years been accustomed to command, and the belief entertained by his followers in his special mission had had its effect upon his manner. Although simple and unassuming in mind, and always ready on his return to the farm to become again the simple worker upon his father's farm, he had yet insensibly acquired the bearing of one born to position and authority. He was much above the ordinary height; and although his figure was slight, it showed signs, which could well be appreciated by the Romans, of great activity and unusual strength. His face was handsome, his forehead lofty, his eyes large and soft, and in the extreme firmness of his mouth and his square chin and jaw were there alone signs of the determination and steadfastness which had made him so formidable a foe to the Romans.

"So you are John of Gamala!" the general said. "We have doubtless nearly crossed swords more than once. You have caused us many a sleepless night, and it seemed to us that you and your bands were ubiquitous. I am glad to meet you, as well are we all. A Roman cherishes no malice against an honorable foe, and such we always found you, and I trust you have no malice for the past."

"None," John said. "I regard you as instruments of God for the punishment of my people. We brought our misfortunes upon ourselves by the rebellion, which would have seemed madness had it not doubtless been the will of God that we should so provoke you and perish. All I ask now is to return to my father's farm and to resume my life there. If I could do that without going to Rome I would gladly do so."

"That can hardly be," Tibellus said. "The rule is that when one appeals to Cæsar, to Cæsar he must go. The case is at once taken out of our hands. Besides, I should have to report the fact to Rome, and Titus may wish to see you, and might be ill-pleased at hearing that you had returned to Galilee without going to see him. Besides, it may be some time before all animosity between the two peoples dies out there, and you might obtain from him an imperial order which would prove a protection to yourself and family against any who might desire to molest you. If for this reason alone it would be well worth your while for you to proceed to Rome."

Three days later Tibellus told John that a ship would sail next morning, and that a centurion in charge of some invalided soldiers would go in her.

"I have arranged for you to go in his charge, and have instructed him to accompany you to the palace of Titus and facilitate your having an interview with him. I have given him a letter to present you to Titus with greetings, saying why I have sent you to him. Here is a purse of money to pay for what you may require on the voyage, and to keep you, if need be, at Rome until you can see Titus, who may possibly be absent. You owe me no thanks," he said as John was about to speak. "Titus would be justly offended were the bearer of his signet-ring sent to him without due care and honor."

That evening Tibellus gave a banquet, at which the general and several officers were present. The total number present was nine, including John and the host, this being the favorite number for what they regarded as small private entertainments. At large banquets hundreds of persons were frequently entertained. After the meal John, at the request of Tibellus, related to the officers the manner of his escapes from Jotapata and Jerusalem, and several of the incidents of the struggle in which he had taken part.

The next morning he and Jonas took their places on board the ship and sailed for Rome.

It was now far in November, and the passage was a boisterous one, and the size of the waves astonished John, accustomed as he was only to the short choppy seas of the Lake of Galilee. Jonas made up his mind that they were lost, and indeed for some days the vessel was in imminent danger. Instead of passing through the traits between Sicily and the mainland of Italy, they were blown far to the west, and finally took shelter in the harbor of Caralis in Sandinia. Here they remained for a week to refit and repair damages, and then sailed across to Portus Augusti and then up the Tiber.

The centurion had done his best to make the voyage a pleasant one to John and his companion. Having been informed that the former was the bearer of a signet-ring of Titus, and would have an audience with him, he was anxious to create as good an impression as possible; but it was not until Caralis was reached that John recovered sufficiently from sea-sickness to take much interest in what was passing round him. The travelers were greatly struck with the quantity of shipping entering and leaving the mouth of the Tiber, the sea being dotted with the sails of the vessels bearing corn from Sardinia, Sicily, and Africa, and products of all kinds from every port in the world.

The sight of Rome impressed him less than he had expected. Of its vastness he could form no opinion; but in strength and beauty it appeared to him inferior to Jerusalem. When he landed he saw how many were the stately palaces and temples; but of the former none were more magnificent than that of Herod. Nor was there one of the Temples to be compared for a moment with that which had so lately stood, the wonder and admiration of the world, upon Mount Moriah.

The centurion procured a commodious lodging for him, and finding that Titus was still in Rome accompanied him the next day to the palace. Upon saying that he was the bearer of a letter to Titus the centurion was shown into the inner apartments, John being left in the great antechamber, which was crowded with officers waiting to see Titus when he came out, to receive orders, pay their respects, or present petitions to him. The centurion soon returned and told John to follow him.

"Titus was very pleased," he whispered, "when he read the letter I brought him, and begged me bring you at once to his presence."

Titus was alone in a small chamber, whose simplicity contrasted strangely with the magnificence of those through which he had passed. He rose from a table at which he had been writing.

"Ah, my good friend," he said, "I am truly glad to see you! I made sure that you were dead. You were not among those who came out and gave themselves up, or among those who were captured when the city was taken, for I had careful inquiry made, thinking it possible that you might have lost my ring, and been unable to obtain access to me; then at last I made sure you had fallen. I am truly glad to see that it is not so."

"I was marvelously preserved then, as at Jotapata," John said, "and escaped, after the Temple had fallen, by a secret passage leading out beyond the wall of circumvallation. As I made my way home I fell into the hands of some slave-dealers, who seized me and my companion, who is my adopted brother, and carried us away to Alexandria, where I was sold. As you had not yet returned to Rome, I thought it better not to produce your signet, which I had fortunately managed to conceal.

"When I heard that you had reached Rome, and had received your triumph, I produced the ring to my master Tibellus, and prayed him to send me and my companion here to you, in order that I might ask for liberty and leave to return to my home. He treated me with the greatest kindness, and but that I had appealed to you would of himself have set us free. It is for this alone that I have come here, to ask you to confirm the freedom he has given me, and to permit me to return to Galilee. Further, if you will give me your order that I and mine may live peacefully without molestation from any, it would add to your favors."

"I will do these certainly," Titus said, "and far more, if you will let me. I shall never forget that you saved my life; and believe me I did my best to save the Temple, which was what I promised you. I did not say that I would save it, merely that I would do my best; but your obstinate countrymen insisted in bringing destruction upon it."

"I know that you did all that was possible," John said, "and that the blame lies with them, and not with you in any way However, it was the will of God that it should be destroyed, and they were the instruments of his will, while they thought they were trying to preserve it."

"But now," Titus said," you must let me do more for you. Have you ambition? I will push you forward to high position and dignity. Do you care for wealth? I have the treasures of Rome in my gift. Would you serve in the army? Many of the Alexandria Jews had high rank in the army of Antony. Two of Cleopatra's best generals were your countrymen. I know your bravery and your military talents, and will gladly push you forward."

"I thank you, Cæsar, for your offers," John said, "which far exceed my deserts, but I would rather pass my life as a tiller of the soil in Galilee. The very name of a Jew at present is hateful in the ear of a Roman. All men who succeed by the favor of a great prince are hated. I should be still more so as a Jew. I should be hated by my own countrymen, as well as yours, for they would regard me as a traitor. There would be no happiness in such a life. A thousand times a home by the Lake of Galilee with a wife and children."

"If such be your determination I will say naught against it," Titus said; "but remember, if at any time you tire of such a life, come to me and I will give you a post of high honor and dignity. There are glorious opportunities for talent and uprightness in our distant dependencies—east and west—where there will be no prejudices against the name of a Jew. However, for the present let that be. To-morrow I will have prepared for you an imperial order to all Roman officers, civil and military, of Galilee and Judea to treat you as a friend of Titus; also the appointment as procurator of the district lying north of the river Hieromax up to the boundary of Chorizin, for a distance of ten miles back from the lake.

"You will not refuse that office, for it will enable you to protect your country people from oppression, and to bring prosperity upon the whole district. Lastly, you will receive with the documents a sum of money. I know that you will not use it on yourself, but it will be long before the land recovers from its wounds. There will be terrible misery and distress, and I should like to think that in the district at least of my friend there are peace and contentment. Less than this Cæsar cannot give to the man who spared his life."

John thanked Titus most heartily for his favors, which would, he saw, insure his family and neighbors from the oppression and tyranny to which a conquered people are exposed at the hands of a rough soldiery. Titus ordered an apartment to be prepared for him in the palace, and begged him to take up his abode there until a vessel should be sailing for Cæsarea. Slaves were told off to attend upon him and to escort him in the city, and everything was done to show the esteem and friendship in which Titus held him. Titus had several interviews with him, and learned now for the first time that he was the John of Gamala who had so long and stoutly opposed the Romans.

"If I had known that," Titus said with a smile, "when you were in my hands, I do not think I should have let you go free, though your captivity would have been an honorable one. When you said that you would not promise to desist from opposing our armies, I thought that one man more or less in the ranks of the enemy would make little difference; but had I know that it was the redoubtable John of Gamala who was in my hands I should hardly have thought myself justified in letting you go free."

John, at the request of Titus, gave him a sketch of the incidents of his life and of the campaign.

"So you have already a lady-love," Titus said when he had finished. "What shall I send her? Better nothing at present," he said, after a moment's thought and a smile, "beyond yourself. That will be the best and most acceptable gift I could send her. Time and your good report may soften the feelings with which doubtless she, like all the rest of your countrywomen, must regard me; though the gods know I would gladly have spared Galilee and Judea from the ruin which has fallen upon them."

In addition to the two documents which he had promised him, Titus thoughtfully gave him another, intended for the perusal of his own countrymen only. It was in the form of a letter, saying to John that he had appointed him procurator of the strip of territory bordering the Lake of Galilee on the east, not from submission on his part, still less at his request, but solely as a proof of his admiration for the stubborn and determined manner in which he had fought throughout the war, and absence of any cruelty practiced upon Romans who fell into his hands, of his esteem for his character, and as a remembrance of the occasion when the two had fought hand to hand alone in the valley going down from Hebron.

The gold was sent directly on board a ship. It was in a box which required four strong men to lift. A centurion, with twenty men, was put on board the ship, with orders to land with John at Cæsarea, and to escort him to his own home, or as near as he might choose them. Titus took a cordial leave of him, and expressed a hope that John would some day change his mind and accept his offer of a post, and that at any rate he hoped that he would from time to time come to Rome to see him.

The voyage to Cæsarea was performed without accident.

"I shall look back at our visit to Rome as a dream," Jonas said one evening as they sat together on the deck of the ship. "to think that I, the goatherd of Jotapata, should have been living in the palace of Cæsar at Rome, with you, the friend of Titus himself! It seems marvelous; but I am weary of the crowded streets, of the noise and bustle, and wealth and color. I long to get rid of this dress, in which I feel as if I were acting a part in a play. Do not you, John?"

"I do, indeed," John replied. "I should never accustom myself to such a life as that. I am longing for a sight of the lake and my dear home, and of those I love, who must be mourning for me as dead."

At Cæsarea a vehicle was procured for the carriage of the chest, and the party then journeyed until they were within sight of Tarichea. John then dismissed his escort with thanks for their attention during the journey, and begged them to go on to the city by themselves. When they were out of sight he and Jonas took off their Roman garments, and put on others they had purchased at Cæsarea, similar to those they were accustomed to wear at home. Then they proceeded with the cart and its driver into Tarichea, and hired a boat to take them up the lake. The boatmen were astonished at the weight of John's chest, and thought that I must contain lead for making into missiles for slingers. It was evening when the boat approached the well-known spot, and John and his companion sprang out on the beach.

"What shall we do with the chest?" one of the boatmen asked.

"We will carry it to that clump of bushes, and pitch it in among them until we want it. None will run off with it, and they certainly would not find it easy to break it open."

This reply confirmed the men in their idea that it could be nothing of value; and after helping John and Jonas to carry the chest to the point indicated, they returned to their boat and rowed away down the lake.

"Now, Jonas, we must be careful," John said, "how we approach the house. It would give them a terrible shock if I came upon them suddenly. I think you had better go up alone and see Isaac, and bring him to me; then we can talk over the best way of breaking it to the others."

It was nearly an hour before Jonas brought Isaac down to the spot where John was standing, a hundred yards away from the house, for he had to wait some time before he could find an opportunity of speaking to him. Jonas had but just broken the news that John was at hand when they reached the spot where he was standing.

"Is it indeed you, my dear young master?" the old man said, falling on John's neck. "This is unlooked for joy indeed. The Lord be praised for his mercies! What will your parents say, they who wept for you for months as dead!"

"They are well, I hope, Isaac?"

"They are shaken, greatly shaken," old Isaac said. "The tempest has passed over them; the destruction of Jerusalem, the woes of our people, and your loss have smitten them to the ground; but now that you have returned it will give them new life."

"And Mary, she is well, I hope, too?" John asked.

"The maiden is not ill, though I cannot say that she is well," Isaac said. "Long after your father and mother and all of us had given up hope she refused to believe that you were dead; even when the others put on mourning she would not do so; but of late I know that though she has never said so, hope has died in her too; her cheeks have grown pale and her eyes heavy, but she still keeps up for the sake of your parents, and we often look and wonder how she can bear herself so bravely."

"And how are we to break it to the old people?" John asked.

Isaac shook his head; the matter was beyond him.

"I should think," Jonas suggested, "that Isaac should go back and break it to them first that I have returned; that I have been a slave among the Romans, and have escaped them. He might say that he has questioned me, and that I said that you certainly did not fall at the siege of Jerusalem, and that I believe that you, like me, were sold as a slave by the Romans. Then you can take me in and let them question me. I will stick to that story for a time, raising some hopes in their breasts, till at last I can signify to Mary that you are alive, and leave it to her to break it to the others."

"That will be the beset way by far," John said. "Yes, that will do excellently well. Now, Isaac, do you go on and do your part. Tell them gently that Jonas has returned, that he has been a slave, and escaped from the Romans, and that, as far as he knows, I am yet alive. Then, when they are prepared, bring him in and let him answer their questions."

The evening meal had been ended before Isaac had left the room to feed with some warm milk a kid whose dam had died. It was while he was engaged upon this duty that Jonas had come upon him. When he entered the room Simon was sitting with the open bible before him at the head of the table, waiting his return to commence the evening prayers.

"What has detained you, Isaac?" he asked. "Surely it is not after all these years you would forget our evening prayers?"

"I was detained," the old man said unsteadily; and at the sound of his voice, the sight of his face as it came within the circle of the light from the lamp, Mary rose suddenly to her feet and stood looking at him.

"What is it?" she asked in a low voice.

"Why," Simon asked calmly, "what has detained you, Isaac?"

"A strange thing has happened," the old man said. "One of our wanderers has returned, not he whom we have hoped and prayed for most, but Jonas. He has been a slave, but escaped and come back to us."

"And what is his news?" Simon asked, rising to his feet; but even more imperative was the unspoken question on Mary's white face and parted lips.

"He gives us hope," Isaac said to her. "So far as he knows John may yet be alive."

"I knew it, I knew it!" Mary said in a voice scarcely above a whisper. "O Lord, I thank thee; why have I doubted thy mercy!" And she stood for a moment with head thrown back and eyes upraised; then she swayed suddenly, and would have fallen had not Isaac ran forward and supported her, until at Martha's cry two of the maids hastened up and placed her on a seat. Some water was held to her lips; she drank a little, and then said faintly, "Tell us more, Isaac."

"I have not much more to tell," he replied. "Jonas says that John certainly did not fall in Jerusalem, as indeed we were told by the young man of his band who returned, and that he believes that, like himself, he was sold as a slave. But Jonas is outside. I thought it better to tell you first; now I will call him in to speak for himself."

When Jonas entered, Martha and Mary were clasped in each other's arms. Miriam, with the tears streaming down her cheeks was repeating aloud one of the Psalms of thanksgiving; while Simon stood with head bent low, and his hands grasping the table, upon which the tears were raining down in heavy drops. It was some little time before they could question Jonas further. Martha and Mary had embraced him as if he had been the son of one, the brother of the other. Simon solemnly blessed him, and welcomed him as one from the dead. Then they gathered round to hear his story.

"John and I both escaped all the dangers of the siege," he said; "we were wounded several times, but never seriously. God seemed to watch over us, and although at the last, of the six hundred men with which we entered Jerusalem there were but twelve who remained alive; we were among them."

"Yes, yes, we knew that," Mary said. "News was brought by a young man of his band who belonged to a village on the lake that twelve of you had escaped together on the day the Temple fell. The others all returned to their homes, but no news ever came of you, and they said that some party of Romans must have killed you; what else could have befallen you? And now we are in February—nearly six months have passed—and no word of you!"

"We were carried off as slaves," Jonas said, "and taken, like Joseph, to be sold in Egypt."

"And have you seen him since?" Simon asked.

"Yes, I saw him in Egypt."

"And he was well then?"

"Quite well," Jonas replied. "I was sent back to Rome, and thence managed to make my way back by ship."

"We must purchase him back," Simon said. "Surely that must be possible! I have money still. I will make the journey myself and buy him."

And he rose to his feet as if to start at once.

"Well, not now," he went on in answer to the hand which Martha laid on his solder, "but tomorrow."

While he was speaking Mary had touched Jonas, gazing into his face, with the same eager question her eyes had asked Isaac. The thought that Jonas was not alone had flashed across her. He nodded slightly and looked toward the door. In a moment she was gone.

"John!" she cried as she ran out of the house, at first in a low tone, but louder and louder as she ran on. "John! John! Where are you?"

A figure stepped out from among the trees, and Mary feel into his arms. A few minutes later she reentered the room.

"Father," she said, going up to Simon, while she took Martha's hand in hers, "do you remember you told me once that when you were a young man you went to hear the preaching of a teacher of the sect of the Essenes whom they afterward slew! You thought he was a good man and a great teacher, and you said he told a parable, and you remembered the very words. I think I remember them now: 'And his father saw him and ran and fell on his neck, and kissed him, and said, Let us be merry, for my son was dead and is alive again; he was lost and is found.' And so, father, is it even unto us."

Martha gave a loud cry and turned to the door, and in another moment was clasped in John's arms. Then his father fell on his neck.

There was no happier household in the land than that which joined in the Psalms of thanksgiving that night. The news spread quickly to the fishermen's cottages, and the neighbors flocked in to congratulate Simon and Martha on the return of their son; and it was long since the strains of the songs of joy had floated out so clear and strong over the water of Galilee, for, for years strains of lamentation and humiliation alone had been on the lips of the Jewish maidens.

After the service of song was over Miriam and the maids loaded the table, while Isaac fetched a skin of the oldest wine from the cellar, and all who had assembled were invited to join the feast.

When the neighbors had retired John asked his father and Isaac to come down with him and Jonas to the side of the lake; to bring up a chest that was lying there. "It is rather too heavy for Jonas and me to carry alone."

"It would have been better, my son, to have asked some of our neighbors; they would gladly have assisted you, and Isaac and I have not between us the strength of one man."

"I know it, father, but I do not wish that any besides ourselves should know that the box is here. We will take a pole and a rope with us, and can adjust the weight so that your portion shall not be beyond your strength."

On arriving at the spot Simon was surprised at seeing a small box, which it would be thought a woman could have lifted with ease.

"Is this the box of which you spoke, John? Surely you want no aid to carry this up?"

"We do indeed, father, as you will see."

With the assistance of Jonas John put the rope round the box and slung it to the pole near one end. He and Jonas then took this end; Simon and Isaac lifted that furthest from the box, so that but a small share of the weight rested upon them. So the chest was carried up to the house.

"What is this you have brought home?" Martha asked as they laid the box down in the principal room.

"It is gold, mother—gold to be used for the relief of the poor and distressed, for those who have been made homeless and fatherless in this war. It was a gift to me, as I will tell you tomorrow; but I need not say that I would not touch one penny of it, for it is Roman gold. But it will place it in our power to do immense good among the poor. We had best bury it just beneath the floor, so that we can readily get at it when we have need."

"It is a great responsibility, my son," Simon said; "but truly there are thousand of homeless and starving families who sought refuge among the hills when their towns and villages were destroyed by the Romans; and with this store of gold, which must be of great value, truly great things can be done toward relieving their necessities."

The next morning John related to his family the various incidents which had befallen him and Jonas since they had last parted; and their surprise was unbounded when he produced the three documents with which he had been furnished by Titus. The letters saying that the favor of Cæsar had been bestowed upon John as a token of admiration only for the bravery with which he had fought, and ordering that all Romans should treat him as one having the favor and friendship of Titus, gave them unbounded satisfaction. That appointing him procurator of the whole district bordering the Lake to the east surprised and almost bewildered them.

"But what are you doing to do, my son? Are you going to leave us and live in a palace, and appear as a Roman officer?"

"I am not thinking of doing that, father," John said with a smile. "For myself I would much rather that this dignity had not been conferred on me by Titus, and I would gladly put this commission with its imperial seal into the fire; but I felt that I cannot do this, for it gives me great power of doing good to our neighbors. I shall be able to protect them from all oppression by Roman soldiers or by tax-gatherers. There is no occasion for me to live in a palace or to wear the garments of a Roman official. The letter of Titus shows that it is to a Jew that he has given this power, and as a Jew I shall use it. While journeying here from Rome I have thought much over the matter. At first I thought of suppressing the order. Then I felt that a power of good had been given into my hands, and that I had no right from selfish reasons to shrink from its execution. Doubtless at first I shall be misunderstood. They will that I, like Josephus, have turned traitor, and have gone over to the Romans. Even were it so, I should have done no more than all the people of Tiberias, Sepphoris, and other cities which submitted to them. But I do not think this feeling will last long. All those who fought with me outside Jerusalem against the Romans know that I was faithful to the cause of my country. The few survivors of the band I led into Jerusalem can testify that I fought until the Temple fell, and that I escaped by my own devices and not from any agreement with the Romans. Moreover, they will in time judge me by my acts. I shall rule, as I said, as a Jew and not as a Roman—rule as did the judges in the old times, sitting under my own fig-tree here and listening to the complaints that may be brought to me, and I trust that wisdom will be given to me by the Lord to judge wisely and justly among them."

"You have decided well, my son," Simon said. "May God's blessing be upon you! What think you, little Mary? How do you like the prospect of being the wife of the ruler of this district?"

"I would rather that he had been the ruler only of this farm," Mary said; "but I see that a great power of good has been given into his hands, and it is not for me to complain."

"That reminds me," Simon said, "of what Martha and I were speaking together last night. You have both waited long; there is no occasion for longer tarrying; the marriage-feast will be prepared, and we will summon our neighbors and friends to assemble here this day week. And now, John, what are you going to do?"

"I am going, father, at once to Hippos, the chief town in the district. I shall see the authorities of the town and the captain of the Roman garrison and lay before them the commission of Cæsar. I shall then issue a proclamation announcing to all people within the limits of the district that have been marked out that I have authority from Rome to judge all matters that may come before me in the district, and that all who have causes of complaint or who have been wronged by any will find me here, ready to hear their cause and to order justice to be rendered to them. I shall also say that I shall shortly make a tour through the district to see for myself into the condition of things and to give aid to such as need it."

Great was the surprise of the Roman and Jewish authorities in Hippos when John produced the imperial commission. There was, however, no doubting or disputing it. The Roman officers at once placed themselves under his orders, and issued proclamations of their own in addition to that of John, notifying the fact to all the inhabitants of the district. Among the Jewish authorities there was at first some feeling of jealousy that this young man should be placed over them; but they felt nevertheless the great benefits that would arise from the protection which one of their own countrymen high in favor of Titus would be able to afford them. When showing his commission John had also produced the letter of

Titus giving his reasons for the nomination, and, indeed, the younger men in the district, many of whom had followed John in his first campaign, and who had hitherto, in accordance with the oath of secrecy taken on enrollment, concealed their knowledge that John of Gamala was the son of Simon, now proclaimed the fact and hailed his appointment with joy.

On the appointed day of marriage of John and Mary took place; and as the news had spread through the country a vast gathering assembled and it was made the occasion of a public demonstration. The preparations which Martha and Mary had made for the feast, ample as they had been, would have availed but little among such a multitude; but Isaac and the men-servants drove in and slaughtered several cattle, and as those who came for the most part bore presents of wine, oil, bread, goats, and other articles, and the neighbors lent their assistance in preparing the feast at the great fires which were lighted along the shore, while Simon contributed all the contents of his wine store, the feast proved ample for all assembled. John and his wife moved among the throng receiving congratulations and good wishes; Mary blushing and tearful with happiness and pride in the honor paid to John; John himself radiant with pleasure and with satisfaction at the thought of the good which the power so strangely conferred upon him would enable him to effect for his neighbors.

After that things went on in their ordinary routine at the farm, save that John was frequently away visiting among the villages of the district, which was some thirty miles long by ten wide. The northern portion was thickly inhabited, but in the south the villages were thick, and the people had suffered greatly from the excursions of the Roman foragers at the time of the siege of Gamala. Many of the villages had been rebuilt since that time, but there was still great distress, heightened by the number of fugitives from the other side of Jordan.

The aid which John gave enabled most of the fugitives in his district to return to their distant villages and to rebuild their homes, where there was now little fear of their being again disturbed. The distress in his own district was also relieved. In some cases money was given, in others lent, to enable the cultivators to till their fields, to replant vineyards, and to purchase flocks. So that in the course of a year the whole district was restored to its normal appearance, and the signs of the destructive war were almost entirely effaced.

Then John was able to settle down in his quiet home. In the morning he worked with his father; in the afternoon he listened to the complaints or petitions of those who came before him, settling disputes between neighbors, hearing from those who considered that they were too hardly pressed upon by the tax-collector, and doing justice to those who were wronged.

Soon after he married, mindful of the doctrines he had heard during his visit among the community of Nazarites by the Dead Sea, John made inquiries, and found that many of the sect who had left the land when the troubles with the Romans commenced had now returned, and were preaching their doctrines more openly than before, now that those of the ancient religion could no longer persecute them.

At Tiberias a considerable community of the sect soon established themselves; and John, going over, persuaded one of their teachers to take up his abode with him for a time and to expound their doctrines to him and his family. He was astonished at the spirit of love, charity, and goodwill which animated the teaching of the Christians—still more at the divine spirit that breathed in the utterances and animated the life of their Master.

The central idea, that God was the God of the whole world, and not, as the Jews had hitherto supposed, a special deity of their own, struck John particularly, and explained many things which had hitherto been difficult for him to understand. It would have been galling to admit as much in the days of Jewish pride and stubbornness; but their spirit was broken now; and John could understand that although as long as the nation had believed in him and served him God had taken a peculiar interest in them and had revealed to them much of his nature and attributes, while the rest of the world had been left to worship false gods, he yet loved all the world, and was now about to extend to all men that knowledge of him hitherto confined to the Jews. Above all, John saw how vastly higher was the idea of God as revealed in the new teaching than that which the Jews had hitherto entertained regarding him.

A month after the arrival of the teacher John and Mary were baptized into the new faith; and a few months later Simon and Martha, who had been harder to convince, also became converts.

When Titus was raised to the imperial throne, John, in compliance with the request he had made him, journeyed to Rome and remained there for a short time as his guest. Titus received him with affection.

"I have every reason to be thankful," John said. "I have been blessed in every way. My parents still survive. I am happy with my wife and children. Your bounty has enabled me to bind up the wounds and relieve the distress caused by the war. My mind has been opened to heavenly teaching, and I try humbly to follow in the steps of that divine teacher, Jesus of Nazareth."

"Ah, you have come to believe in him!" Titus said. "There are many of his creed here in Rome, and they say that they are even on the increase. I would gladly hear from you something of him. I have heard somewhat of him from Josephus, who for three years dwelt among the Essenes, and who has spoken to me highly of purity of life, the enlightenment, and religious fervor of that sect, to which, I believe, he himself secretly inclines, although, from the desire not to offend his countrymen, he makes no open confession of faith."

John, before he left, explained to the emperor the teachings of his Master, and it may be that the wisdom, humanity, and mildness which Titus displayed in the course of his reign was in no small degree the result of the lesson which he learned from John.

The latter came no more to Rome, but to the end of his life dwelt on the shore of Galilee, wisely governing his little district after the manner of the judges of old.

Jonas never left his friend. He married the daughter of one of the fishermen, and lived in a small house Simon built for him close to his own. At the death of the latter he become John's right hand on the farm, and remained his friend and brother to the end.

THE MISSION OF GREAT CHRISTIAN BOOKS

The ministry of Great Christian Books was established to glorify The Lord Jesus Christ and to be used by Him to expand and edify the kingdom of God while we occupy and anticipate Christ's glorious return. Great Christian Books will seek to accomplish this mission by publishing Gospel literature which is biblically faithful, relevant, and practically applicable to many of the serious spiritual needs of mankind upon the beginning of this new millennium. To do so we will always seek to boldly incorporate the truths of Scripture, especially those which were largely articulated as a body of theology during the Protestant Reformation of the sixteenth century and ensuing years. We gladly join our voice in the proclamations of— Scripture Alone, Faith Alone, Grace Alone, Christ Alone, and God's Glory Alone!

Our ministry seeks the blessing of our God as we seek His face to both confirm and support our labors for Him. Our prayers for this work can be summarized by two verses from the Book of Psalms:

"...let the beauty of the LORD our God be upon us, And establish the work of our hands for us; Yes, establish the work of our hands." —Psalm 90:17

"Not unto us, O LORD, not unto us, but to your name give glory." —Psalm 115:1

Great Christian Books appreciates the financial support of anyone who shares our burden and vision for publishing literature which combines sound Bible doctrine and practical exhortation in an age when too few so-called "Christian" publications do the same. We thank you in advance for any assistance you can give us in our labors to fulfill this important mission. May God bless you.

For a catalog of other great
Christian books including
additional titles by
G. A. Henty —

contact us in
any of the following ways:

write us at:
Great Christian Books
160 37th Street
Lindenhurst, NY 11757

call us at:
(631) 956-0998

find us online:
www.greatchristianbooks.com

email us at:
mail@greatchristianbooks.com

www.ingramcontent.com/pod-product-compliance
Lightning Source LLC
Chambersburg PA
CBHW030153070426
42447CB00032B/920